TRANSFORMING WORKPLACE CULTURES

Insights from Great Place to Work® Institute's first 25 years

Edited by Robert Levering

Edited by Robert Levering, Co-Founder

Jennifer Amozorrutia
Prasenjit Bhattacharya
Horacio Bolaños
Leslie Caccamese
Trish Dagg
Gilberto Dondé
Palle Ellemann
Ana Maria Gubbins
Frank Hauser
Williams Johnson
José Tolovi Jr.
Michael Katz
Sandrine Lage
Amy Lyman, Co-Founder
Milton Moskowitz
Lisa Ratner
Tobias Schmidtner
Raciel Sosa
Adriana Souza
Chris Taylor

GREAT PLACE TO WORK®

Building a better society by helping companies transform their workplaces.

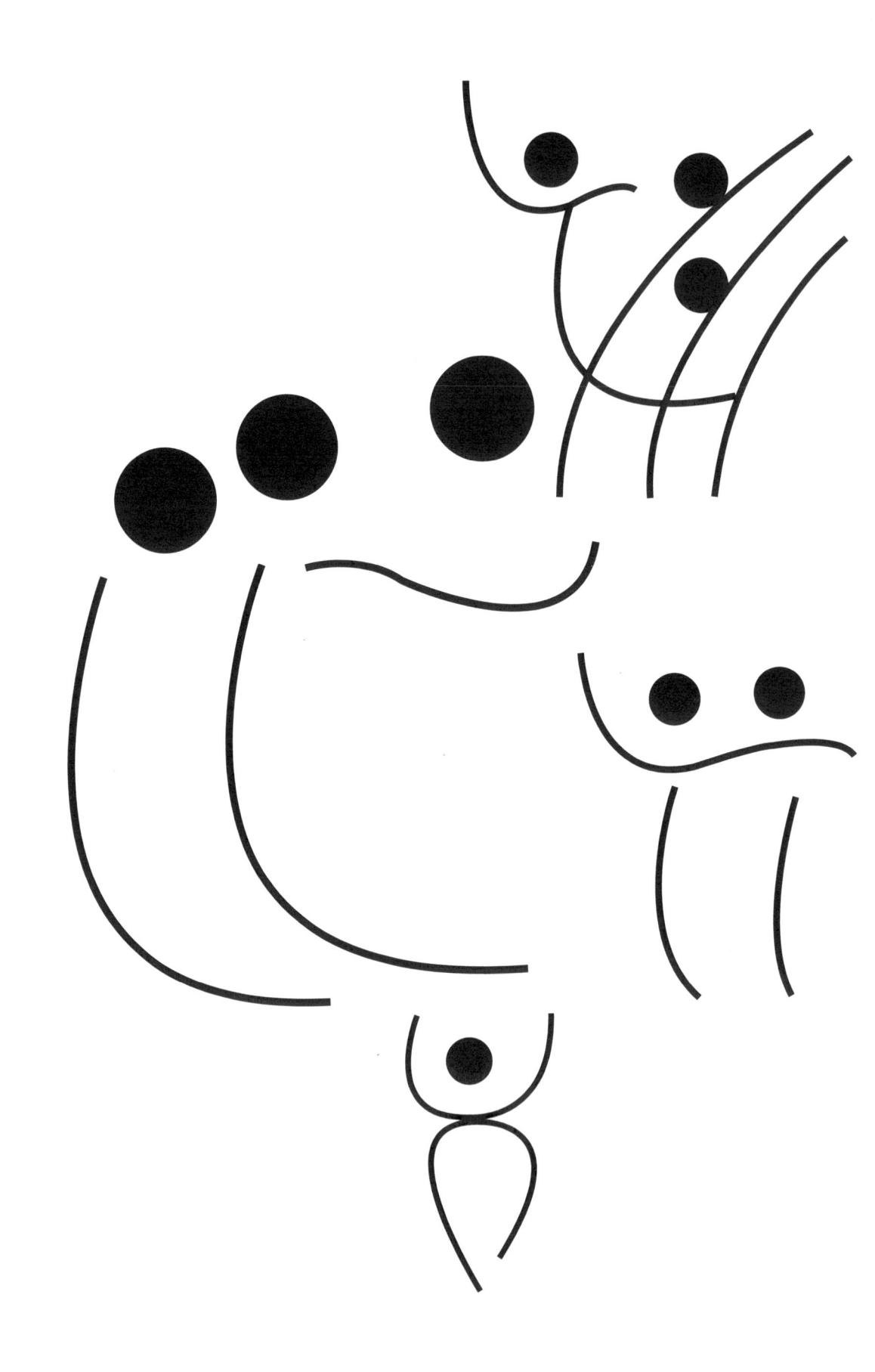

THIS BOOK IS DEDICATED TO

those people who have created amazing workplaces which inspire us and so many others around the world

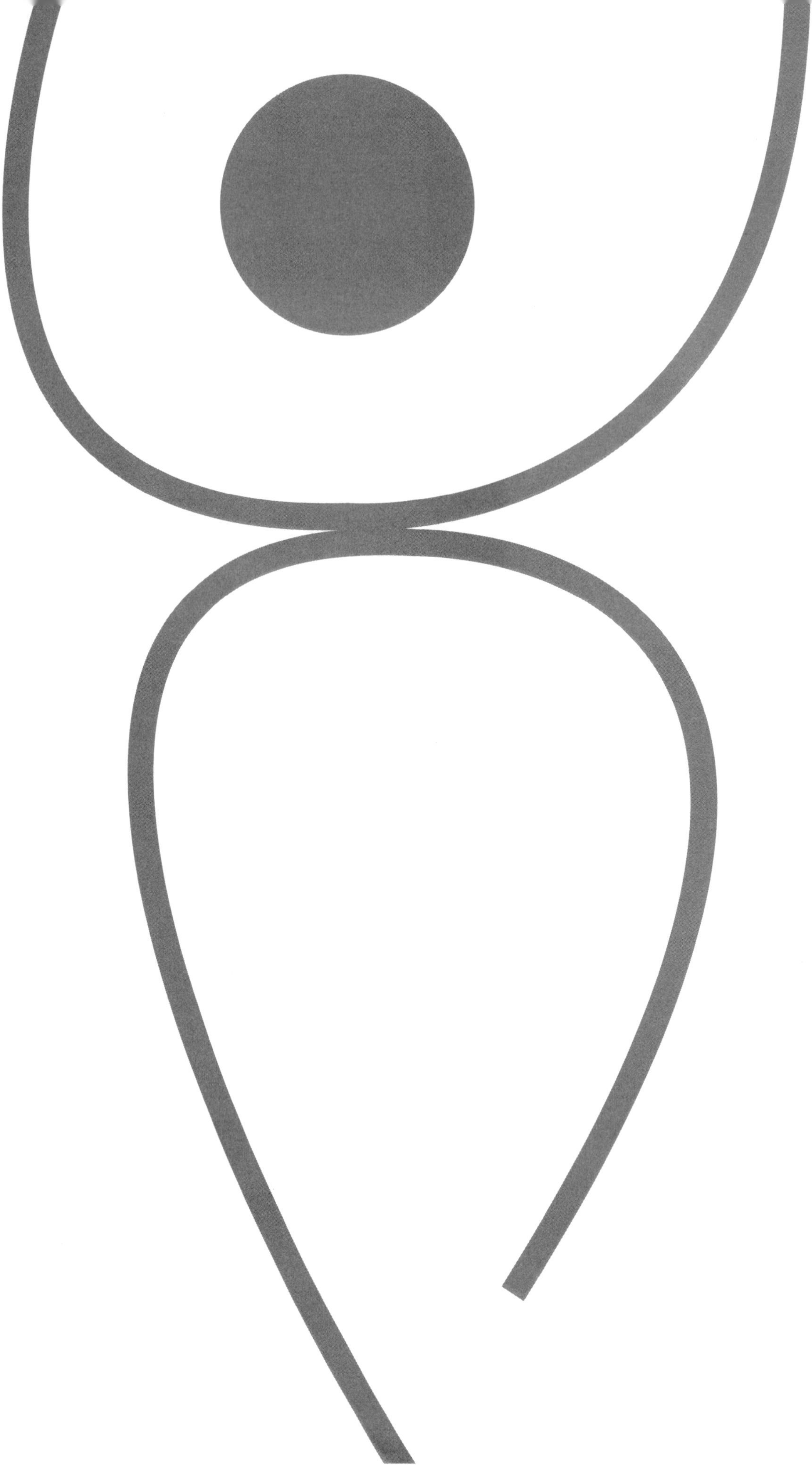

THE GREAT PLACE TO WORK
MOVEMENT ENTERS
A **NEW DECADE**

Book subtitles often mislead readers because publishers sometimes are willing to sacrifice accuracy for increased sales. Happily, the subtitle for this volume tells you exactly what to expect: "Insights from Great Place to Work® Institute's first 25 years." This is indeed a collection of writings spanning a quarter of a century from an organization whose name describes its focus. What the subtitle doesn't reveal is the global nature of the book. Its 20 authors offer perspectives from five different continents.

We believe you will find much in these essays to be thought provoking. But we also sincerely hope that you encounter some ideas that can be of use. The book will have accomplished its purpose if you apply some of these insights to your own workplace. It would mean that this book has helped fulfill the Institute's raison d'etre as articulated by our mission statement: "Building a better society by helping companies transform their workplaces."

We realize that references to a corporate mission statement are normally greeted with skepticism, if not with outright cynicism. As a rule, they represent well-meaning, but often seemingly irrelevant, attempts to convince employees and/or customers that an organization has a loftier purpose than achieving higher profits. (See Milton Moskowitz's perceptive article "Trumpeting the New Values," written in 1983 when such statements were first becoming the vogue.) But we believe that our Institute's mission statement actually does accurately represent who we are and what we do today, many years after it was first penned by co-founder Amy Lyman and me.

Not only does our organization have a social mission, we view ourselves as serving a social change movement — a movement with the audacious goal of making every organization a great place to work. We think we played a major role in setting this movement in motion by introducing Best Workplaces lists throughout the globe. But today this movement goes far beyond our efforts and now encompasses many evangelists, especially people associated with the hundreds of companies a year that we select for our lists.

For too long, most people's experience of the workplace has been one of alienation and dissatisfaction. It's true that most employees typically enjoy at least some of the tasks they perform during their work days. And they often find pleasure socializing with their coworkers. Yet the overall experience of the workplace is rarely uplifting because people regularly feel treated as if they were replaceable parts of a machine, as numbers, as automatons. At times employees make individual protests or even form unions. But most simply accept a dehumanized workplace as normal, as the way things are, as a devil's bargain where you sell your soul for a paycheck. Thus, for many people, life begins after 5 pm, after the work day, when you can be with family or friends and do activities that you feel are enriching.

But the workplace doesn't have to be like that, and we are proud to be part of a movement of people who are dedicated to changing what is a demoralizing reality for far too many workers. We are encouraged by the progress achieved since the early 1980s when my fellow journalist Milton Moskowitz and I first embarked on a quest to write a book entitled *100 Best Companies to Work for in America*. We thought it was a great title for a book, but we anticipated that we would only be able to identify 100 companies that were the best of a pretty sorry lot.

What we discovered amazed us. Our travels took us to companies that were not merely better than others. We found some truly great places to work — remarkable organizations where the people we interviewed raved about their workplace environments and talked glowingly about the relationships between management and employees. We felt like explorers who had stumbled on new territory. No one had written about these places before, nor had anyone made any attempt to investigate what made them tick.

Looking back from this vantage point a quarter century later, I would suggest that the publication of that book in 1984 marked the beginning point of the great place to work movement. The book was a hit, making *The New York Times* bestseller list almost overnight. People were genuinely curious to read about what went on inside these companies. But much more importantly, the book led many people to make changes in their own companies. After satisfying their initial curiosity about other firms, people begin asking questions about their own workplaces. They wonder how their own firms compare with "the

Best." In some cases, they are inspired to apply some of the policies or practices they learn about. In other cases, managers decide to benchmark their workplace practices with "the Best." In still other cases, company leaders decide that their own firms are worthy candidates and participate in the list process themselves.

We hear many such stories every time we produce a list anywhere in the world (currently in more than 40 countries). We're certain there are countless other examples that we never hear about. Once people within companies start on this path, we've found that they have an insatiable appetite to make their workplaces better. They want to know whether creating a great workplace will help the bottom line. (It usually does, as several articles in this book demonstrate.) They want to get together with others who have also been bit by the great workplace bug. (We can see that from the popularity of our award events and conferences and constantly hear of many other networking efforts that companies do with each other.) Above all, as is true of business people the world over, they want practical advice about how to do it.

In this book you will hear, not abstract ideals, but inspiring stories and practical tips from enthusiastic adherents of great workplaces from Portugal to Australia, from the US to Argentina, from Mexico to India. Brazil's Jose Tolovi Jr. tells about how great workplaces handle crises. Italy's Gilberto Dondé talks about the impact of workplace culture on creativity and innovation, and Australia's Trish Dagg and Chris Taylor explain how that country's best firms keep employee loyalty during tough times.

Why do these lists provoke such reactions? After all, there are dozens of business rankings produced every year that have no discernable impact beyond possibly bumping up magazine sales. I think there are three interrelated factors, each of which contributes to the creation of this particular social change movement:

First, our lists take a populist and inclusive approach. Instead of looking at business from the top down, they look at organizations from the bottom up. That is, these lists adopt the employee perspective rather than that of investors or managers, which is the viewpoint of 99.9% of other articles or books that appear in the business press. Significantly, our "employee perspective" includes managers as well as rank-and-file workers. After all, managers are employees of organizations, too. The quality of the workplace environment impacts managers professionally and personally just as much as it does nonmanagers. By breaking down the usual demarcation line between management and labor, our approach encourages people to view their organizations with fresh eyes. For people to embark on any kind of change process, they need to alter their usual way of looking at the world. This is precisely what happens with these lists.

Second, although we look at the workplace from the employee viewpoint, we share little in common with others who also look at organizations from that perspective. Labor reporters, union organizers and academics almost always focus on what is wrong with particularly bad workplaces. By contrast, we tell positive stories of what is right about exemplary ones. Social change movements typically respond to the perceived ills of society, and most try to eradicate those problems by directing attention to them. This frequently involves confrontations with those in authority who are deemed to be responsible for creating them. Union movements, for instance, have produced great changes by focusing on low or exploitative wages and poor working conditions and making demands on the management/owners. However, social change also can occur by focusing on the positive and trying to get all interested parties to move in that direction. This is generally true of the current ecology movement that seeks to involve the public generally in going green. Our movement to create great places to work stands in that tradition.

Finally, any social change movement must offer hope, a vision for change. Our lists shine a bright light on the best workplaces, providing a very tangible target at which everyone else can aim their efforts. People often react by saying: "If these companies, which encompass virtually every industry, size, and nationality, can do it, why can't we?" Our Institute has even raised the ante by putting forth a model of an ideal workplace, what we call a "great place to work," with trust as its defining characteristic. This model and the importance of trust are spelled out in several articles in this book.

Because this movement revolves around an ideal, those who are part of it realize that they always can make improvements to their workplaces. One can always do things to increase the level of trust.

This book aims to help you do just that so you can join us in the great place to work movement.

Robert Levering

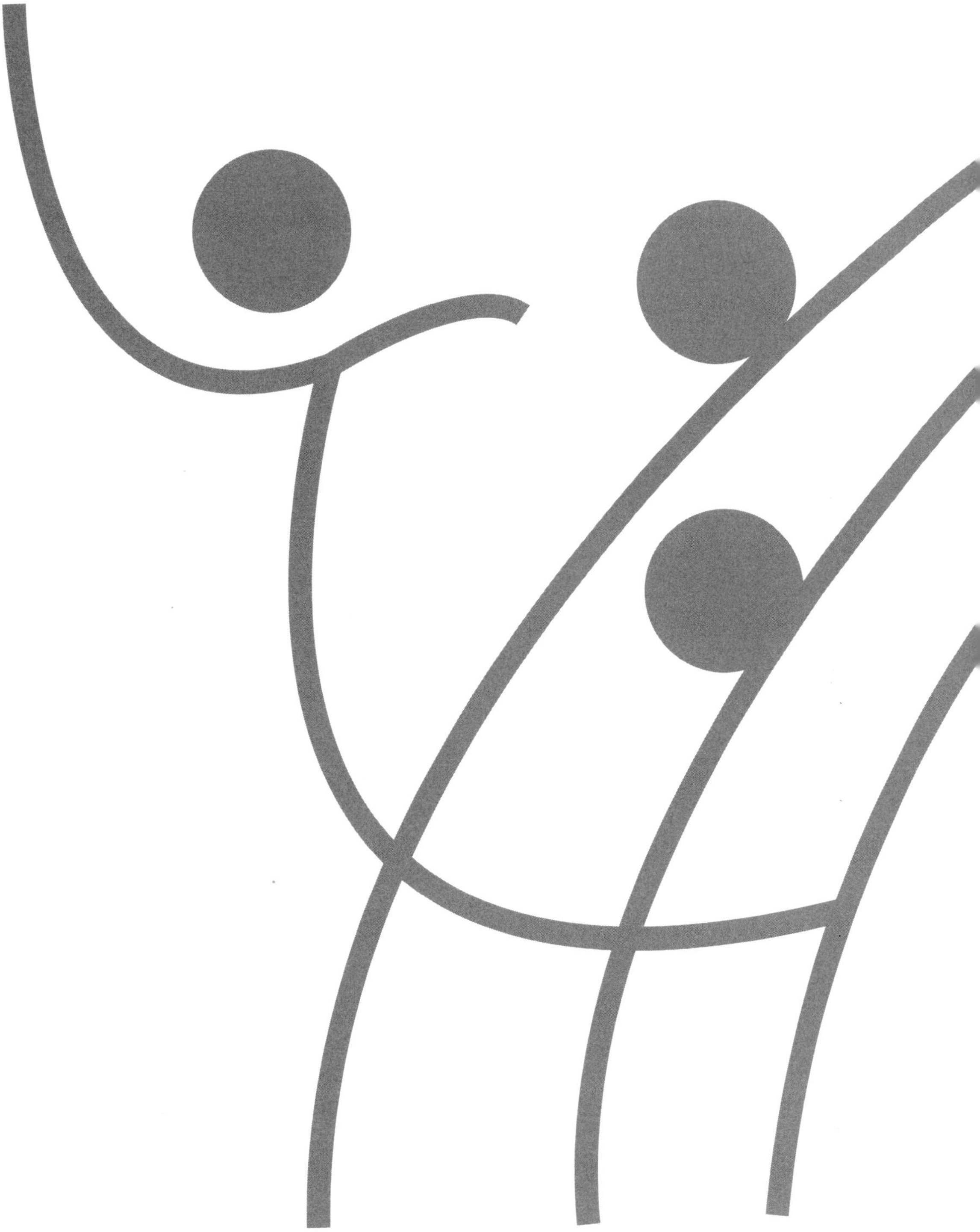

17   WHERE IT ALL BEGAN

67   IMPORTANCE OF TRUST

CONTENTS

117   MODELS FOR CHANGE AND GLOBAL PERSPECTIVES

118   Great Place to Work® Model
166   Giftwork®
180   Global Perspectives

223   TRUST MAKES COMPANIES STRONGER AND MORE ABLE TO HANDLE BAD TIMES

224   The Bottom Line
282   Managing in Difficult Times

305   BUILDING A BETTER SOCIETY

347   INDEX OF ALL ARTICLES

WHERE IT ALL
BEGAN

1984

THE 100 **BEST COMPANIES** TO WORK FOR IN **AMERICA**

By **Robert Levering**, **Milton Moskowitz** and **Michael Katz**

[ADDISON-WESLEY]

Finding a good place to work is not easy. It's not easy for a job hunter, and it wasn't easy for us.

Over the years everyone hears about great places to work—that such-and-such a company has a country club for employees, that a certain firm has such a terrific profit-sharing plan, that a $5-an-hour warehouseman retired with a half-million dollars, or that some corporations treat their people so well that executive recruiters find it impossible to lure them away. But how do you go about finding America's superlative employers?

We had some ideas to begin with. One of us covered the business scene for more than 25 years. All three of us have worked together to produce *Everybody's Business: An Almanac*, a book published by Harper & Row in 1980, which profiled 317 large companies.

Our previous research made us painfully aware that we were entering unexplored territory. It's

The roots of Great Place to Work® Institute can be traced directly to the first edition of *The 100 Best Companies to Work for in America*, published in 1984. Here is the original introduction to that book, which was the first attempt to rate companies based on the quality of their workplace cultures.

odd — but telling — that American companies are rarely examined from the standpoint of their employees. The literature of business is rich with stories about companies and analyses of their operations. The *Wall Street Journal* chronicles these activities so well that it has become the largest selling daily newspaper in the nation. During the course of a year, *BusinessWeek, Forbes, and Fortune* publish 103 issues that are crammed with lists, tables, and charts tracking the progress of companies in a multitude of categories. And there are hundreds of trade magazines that rank, grade, and otherwise evaluate companies in their industrial settings: biggest hotels, biggest candy makers, biggest airlines, and on and on.

Yet none of these sources regularly spotlight the human condition inside business. They don't, as a rule, tell how employees are treated. They don't discuss which companies have the best benefit programs. They hardly ever do company-by-company comparisons of workplace environments.

We knew we had to cast a wider net to confirm our hunches and inspire new ones. If a company is a good place to work, its employees make no secret of it. Talking about where you work is one of the most common pastimes in America (and who isn't at least curious about whether the grass is greener somewhere else?). The better employers usually acquire a good reputation within their communities and within their industries. We realized that, at first, reputation would have to be our guide, so we resorted to the grapevine.

We asked all kinds of people to recommend great places to work: friends, relatives, executive recruiters, management consultants, market researchers, publishers, public relations counselors, business school teachers, newspaper reporters, magazine editors, radio and TV news staffers, advertising agency employees. We literally solicited prospects from everyone we met, including doctors and dentists we visited. A notice that we were looking for superior workplaces appeared in three widely circulated business publications. We rarely conducted interviews inside a company without asking the people we were talking with for additional recommendations.

After we had compiled a list of 350 candidates, we wrote to all of them for information about themselves and their employee policies. We received a wide range of responses. Some sent elaborate descriptions of their employee philosophy; at the other extreme was a terse letter informing us that the company was already besieged with job applicants and that the last thing they need was more attention of this kind; still others, suspecting a vanity press venture, told us they chose "not to participate."

Sifting through this material and listening to what people told us, we narrowed our candidate roster to 135 companies. But we quickly realized that the material was thin and rather lifeless, and that the only way to get in-depth information and lend substance to hearsay was to look for ourselves at every company on our list. We took a deep breath and telephoned our travel agents.

We crisscrossed the country for the better part of the year, visiting 114 companies in 27 different states— from a textile mill in South Carolina to a plywood co-op in Oregon, from banks on Wall Street to oil companies in Texas. In between plastic trays of airline food, we settled down to lengthy conversations with employees, from the factory floor to the executive suite. We typically interviewed at least half a dozen people at each company, and sometimes we talked with several dozen. We made a point of asking the companies to set up interviews with people who had previously worked elsewhere. We found group interviews to be particularly useful, because comments by one person would spark reaction from another.

It was heartening to discover how well-earned are the reputations of the companies on our list; people really like to work at these places. Employee satisfaction is a factor you can't measure by reading company pamphlets. It's one thing to listen to presidents or chairmen talk about the great companies they head; they do it all the time. It's something else to talk, as we did, to the head of the mailroom at Time Inc., or an usher at the Los Angeles Dodgers stadium, and to see the pride they felt about working for the companies.

People are proud to work for companies that treat them well. They become linked to these companies in more than just an employer/employee relationship. It's the presence of this feeling more than any other, perhaps, that sets these 100 companies apart from the great mass of companies in America.

Our methods were journalistic rather than scientific. We did not try to impose a preconceived set of standards. The firms vary too much for systematic comparison. Working in a bank in Southern California is very different from working in a steel mill in Indiana. And IBM, with over 20,000 U.S. employees, is a world apart from Celestial Seasonings, with about 200 workers.

Despite the discovery, almost everyone of the "100 Best" has something distinctive to offer its employees. At some the benefits are very tangible, from the huge fortunes attainable at Trammell Crow to the 25-cent gourmet lunch prepared by a French chef at Merle Norman Cosmetics or the million-dollar employee center with swimming pools, Jacuzzi, and handball courts at ROLM. Other places, like Gore and Kollmorgen, offer unusual management styles. Each company is unique, but there were certain themes we heard over and over again, and the urge to draw a kind of composite picture of the ideal company is irresistible. Beyond good pay and strong benefits, such a company would:

• Make people feel that they are part of a team or, in some cases, a family.

• Encourage open communication, informing its people of new developments and encouraging them to offer suggestions and complaints.

• Promote from within; let its own people bid for jobs before hiring outsiders.

• Stress quality, enabling people to feel pride in their products or services they are providing.

• Allow its employees to share in the profits, through profit-sharing or stock ownership or both.

• Reduce the distinction of rank between the top management and those in entry-level jobs; put everyone on the first-name basis; bar executive dining rooms and executive perks for high-level people.

• Devote attention and resources to creating as pleasant a workplace environment as possible; hire good architects.

• Encourage its employees to be active in community service by giving money to organizations in which employees participate.

• Help employees save by matching the funds they save.

• Try not to lay off people without first making an effort to place them in other jobs either within the company or elsewhere.

• Care enough about the health of its employees to provide physical fitness centers and regular exercise and medical programs.

- Expand the skills of its people through training programs and reimbursement or tuition from outside courses.

We found, in general, that small companies are better than big companies—as places to work. So you will find here some companies you may never have heard of, like Odetics or Moog. The big companies on our roster have maintained many small-company traits: they break down their operations into small units, they push responsibility down into the ranks, they don't manage people. We were pleased also to find three divisions of large companies that qualified (though their parent companies didn't): Bell Labs (American Telephone & Telegraph), Physio-Control (Eli Lilly), and Westin Hotels (United Airlines).

Midway though our process the Thomas Peters/Robert Waterman book, *In Search of Excellence*, was published. We examined their list of "excellent" companies with interest to see how it compared with our "100 Best." Finding some overlap but also significant divergences, we observed that management for profits, growth, and contented stockholders does not always yield a good place to work. We rejected many companies to which they gave accolades — Boeing, National Semiconductor, Frito-Lay, and McDonald's (the next article), to name a few.

By the time we completed our research we had gained a better understanding of the difference between the traditional employer/employee relationship, which is often adversarial, and the kinds of practices we encountered on our journey. We feel that the "100 Best" may be part of the first wave in a major change that will affect for the better the way all of us think of our jobs and conduct our business. A phrase that expresses this change is "beyond technique." Whether a technique is drawn from a management handbook or an organization psychologist, the whole framework tends to be manipulative: "we" are looking for a way to make "them" work harder or do something we want them to do. (One of the most alienated groups of employees we met was a Japanese-style quality circle at a Honeywell bomb factory in Minneapolis.) Among the "100 Best" we found many firms that have transcended that manipulative framework and achieved a sense that "we are all in it together." This unwritten pact among employees often begins with one or more key individuals who genuinely care about the quality of the experience of everyone in the company.

It can be argued that both conventional managerial techniques and the innovative practices described in this book enhance productivity and create a healthy economy. But the "100 Best" offer an added benefit of such high value that it's difficult to place on the same scale: a working life for thousands of people really worth living and worth looking forward to every day.

1984

BEYOND **GOOD** POLICIES AND **PRACTICES**

By **Robert Levering**, **Milton Moskowitz** and **Michael Katz**

[ADDISON-WESLEY]

In this epilogue to the first edition of the 100 Best book, the authors explain how being a great workplace requires more than having good policies and practices. The example they chose, McDonald's, has made significant changes since this was written and has earned a spot on a number of the Institute's Best Workplace lists in Denmark (2002); Norway, Chile (2004); Ireland (2005); Peru and Denmark (2006); Norway and U.K. (2008); Ecuador, Netherlands, Mexico, and Brazil (2007).

How can a company that has a vice-president for individuality *not* be a good place to work? McDonald's, the world's largest restaurant business, has such a position. It's filled by the company's former personnel director, James Kuhn, who's described as a "free spirit." His mission is to help employees escape the deadening hand of bureaucracy. He tries to loosen things up.

Kuhn works out of McDonald's headquarters at Oak Brook, Illinois, a suburb 42 miles west of Chicago's Loop on the way to Aurora. Having a vice-president for individuality is not the only unusual aspect of work life at McDonald's headquarters. It's a highly revved-up place where people seem to enjoy working long hours, a company for workaholic cheerleaders. And these people know they do not need an MA or MBA. or PhD to get to the top. McDonald's does not recruit at graduate business schools. The route to the top can start on the firing line in a McDonald's store, serving Big Macs, bagging fries, making milk shakes. Fred L. Turner and Michael R. Quinlan, who were chairman and president, respectively, in 1983, did work their way up from the bottom: Turner from a grill station, Quinlan from the mailroom.

We visited McDonald's because people who had once worked in staff positions at Oak Brook strongly recommended the company to us. The people we met there praised it effusively. Ray Mines, one of the highest-ranking blacks in the company (in 1983 he was on the nine rectors of national operations), told us how it is to work at McDonald's: "First you have to get McDonalidized. They take all the blood out of your veins and put ketchup in them. That's the truth. If you work hard, you can make it here. McDonald's is a very big corporation, but you're not a number. They know your name."

Helen Farrell joined McDonald's in 1973 after having taught at a community college in Nebraska. Hired as a paralegal staffer, she recalls that in her first month at McDonald's, she had a logistical problem in getting her two children transported from Texas, where they were with their father, to Chicago. She couldn't afford the airfare, and the bus and train schedules were complicated. She noticed from a posted schedule that the McDonald's plane was due to fly from Texas to Chicago — and so she called Ray Kroc's office (Kroc founded McDonald's) to ask whether her children could hitch a ride. Twenty minutes later Kroc himself called back to ask, "Now what's this about those children in Texas?" After she explained the situation, he said, "Have those kids at Love Field, and they'll be picked up." Farrell learned later that the plane's schedule had been changed to fly directly from Florida to Chicago without stopping in Texas. But Kroc rerouted it to pick up her children. "I'm going to do an awful lot for a company that does that for a nobody," Farrell told us.

McDonald's does a lot for people who hang in there with the company. It has a strong array of benefit programs—profit-sharing (which typically augments your pay by more than 10 percent a year); an investment savings plan; a free physical exam every other year if you're under age 35, every year if you're over 35; a three-month sabbatical after 10 years' service. Some 50 employees are saluted annually for outstanding achievements. They receive the President's Awards, which, aside from prestige attached to them, come with a cash bonus equal to one-third of their pay.

All right, if it's so good, why isn't McDonald's one of the 100 best companies to work for in America? It certainly makes every list of the best-managed companies in the nation. It failed to qualify because we found, in checking at the local level where most employees work, that a McDonald's job is not an uplifting experience; it's certainly not a "people first" place.

McDonald's is the largest employer of teenagers in the country, and the profit squeezed out of the business by the parent corporation and the franchisees who own three-quarters of the outlets depends crucially on low wages (as low as possible) and an assembly-line operation that leaves the employees with little or no free time to think. Here are some comments given to us by teenagers working in McDonald's stores in California:

- "McDonald's is a place where you work hard for little money. The one I worked at would only allow you a small French fries, a small drink, and a large hamburger for six hours of work."

- "The starting pay is $3.35 an hour. Every three months the employee gets reviewed to see if you get a five-cent, ten-cent, or fifteen-cent raise."

- "They work you to death for cheap pay."
- "Kids hate the job but they need the money."
- "People leave all the time because the pay is low and lousy for the amount of work they put you through."

The McDonald's people at Oak Brook do not deny that the pay at the crew level is low. Nor do they deny that the kids have to work to a routine and are watched over carefully by their supervisors. What they say, in defense, is that this job is actually the first work experience for these teenagers, and the discipline will stand them in good stead. They claim that many teenagers work for McDonald's in high school and later return as full-timers. They insist that if you take all the hard stuff in the beginning and stay for the long haul, the rewards will be great. And then there is this ultimate justification: McDonald's creates jobs. Lee Dunham, operation of six McDonald's stores in New York City Harlem area, says, "We give jobs to 400 people who otherwise wouldn't have them."

We debated among ourselves whether McDonald's belonged on our roster, deciding in the end that for most of the people who work for the company and its franchisees (well over 250,000), it's dehumanizing, similar to the experience Charlie Chaplin encountered in *Modern Times*. We believe it's also true that for most of them, it leads nowhere. Peggy Stinnett, a member of the school board in Oakland, California, summed up what teenagers get from McDonald's in an interview with Seth Rosenfeld at Pacific News Service: "At the end of the semester, they're going to have a little experience at McDonald's and that's not going to buy them much."

In searching for good places to work, we wanted to select companies that are good for people in the lower ranks as well as in management. We clearly did not get to every last outpost of every company in this book, but all of the ones we finally selected did have in place a people orientation that was intended to flow through all the ranks, from top to bottom. McDonald's, on the other hand, seemed to embrace a system geared to exploiting people in the lower ranks.

1984

WORKING FOR **THE BEST**

By **Robert Levering** and **Milton Moskowitz**

[SAN FRANCISCO FOCUS]

It's soul-searching time in American business. Gone is the era when an executive could tally a company's performance merely by tallying its account books. And, while profit is still, literally, the bottom line, companies are now searching for better ways to work with their employees and are beginning to understand that profits themselves may hinge partially on job satisfaction.

Does this mean we can soon expect a sauna in every office building, picnics in the Rockies and vacations in the Alps, equality in the workplace, and security à la Japanese corporations? Not necessarily, since the definition of "ideal working conditions" differs among people, and old ways of treating employees die hard. But a trend is evident, signaled by a recent outpouring of books, articles, and speeches. The crowning achievement was, of course, last year's *In Search of Excellence*, by Thomas J. Peters and Robert H. Waterman Jr., a $19.95 book that stayed on the bestseller list for more than a year and immediately shot to the top

It's remarkable to read the descriptions of these companies that appeared in the 1984 edition of *The 100 Best Companies to Work for in America*. Not only are some of the perks listed here as appealing as they were a quarter century ago, but so is the overall atmosphere of these companies. Three of these companies - ROLM, Tandem Computers, and Viking Freight — were later aquired by other firms — IBM, HP, and Fedex, respectively — which have also appeared on our lists.

of the paperback bestseller list when it appeared this spring in an $8.95 version.

Sparks off this anvil continue to fly. For two years now *Fortune*, renowned for its Fortune 500 roster that ranks companies by such mundane factors as sales and profits, has been surveying thousands of executives to yield the rankings of "America's most admired corporations." And the Tarrytown Center in Tarrytown, New York, presided over by Robert L. Schwartz, has come up with the concept of the "Tarrytown 100," an assemblage of people, nearly all of them in the business world, who are unconventional, innovative, or socially conscious.

The rising tide of new lists and literature reflects a widespread disappointment and dissatisfaction with corporate performance in American society. *In Search of Excellence* touched a nerve because its many examples of business excellence contrasted sharply with the pervasive mediocrity that characterizes much of American corporate behavior. So board chairs and presidents all over the country have ordered their subordinates to read it, hoping that some of the lessons would rub off.

As we see it, two strands are now being joined in the new literature. Self improvement has always been a strong strain in American life. We have produced a steady stream of preachers, soothsayers, cheerleaders, and politicians who have talked about what people could do to improve themselves. Salespeople, from itinerant peddlers to pitchmen on TV commercials, have seduced American consumers with the "it's-good-for-you" message. And, on the other side of the coin, we have a long history of social protest directed against the business establishment, especially "big business." Companies have been perceived as exploiters of working people and communities. They have been ridiculed, satirized, and attacked (and regulated) for pursuing their private, selfish aims with complete disregard for the public interest.

So the new message is that Americans can improve themselves by changing business from a heartless, hierarchical affair to a humanistic, open arena where people are valued and encouraged to be entrepreneurial. And the clincher is that U.S. business had better opt for these changes if it doesn't want to be relegated to the dustbin of industrial history by the Japanese and other more resourceful competitors.

As these sour mashes of discontent have been fermenting, we, along with Michael Katz, have been working on our own addition to the literature. A sequel to our previous work, *Everybody's Business: An Almanac*, this one is called the *100 Best Companies to Work for in America* (published this spring by Addison-Wesley). Our base was the San Francisco Bay Area, because we live here, but we scoured the country looking for candidates—and we personally visited well over a hundred companies in twenty-nine states before we came up with our final roster.

A point to keep in mind about the books that preceded ours is that they were usually written by management consultants. That doesn't mean they are bad books; on the contrary, we think they are good—and they certainly stimulated our thinking. But our methods were journalistic, and we approached the subject of what constitutes a good company from the standpoint of employees, not management.

We think a phrase that aptly expresses our approach is "beyond technique." Whether a technique is drawn out from a management handbook or an organization psychologist, the framework tends to be manipulative: "we" are looking for a way to get "them" to work

The rising tide of new lists and literature reflects a widespread disappointment and dissatisfaction with corporate performance in American society.

harder or do something we want them to do. In this framework, of course, "we" represents management, "them" the great mass of employees. We hoped to find companies that transcend the traditional framework—companies where an unwritten pact said "we are all in it together." Very simply, we wanted to locate firms where employees are not only happy but intensely proud to be working there.

We selected a Bay Area firm, Palo Alto-based Hewlett-Packard, for our list on the ten best companies to work for in the United States. Founded in 1938 in the proverbial garage by two then-recent Stanford University engineering graduates, Hewlett-Packard has grown to be the largest maker of sophisticated electronic measurement and testing instruments and the second largest manufacturer of minicomputers. It has annual sales of over $3 billion and employs more than seventy thousand people worldwide. Its financial success has not taken place at the expense of its working environment, however. Indeed, many who work there claim that its success is due in no small part to how the employees are treated. H-P provides a superlative workplace by almost any standard: high pay, super benefits, a relaxed, egalitarian environment and job security stemming from an unwritten no-layoff policy.

In terms of pay, for instance, H-P aims to pay 5 to 10 percent higher than similar high-tech firms, or roughly, equivalent to the top five to ten companies of any type in the United States. In addition to base pay, H-P offers a cash profit-sharing plan, equal to about 12 percent of the firm's pretax profits. In recent years, this has meant an additional 7 percent of income per year for each employee. H-P also picks up 100 percent of each employee's medical and dental insurance. For those who wish to buy H-P stock, the company kicks in one dollar for every three dollars put up by employees.

H-P employees also have access to a dozen different recreation areas throughout the world—an outgrowth of the traditional annual company picnic. To accommodate the picnic, H-P bought Little Basin Park in the Santa Cruz Mountains in 1962. Since then the company has purchased three recreation areas in Colorado, one in the Pocono Mountains of Pennsylvania, a lake resort in Scotland, and a ski-chalet complex in the German Alps. H-P employees can make reservations to vacation at any of these locations.

At some firms, employees do not have to travel for recreation. One of H-P's Silicon Valley neighbors, ROLM, has created a recreation area at its corporate headquarters. ROLM manufactures telephone switchboard equipment. Some have described the company's Santa Clara headquarters (located a few blocks from Marriott's Great America) as a cross between a college campus and a country club. In the middle of the complex administrative and manufacturing buildings is ROLM's million-dollar recreation center. The day we visited, an aerobics class was being conducted in the center, while other employees were lounging around one of the two swimming pools. Employees were also taking advantage of the center's Jacuzzi and steam room, while others were playing racquetball.

Making a good working environment is an explicit corporate goal at ROLM. The company is the only one in the United States with a "Great Place to Work®" department. Besides the physical fitness center, ROLM offers an unsurpassed sabbatical program. After six years on the job, ROLM employees can take three months off at full pay. This paid sabbatical is in addition to the regular vacation program.

In Search of Excellence **touched a nerve because its many examples of business excellence contrasted sharply with the pervasive mediocrity that characterizes much of American corporate behavior.**

Another Silicon Valley firm with a paid sabbatical is Tandem Computer, a Cupertino-based maker of fail-safe computer systems for large businesses. Tandem employees qualify for six weeks off at full pay after just four years of service. Tandem fosters an egalitarian atmosphere. The company's founder and chairman, Jimmy Treybig, once explained the philosophy behind the firm's policies: "We are trying to create a condition of equality among the people here." There are no reserved parking places for top executives, nor are there time clocks or organization charts. A premium is placed on flexibility. One software programmer who has worked with several other firms appreciates Tandem's lack of bureaucracy. "People stay off my back here," he told us. "I don't like meetings and I don't like memos. At Tandem I don't get any memos, and I only go to one meeting a week."

Intel, on the other hand, believes in meetings. A manufacturer of semiconductor chips that form the innards of personal computers and other electronic products, Intel is militantly egalitarian, like Tandem and many other Silicon Valley firms. There are no reserved parking spots for top executives nor any executive dining rooms. But Intel is not for the free spirit. There is no flextime" at Intel. Everyone is expected to be at work at 8:00 a.m. Dr. Robert Noyce, cofounder of the company, once explained, "It is another way of saying to people that they're valuable to us. How can we do our work if they're not here? Intel is the only place I ever worked where an 8:00 a.m. meeting starts at 8:00 a.m."

It's a high-pressure environment for those who like to knock heads with other brainy people. Intel attracts people who like being challenged. As one former Intel executive said, "There are no sissies at Intel." The firm rewards those who can keep up with the pace. During the recession of 1981-

82, Intel chose not to lay off any people at the time when many of the other chip makers were laying off hundreds of employees. Instead, Intel asked everyone to take salary cuts graduated by income. Intel also allows employees with seven years on the job to apply for six months off, with pay, for public service, teaching, or exceptional education opportunities.

Apple computer is considered by many younger people in Silicon Valley to be a superb workplace, partly because of its reputation as a counter-corporate culture. Vice-presidents often show up at the office in jeans and T-shirts. They talk of how new management hired from other companies must go through a process of being "Appleized," meaning learning how to relate to other employees in a nontraditional, egalitarian way. As one Apple vice-president explained, "We're looking for people who are coaches and team builders and expanders, not controllers of people."

The company's beliefs are summed up in its "Apple Values," a statement of the company's philosophy handed out to all employees. One section reads: "Quality/Excellence. We care about what we do. We build into Apple products a level of quality, performance, and value that will earn the respect and loyalty of our customers." Another Apple value says: "We offer superior products that fill real needs and provide lasting value. We are genuinely interested in solving customer problems and will not compromise our ethics or integrity in the name of profit."

Apple offers an unusual benefit to all employees: an Apple 11e computer. After two months on the job, employees are loaned the machine (with disk drive and monitor). When they have been with the company for a full year, the company is theirs, no strings attached.

> There are other factors besides good communications, good pay, and benefits that attract people. Employees are proud to work for companies that make efforts to be active in their communities.

The Apple 11e is a nice benefit, but stock options have been the real bonanza for many of Apple's employees. While many corporations provide stock options for only its top executives, Apple offers them to all. Some three hundred of Apple's early employees are said to have become millionaires from their holdings in Apple stock.

A few miles from Apple's headquarters is the Cupertino home of Advanced Micro Devices, a manufacturer of semiconductors, whose president typifies the self-made Silicon Valley millionaire. Jerry Sanders is one of the area's folk heroes, complete with loud clothes, gold chains, and a bunch of fancy cars including a Rolls Royce Corniche convertible and a Ferrari.

Like other admired employers, Sanders believes in sharing the wealth. AMD's annual Christmas party, for instance, is something to behold. Last year's was held at the Moscone Center in San Francisco. *The Examiner* said it out-dazzled "even Hollywood's tribute to the Queen of England" earlier in the year. The convention hall was decked with 24,000 giant balloons and hundreds of Christmas trees and poinsettias. The feast, for some 4,000 AMDers and their guests, included 8,000 pounds of seafood, 1 1/2 tons of roast beef, 16,000 pastries and 500 gallons of ice cream. Sanders himself rode into the hall in a sleigh. He was quoted as justifying the huge expense by saying: "The bottom line is people are not just machines. I believe people make the difference. And I believe they will do an extraordinary job if fairly treated."

Not all the local companies in our books are high tech. Viking Freight System's trucks haul freight throughout the West. Unlike most major truckers, Viking drivers don't belong to the Teamsters union. The company has managed to keep out organized labor by paying union scale and offering comparable benefits. Employees are paid bonuses based on their previous month's profits. Bonus checks often range from $15 to $200 a month on top of the regular salaries. In addition, the company offers bonuses for attendance and punctuality. So, for instance, those who are not late or absent more than three times within six months receive bonuses ranging from thirty to forty cents an hour.

The bonus checks are handed out at monthly meetings held at each of the company's thirty truck terminals. These meeting are crucial to Viking's maintaining a small company/family feeling, according to founder and president Richard Bangham. Either Bangham or one of the top corporate officers chairs the monthly gatherings. "Almost anything is discussed, from a driver complaining about a faulty heater on a truck to someone having a problem with collecting health insurance benefits," Bangham explains.

There are other factors besides good communications, good pay, and benefits that attract people. We found that employees are proud to work for companies that make efforts to be active in their communities. San Francisco's Levi Strauss has long exhibited a sense of social responsibility and has been generous in supporting the social and cultural needs of communities in which its plants are located. It also has an unusual plan to encourage employees to be active in their communities through its Social Benefits Program. If an employee participates in a community organization for at least a year, the firm may contribute to the group through the Levi Strauss Foundation. Those who serve the board of directors of the community group can get grants ranging from $500 to $1,500 for the organization.

Levi's social consciousness extends even to its neighbors. The corporate headquarters complex

The new message is that Americans can improve themselves by changing business from a heartless, hierarchical affair to a humanistic, open arena where people are valued and encouraged to be entrepreneurial.

occupies 8.2 acres at the foot of Telegraph Hill, just off the Embarcadero. The five low-slung, red brick buildings (none higher than seven stories) are places in a setting of green lawns, a huge open plaza, streams, waterfall, and wildflowers. It is often called "Levi Strauss University." As a courtesy to residents living in the hills above Levi's Plaza, the window blinds facing west are drawn every day at 4:00 p.m. to keep any glare from interfering with the residents' view of the bay.

Thus the new corporate soul-searchers continue to expand the meaning of business "excellence." We can only wait to see what forms that expansion might take in the coming decades.

1985

THE 100 BEST COMPANIES TO WORK FOR: ONE YEAR LATER

By **Robert Levering** and **Milton Moskowitz**

[CALIFORNIA BUSINESS]

Companies never stand still. They are changing everyday—and since the May 1984 publication of our book *The 100 Best Companies to Work for in America*, we have carefully monitored the advances and setbacks of the companies on our original roster.

We compiled our original roster after crisscrossing the country for two years, visiting companies in 27 different states—from steel mills in Ohio to oil companies in Texas, from an investment bank on Wall Street to a lingerie manufacturer in Los Angeles. All the travel and the hundreds of face-to-face interviews were essential because we discovered that we had ventured into unexplored territory. Despite the explosion of news about business, precious little has been written about the human condition inside corporate walls.

In compiling our roster, we rated companies on five factors: pay, benefits, job security, chance to move up, and ambience. The first four are self

In 1985, Milton and Robert wrote this piece for *California Business*, a regional business publication, describing why they added six new companies — and dropped six others — in the paperback edition of the book. Particularly instructive is their discussion of why Walt Disney did not make the list again.

explanatory; and the fifth was our code word for unique qualities that a company has—styles of working (or playing) that set it apart from all others. We had a rating system that went from one star (at the lowest) to five stars (at the top). But the "measurement" that meant the most to us was an intangible one. We had to hear from the employees themselves that they liked working in these companies. Our bottom line then was the employees' opinion.

Our book apparently struck a chord. Soon after its publication, we were deluged by letters from all parts of the country, most of them approving our choices but some questioning why their company wasn't included, others disputing some of our selections, and a handful congratulating us for not including their companies (two letters from employees of the American Broadcasting Cos. were notable in this latter respect).

We also welcomed the nominations of new candidates. We had specifically invited such nominations in the closing lines of our book. And we received many.

As a result, after New American Library acquired the paperback rights to our book and planned to issue it as a Plume edition in May, 1985, we decided that rather than regulate the hardcover edition, line-for-line and word-for-word, it would make sense to recast it in light of the new information before us. And this is precisely what we did.

So the Plume paperback now showing up in bookstores is not the same book that appeared a year ago. In addition to updating all the facts and figures, we made substantive changes, based on visits we made to new and old companies.

We replaced six of our original choices with new ones. The companies that appeared in the first edition but failed to make the new one are: Borg-

Warner, Walt Disney Productions, Hospital Corps. of America, Merck, Philip Morris, and Ralston Purina. The companies that replaced them are: Federal Express, Fischer-Price Toys, Northrop, Recreational Equipment (REI), Remington Products, and Steelcase.

Of the 100 companies on our original roster, 82 were publicly owned. The six that are being dropped are all companies from this group. Their stock is traded publicly. Of the six additions, two—Federal Express and Northrop—are public companies. Two—Remington Products and Steelcase—are privately owned. One, Fischer-Price, is a subsidiary of Quaker Oats, which was rejected by us. It didn't surprise us that a company could have a different culture from its parent. In our first go-around, Seattle-based Westin Hotel made our list, but not its parent, UAL (which also owns United Airlines); Physio-Control, also in the Seattle area, is also one of the "100 Best," but not its parent, Eli Lilly; and we included Bell Laboratories, but, certainly not its parent, AT&T.

We look for companies that are bringing out the best in their people. And we feel that the best guides to those companies are the employees themselves.

A Businesslike Co-op

Recreational Equipment Inc.—better known as REI—becomes the second cooperative on our list. The first is Linnton Plywood, a workers' cooperative in Oregon. REI is the nation's largest consumer cooperative, selling outdoor clothing and gear in 10 stores and through a mail-order catalog. Sales in 1984 were $94 million. REI is another Seattle-based outfit, but has a strong presence in California, with a Berkeley store that does $12 million a year, plus other stores in Carson and Orange. A new REI was slated to open in early 1985 in Sacramento, and the 12th store will debut in Cupertino in the fall.

REI is the perfect example of the kind of company we looked for. It's not the most sensational payer in the world, but the people who work there get a bang out of being there, happy to be selling topnotch outdoor equipment to backpacking customers who know the difference. The customer should be happy, too. REI members received a cash dividend last year equal to 12.7 percent of what they bought from the cooperative during the year. REI is a cooperative that runs a businesslike show; and it always ends up with a profit on its operations.

Northrop Joins The List

California continues to lead the country, with 18 companies based here. The latest addition to the California contingent is Northrop, the big military contractor with nearly 20,000 employees in Southern California. It was recommended to us as the best aerospace firm to work for. For years the company has had as its slogan: "Northrop is a good place to work." It has even plastered that slogan on recruiting billboards that can be seen near Los Angeles International Airport.

That slogan is a reality, according to both assembly-line workers at Northrop's huge fighter aircraft plant in El Segundo and professional employees at a nearby electronics facility. They talked about non-hierarchical family atmosphere at Northrop—characteristic of many of the best workplaces. Although non-union, Northrop pay wages comparable to its unionized competitors, and it provides an impressive galaxy of benefits. Most notable is a generous savings plan where the company matches money an employee sets aside, up to 8 percent of his or her income. A full 21 percent of Northrop stock is held by the savings plan.

To add deserving companies like Northrop to our list, we had to drop ones we had originally picked. That was much more difficult. We literally agonized over each decision. Our criterion, we should emphasize, was not a falloff in sales or profits. We hold that companies should be good for their people—in bad times and good. Our criterion was a falloff in the humanistic values that had landed them on our roster in the first place.

One California company that we found still passed muster is Olga, the Van Nuys-based women's undergarment manufacturer that was acquired during 1984 by Warnaco. It still retains the family feeling that has been a central part of the company since its founding more than 40 years ago by Jan and Olga Erteszek.

Our criterion for dropping a company was not a falloff in sales or profits, but in the humanistic values that had landed companies on our roster in the first place.

Dropping Disney

Walt Disney was a particularly difficult company to drop. How can you criticize Mickey Mouse? But we were forced to reevaluate Disney because of the 22-day strike at Disneyland in the summer of 1984. A few months after the strike had been settled (with a two-year wage freeze and a different pay scale for new hires), we visited the park. We found out almost immediately that indeed things had changed at Disney.

Unlike our first visit, when the management encouraged us to interview anyone we wished, we were expressly forbidden full access to workers. We did, however, manage to talk with a wide variety of employees. Disneyland still has its attractiveness. Mark Hays, a monorail guide, said, "Where else can you earn over $20,000 a year to smile and be happy? They are paying me to be myself." But, he added, "I think the strike has changed everybody's attitude. It took away the pixie-dust aspect. It makes it seem more like a regular company."

Hays was much less critical than most of the others we talked with. A Frontier-land employee who did not want his name used said Disneyland has "lost the family touch. It emphasizes profits more than the products."

Sue Kemp, a 13-year Disneyland veteran who works at the Candy Palace on Main Street, put it this way. "It used to be fun; now it's just a job. It's no longer one big happy family." One of the strike leaders, Kemp insisted, that "supervisors and the upper management don't care about hourly people." It was a sentiment we heard again and again.

During the strike, one of the placards read: "Disneyland: Walt's Dying Dream." To those who had worked at the park for a number of years, that placard says it all. The firm's new top executives have a big job ahead of them if they want to recapture the part of Walt's dream that has made Disney a special place for the people working there.

Safety Concerns At AMD

A company cannot be a good place to work if employees fear for their own health and safety on the job. That's why we were deeply concerned about the implications of an article in the *San Jose Mercury-News* about the Advanced Micro Devices, a Silicon Valley chip maker. The article detailed charges made by eight former AMD employees who claim disabilities from working in AMD wafer fabrication facilities.

We spent the better part of the week trying to ascertain whether AMD (and other semiconductor manufacturers) pose significant health hazards to their employees. We simply were not persuaded that working at AMD was dangerous to one's health. We found ourselves impressed with the elaborate health and safety programs in place at AMD and the "safety at any cost" attitude of senior company officials. And after talking with employees at random in a company cafeteria, we found that workers had a high regard for the safety training and precautions at AMD. We found it notable that several who had worked at other chip makers considered AMD's safety programs to be superior to others. We will, of course, follow with interest the disposition of the litigation on the eight cases cited in the *Mercury* article. But we don't think it is in our province to consider AMD guilty in the meantime.

Levi's Corporate Responsibility

We also confronted a tough decision in Levi Strauss. The San Francisco-based apparel maker enjoys an almost legendary reputation for corporate social responsibility, one of the features that cinched its selection in the first place. And indeed during 1984 this reputation was confirmed by the winning of two major awards. Levi's captured the Wien Prize given annually by Colombia University business school to recognize a company with an outstanding record in social responsibility. It also received the White House Award for Corporate Volunteerism—the only company so honored in 1984.

On the other hand, the social consciousness symbolized by these awards may be a legacy of a past that is disappearing. Levi Strauss is in the midst of a painful transition from a jeans-dominated company to a diversified house that makes all kinds of clothing, including fashion lines and garments that do not bear the Levi's name. How painful is easy to see from the figures. In fiscal 1984, Levi's profits plunged 79 percent to $41.4 million, its worst showing since 1974. The company closed 20 plants across the United

> The strike has changed everybody's attitude. It took away the pixie-dust aspect. It makes it seem more like a regular company.

States. Five thousand people lost their jobs. How can such a company be a good place to work?

We decided that it is, after talking to numerous Levi people, (including some ex-employees), although we do not give it as high marks as we did in the first edition. The company certainly ranks at the bottom now in job security, and it's now only average in ambience. Oldtimers are certainly bitter over some of the mindless bureaucracy creeping into the company.

We were impressed, though, with the good feelings employees still have about Levi Strauss. It may not be the same euphoria as that in evidence during the late 1970s, but the people working there still look upon their company as one that has high ethical standards and one that will not go back on any long tradition of caring for its employees. This feeling was even manifested in the communities where plants were closed. Levi's put together an exemplary termination package that included a minimum of 13 weeks, maintenance of health insurance for an additional three to sixth months, one week's severance pay for each year of service, and an outplacement office to help people get new jobs. In at least two plants, employees were so pleased with this package that they broke into applause when the terms were announced. And at the Memphis plant, 539 employees who were about to be rendered jobless personally signed a letter thanking the company "for the package you put together for us," adding, " We are proud to have been part of Levi Strauss."

With testimonials of that kind, we found it impossible to eliminate Levi Strauss from our roster. It may be going through a rough time, but it still stands well above the great mass of companies in the nation as a nourishing workplace.

Our standards have remained the same. Above all, we look for the special feeling that exists where management and employees work together rather than square off in "we vs. them" confrontations. We look for companies that are bringing out the best in their people. And we feel that the best guides to those companies are the employees themselves.

1988

WHAT MAKES SOME EMPLOYERS SO GOOD — AND MOST SO BAD

By **Robert Levering**

[RANDOM HOUSE]

A Great Place to Work: What makes some employers so good and most so bad, laid the bedrock of the Great Place to Work® Intitute's work. In the introduction, Robert details the methodology and offers a strong plea for the social significance of great workplaces. This notion is reflected in the Institute's vision statement composed by Robert and cofounder Amy Lyman soon after they founded the company: "Building a better society by helping companies transform their workplaces."

Nearly six years ago, I started interviewing employees in their offices, factories, and cafeterias for the book *The 100 Best Companies to Work for in America*. As the book's title suggests, my coauthors, Milton Moskowitz and Michael Katz, and I sought to identify the best employers of the land. In all, we visited about 125 companies in 30 states and talked with hundreds and hundreds of employees about their workplaces. When we first started, we weren't sure what we should find. My impression, based on more than a decade as a business and labor journalist, was that most companies are pretty lousy to work for. I assumed that working for a company, especially a large one, implies a Faustian bargain— security and/or money for a piece of your soul. That conviction came early in life, when overhearing my father talk about work life at a major airline, where he worked for forty years. My own work experiences had further soured me on the possibilities of an uplifting working environment.

My longest employment (six years) had been with a weekly newspaper in San Francisco. Employee turnover there was almost 100 percent a year. At one point, the entire nonmanagerial staff went out on strike over the working conditions and lack of job security. In the end, I was fired for objecting to another employee's being terminated for refusing to do more work for less pay.

Several of my friends or acquaintances have reported similar—or worse—encounters with their employers. Those stories have been the exception. More typical have been the off-hand comments with which people indicate a feeling of alienation at work. Most people I've known have eventually found themselves making unpleasant compromises, ones that affect their feelings of self-worth. It's seen as part of the job.

Many social observers have reinforced these subjective impressions. In his bestseller *Working*, Studs Terkel relates interview with more than a hundred people talking about the working careers. They paint a picture of a workplace full of "daily humiliations." What's especially depressing is that most of Terkel's people say they want to do a good job; they want to feel pride in their work. But such yearnings rarely can be fulfilled in the contemporary American workplace.

Another keen social commentator, pollster Daniel Yankelovich, has gathered some impressive statistical evidence showing that if anything, the workplace is getting worse. In a survey conducted in the late 1960s, Yankelovich found that more than half the respondents felt they got personal fulfillment from their job; by 1980 when the same question was asked in another survey, only 27 percent were able to say that their job turned them on. Despite these figures, Yankelovich, like Studs Terkel, discovered that most Americans still want to do a good job. Over half of all working

When there's a mismatch between what most of us want to do during our working hours and what we are allowed to do in our workplace, the discrepancy translates to a profound feeling of alienation.

Americans still endorse the work ethic, agreeing with the statement "I have an inner need to do the very best job possible, regardless of pay." There's a mismatch, then, between what most of us want to do during our working hours and what we are allowed to do in our workplace. This discrepancy translates, on a personal level, to a profound feeling of alienation. Socially, it represents a tragic waste of human energy.

I was surprised, therefore, when our research for *The 100 Best Companies to Work for in America* led us to some really terrific places to work— where the experience of work was fulfilling rather than alienating. Especially convincing were the positive comments made by people whom you would not expect to be singing praises of their employer—secretaries at Goldman Sachs in New York City, steelworkers in a Nucor mill in Utah, electronics assembly-line workers at Tektronix in Oregon, insurance clerks at Northwestern Mutual Life in Wisconsin. Employees talk about a "people orientation" and sense of community (sometimes called "family") at especially good workplaces.

To examine the phenomenon of good workplaces for this book, I have relied first and foremost on interviews with employees. Their observations form the backbone of the book. It is their experience at work that this book aims to explain.

After completing *The 100 Best Companies to Work for in America*, I revisited twenty especially good workplaces (the best of the best, if you will). In addition to further interviews with lower-level employees, I made a point to talk with the top officers and, where possible, the founders. I wanted to find out why and how they thought their companies had become great places to work. Among the people whose insights I obtained were top executives and/or founders of the following companies: Advanced Micro Devices; Delta Air

Lines; Electro Scientific; Federal Express; Goldman Sachs; W.L. Gore; Hallmark Cards; Hewlett-Packard; Marion Labs; 3M; J.P. Morgan; Northwestern Mutual Life; Olga; Pitney Bowes; Preston Trucking; Publix Super Markets; Quad/Graphics; ROLM; Tandem Computers; and Tektronix. The fifty transcribed interviews that resulted and the follow-up visits to those companies provide much of the material presented in this book. Nearly half of this book, in fact, is devoted to detailed descriptions and analyses of the workplace practices at seven of these firms.

To place the phenomenon of good workplace into a broader context, I have read widely about workplace and work-related issues. This has included more than three hundred volumes of management theory, industrial psychology and sociology, economic history, and social and moral philosophy, as well as more than a thousand articles from newspapers, magazines, and professional journals about contemporary workplace issues.

Much of this reading has concentrated on one simple question: Why are most workplaces so bad? Part of the answer can be found by examining the roots of American management styles, especially the ideas of influential management thinkers. It's not enough to criticize others, however. So this book also puts forward an alternative analysis of the workplace that may have some relevance to those interested in a nonmanipulative approach to managing.

It is my hope that the information and analyses in this book can assist those with practical concerns. With an awareness of what makes for a good employer, job seekers can have a better idea of what to look for in a workplace. They would know which questions o ask and which types of employers to avoid. Those with jobs could get some notions about how to improve their own working situations. And more important, having a clearer idea of the characteristics of a good workplace can help shed light on the daily experience of working for an organization. It can help people get a fix on what is possible to expect from their workplace.

This exercise may also be of great help to well-meaning employers. If they can be shown what makes an organization a Great Place to Work®, they might be able to recreate the conditions. Or at least make a stab at it. They would have some tools for analyzing what is wrong with their own workplace.

No discussion of this phenomenon would be complete without an attempt to spell out some of the social implications inherent in the notion of a great workplace. This is, after all, a nation of employees. Just as most Americans consider themselves middle class, most also think of themselves as employees. Indeed, less than 10 percent of the U.S. work force is self-employed. The rest work for companies, government agencies, or nonprofit concerns. So the quality of life within organizations not only has a major impact on each of us personally but on the society as a whole. How we treat each other during our working hours defines what kind of society we have.

Good workplaces provide beacons in a fog of mediocrity and insensitivity. They offer a different version from the dog-eat-dog, each-man-for-himself, free-the-entrepreneur philosophy that enjoys widespread currency today. A great workplace is one where everyone, employees and management, is pulling together. It makes the workers feel better. It makes the managers feel better about the roles they play. And it helps society in general. In short, the attitudes implicit in this volume can do much to revitalize, and possible even transform, American society.

1993

THE 100 BEST COMPANIES TO WORK FOR IN AMERICA (SECOND EDITION)

By **Robert Levering** and Milton Moskowitz

[DOUBLEDAY]

Found in all parts of the country and in all types of industry, [these 100 companies] represent a signal departure from the hierarchical, authoritarian workplace that has prevailed for so long in American business. But they are also exceptional rather than typical. They stand out because they are so different. Most companies still offer dreadful work environment. This is true today, just as it was true in 1984 when we originally identified and described the nation's bet workplaces in the first edition of *The 100 Best Companies to Work For in America.*

In our new search to find companies with exceptional workplaces, we have reached conclusions that run counter to much of the current wisdom about the American workplace. We found that even as the workplace has become traumatized by layoffs, job burnout, and shifting of more health insurance costs to the employee, the very best workplace have become better.

In this excerpt from the introduction of the 1993 edition of the 100 Best book, Robert and Milton describe how the American workplace had changed during the previous decade. As you will see, they found numerous positive developments, including the impact of the quality movement and the influx of women into the workforce.

There were many more viable candidates for this book than for our list a decade ago. We had more than 400 nominations to begin with, more than double the last time. The 100 companies profiled in this book may account for only a small fraction of the total U.S. work force, but as exemplars they represent a growing force. They are magnets for people looking for meaningful work. They are models for companies trying to get it right. In those two important senses, they may herald the future.

Why are there better workplaces today—and more of them? One reason is adversity, which often brings out the best in people—and companies. American companies have been whipsawed in an increasingly competitive global environment. The quality of products turned out by American companies has been questioned, even held up to scorn. It wasn't until recent years that the perception sunk in that poor products may have something to do with bad workplaces, where employees were abused or ignored and considered little more than a cost of doing business. We have seen company after company where the quality movement has taken hold, which is often a key ingredient in the transition to a better workplace. (The quality movement is no panacea, however, as we have also seen workplaces that have changed little or have gotten worse after the introduction of quality processes.) Other factors which have contributed to an improvement in the quality of the workplace have been advancement of women and minorities into management ranks (they bring a fresh perspective to the work at hand), incorporation of environmental needs (workers need to breathe fresh air, too), and a greater health consciousness (reflected in gleaming fitness centers and health education programs). It's difficult to believe that it has taken so long, but at last we see companies which have actually posted it as a goal to become a good workplace.

That kind of attitude was simply not in place in the early 1980s when we set out on our mission to find exceptional workplaces.

We have noted positive changes in five key areas:

More employee participation. A rarity in the early 1980s, genuine employee involvement in decision-making about their job is a reality among the companies in this book. Ironically, this change has often occurred because of layoffs. With fewer supervisors, many companies have been forced to reorganize how work is accomplished. In some cases, the quality movement—the current management buzzword—has provided specific techniques for increasing employee participation.

More sensitivity to work/family issues. Many of the companies in this book have made tremendous strides towards dealing with the problems of working mothers and fathers, offering a variety of childcare options and flexible work schedules.

More two-way communication. Accessibility of the top executives is much more common today than in the early 1980s. Even many large firms offer employees opportunities to ask questions—and get answers—directly from their CEOs.

More sharing of the wealth. Profit-sharing and gain-sharing programs have increased dramatically, as have ESOPs (employee stock ownership plans). Some companies are even extending stock options, typically reserved for a handful of top executives, to everyone in the ranks.

More fun. Finally we saw many more companies where having fun seems to be part of the corporate mission. Fun is not inconsistent with operating a serious, profit-making business. Watch out for companies where there is no sense of humor.

There is a more fundamental characteristic of the new workplace style than quality teams, flextime, or profit-sharing plans. In the best workplace, employees trust their managers, and the managers trust their employees. The trust is reflected in numerous ways: no time clocks, meetings where employees have a chance to register their concerns, job posting (so that employees have first crack at openings), constant training (so that employees can learn new skills), and employee committees empowered to make changes in policies, recommend new pay rates, or allocate the corporate charity dollars. Trust, in the workplace, simply means that employees are treated as partners and recognized as having something to contribute beyond brawn or manual dexterity or strong legs and arms.

There is more trust today because the authoritarian workstyle that has long been the standard operating procedure in American business has failed. It hasn't worked for employees, and it hasn't worked for employers. And that failure is at the root of the poor performance of American companies and the massive layoffs of the late 1980s and early 1990s. When management becomes disconnected from the people who work in the company, it becomes easy to fire them. And when workers are disconnected from what they are doing, it comes easy for them not to care about the product or service they're delivering.

This failure has impelled companies to look for other options. It is our hope that by providing these concrete examples, employees and employers alike will see that this new workstyle is not only possible but realistic and practical. This is true whether your company is big or small, old or young, high-tech or no-tech. The new workstyle reflected in this book may be a harbinger of the American workplace in the next century.

1997

THE **FIRST** LIST

By **José Tolovi Jr.**

[EXAME]

Everybody found it a great idea. Whenever we showed the Great Place to Work® model, everybody agreed it was clear and very easy to understand. However, the presentation was not enough to convince companies to participate in getting on a list that, to be really honest, nobody understood very well. People knew about the other lists of the biggest companies that have been published for years by a number of newspapers and magazines worldwide. Those lists were easy to understand: Revenue and business performance.

But a list that takes into account the employees' opinion, and then the elaborate system of ranking ... this was something abstract and somewhat fearful: "Should I take the risk? I, the company's CEO, and my human resource director find our company great, but do my employees think so? What if we participate and fail to make the list?"

Many people assume that *Fortune* in the United States published the first of the Institute's many annual magazine lists of Best Workplaces. Not so. The first such list was published in Brazil in 1997, several months before the first one appeared in *Fortune*. In this retrospective piece written in 2008, José Tolovi Jr. recounts the story behind that first list. Tolovi serves as global CEO for Great Place to Work®.

Questions like these crossed the minds of the executives, CEOs, and shareholders of the companies invited to presentations. The point of reference we had was Robert Levering's book, *The 100 Best Companies to Work for in America*, a bestseller published in 1984. This was a good reference, but there were magazines or newspapers then, supporting the list. Well, after a marathon of phone calls and personal contacts, carried out by Exame magazine's editor, we were finally able to convince 78 companies to participate in our evaluation.

Almost all of these companies decided to participate based on the personal credibility of those involved in the project. At that time, the Great Place to Work® Institute had been founded only four years earlier, and only operated in the United States. We put the list together and published it in October 1997 as a special edition with The 30 Best Companies to Work for in Brazil. The magazine *Fortune* would publish the first American 100 Best Companies to Work for list in January 1998.

Our first list had a very good response. The edition was sold out in the newsstands. Young people that were looking for their first job, or a job offering them better opportunities bought all the copies and started to send their résumés to the companies in the list. The qualifying companies started to understand how deeply effective the list was and how important it could be for their businesses. Other companies started to ask themselves why they were not on that list and what they should do to be part of it. And, from that first year on, the number of companies interested in competing with other companies and being part of our lists has continuously increased, not only in Brazil and the United States, but also in Portugal, then in Chile, Denmark, the United Kingdom, and Italy. Soon after, Mexico, Argentina, and Korea joined, and today there are a total of 30 countries with 10 other prospective ones in the next years, where companies compete to be on lists of best workplaces.

We have always conducted our lists, in every country, using the same methodology that was developed by Robert Levering. It is important to highlight how this methodology was developed: Interviews with employees from numerous companies were conducted, and the statements that people made when referring to good work environments were collected. Those statements were homogenized, classified, and clustered in sets, that led to dimensions that measured Trust, Pride, and Camaraderie. Because the Trust set was the most significant, in terms of number of the employees' statements, this dimension was divided into Credibility, Respect, and Fairness. Today, therefore, we evaluate the employees' opinion worldwide through a survey that contains approximately 12 statements for each dimension: Credibility, Respect, Fairness, Pride, and Camaraderie, which we named the GPTW® Trust Index©. Employees answer whether they believe that each statement is true or not for their company. As reported, the Great Place to Work® model is based on the observations of people in their everyday life at work. This is not a conceptual or theoretical model, but rather a pragmatic model that is continuously reevaluated, as we survey over 3,000 companies each year.

In addition to the survey with employees, we also conduct a survey with the companies in order to understand how they manage people and what they do to maintain an atmosphere of trust. Recently, Robert Levering brought us one more view in understanding the best work environments. By analyzing year by year the practices of the Best Companies, Robert formulated what we call "The 9 Cultural Practices of the Best Companies to Work for." These are the nine people-management areas, which the Best Companies consistently perform well in to reach incredible results. These areas are the following: Select and welcome new employees; Inspire people for the company's excellence and values; Always say the truth; Listen to people with genuine interest; Thank the collaborators' good performance and dedication; Empower employees, both professionally and personally; Take care of people as individuals; Celebrate the corporate and personal victories; and Share the company's internal and external gains. The analysis of these practices, using our instrument, the GPTW® Culture Audit©, allows us to identify needs and strengths of companies and support the transformations that they want to accomplish in their work environment.

Eleven years have passed, and during that period we witnessed how companies have evolved. The human resources director of a company that always makes the Brazilian lists disclosed to us that, thanks to the movement created by the publication of the lists and the Institute's work, the human resources area has become a subject of interest for the company's executive board of directors. I believe this is happening to many organizations, prompting the continued selection of the best companies in more and more countries and with increasingly significant lists. This is a hard work, implying high responsibility, that occurs every single day somewhere in the world, and, I am sure, we are thereby contributing to the development of better, healthier, more sustainable companies, and as a result, to the construction of a better, more fair society.

2007

WE **LOVE OUR JOBS.**
JUST ASK US.

By **Milton Moskowitz**

[THE NEW YORK TIMES]

Twenty-five years ago, I started to work on a book whose optimistic title was *The 100 Best Companies to Work for in America*. I say optimistic because my writing partner, Robert Levering, and I weren't sure we could find 100 worthy workplaces.

We assembled a list of 350 people and wrote all of them, requesting benefits booklets, corporate histories, and any other information about their practices. But after a slogging through these materials, we realized that we were looking at a very dull book.

We decided that the only way to salvage the project was to hit the road and interview a range of employees to find out what they thought of their employers. We pared our candidates list to 135 and, splitting up, crisscrossed the country for more than a year visiting all of these companies, from a textile mill in South Carolina to a plywood co-op in Oregon, from banks on Wall Street to oil drillers in Texas.

Milton wrote this retrospective piece for *The New York Times* in 2007. He describes the journey that he and Robert Levering have been on since they started researching the first book *The 100 Best Companies to Work for in America*. Milton has been a professional business journalist for nearly 60 years.

We talked to dozens of employees and came away with a rich lode of anecdotes. We had found the key to determining a good workplace: ask the people who work there.

When our book first appeared, in May 1984, it became a best seller. We now do the survey annually for *Fortune* magazine, although we no longer need to visit candidate companies personally. We now put a 57-question survey into the hands of 400 randomly selected employees at each company. But the principle remains the same: employees are, in effect, voting their companies onto the list. Last year we fielded replies from 105,000 employees at 446 companies with at least 1,000 employees.

As a result of our surveys, people are always asking me what makes for a good workplace. Early on, Robert and I came up with this definition: A good workplace is one where management trusts the employees and where employees trust the management.

Of course, there's more to it than that. We do evaluate companies on various attributes—communication, training, recognition and rewards, pay and benefits, fairness, camaraderie, celebrations. But our primary measuring rod is the employee response to the survey, including voluntary comments.

Employees enter yes-or-no responses as to whether they agree with statements like these: "I feel I get a fair share of the profits of this organization," "I am proud to tell others I work here," and "There is a minimum of politicking and backstabbing here."

A not-so-surprising lesson is that it takes more than high pay and lavish benefits to make a work force happy. Employees tell us how important it is to work for a company whose culture embraces fairness, teamwork, education, fun, and contributions to society. And they thrive on being engaged in the company's mission.

Continental Airlines, for example surged onto our list after Gordon M. Bethune, the chief executive, began handing out $65 monthly bonuses to everybody when the airline ranked among the top five in on-time arrivals. Then he upped the ante, giving every employee $100 when Continental ranked No. 1 in on-time arrivals.

Employees at the biotech firm **Genentech** say they are proud to work for a company that has come up with three drugs that are effective against cancer.

Care providers at **Bright Horizons Family Solutions**, which runs more than 500 child care centers at work sites across the country, do not receive rich pay packages—teachers make $25,000 a year—but here is what some of its employees say about working there:

"I have made friends that will last for a lifetime."

"We care passionately about what we do."

I do not want to leave the impression that pay and benefits are unimportant. The companies on our list offer spectacular benefits. As most employees are being asked to shoulder more of their health insurance bills, 16 companies on our current list pay 100 percent of the health insurance premium.'

Google, in the No. 1 position on the current list, has an array of mind-boggling benefits, including a $5,000 subsidy for buying a hybrid car, free on-site washers and dryers, a $500 voucher for takeout food after the birth of a child, an annual all-expenses-paid ski trip, free Wi-Fi-equipped shuttles to pick up and drop off employees, and 17 restaurants with free food.

Perhaps the most memorable benefits I can recall come from **Kingston Technology**, a maker of company memory devices in Fountain Valley, Calif. Kingston was founded by two Taiwanese immigrants, John Tu and David Sun, who sold 80 percent of the company in 1996 to SoftBank of Japan for $1.5 billion. They felt that it was only right to share the proceeds with their employees. So they awarded bonuses that averaged out to $130,000 for each of the 550 workers.

Does sharing the wealth with employees pay off? Well, since the bonuses, Kingston's sales have nearly tripled, to $3.8 billion, and its work force has increased sixfold, to 3,300. And Mr. Sun and Mr. Tu are again 100 percent owners of the company. In 1999, after SoftBank had trouble digesting the acquisition, they bought back the 80 percent stake for $450 million. The stage is set for a second round of lightning. Kingston is now looking for hardware and software engineers and sales representatives.

IMPORTANCE OF
TRUST

2004

EVEN A **PRISON** CAN BE A GREAT **WORKPLACE**

By **Robert Levering**

[CORRECTIONS MAGAZINE]

Every year, Fortune magazine publishes a list of the *"100 Best Companies to Work for"*. It is one of the magazine's most popular issues of the year. People love to read about potential employers where the grass may be greener. And managers find they can pick up tips that they might be able to apply to their organizations to make them better places to work.

To date, none of the organizations on the *Fortune* list has been a correctional facility. But that does not mean that a correctional facility could not make a list of the nation's best employers. In fact, as the coauthor of the *Fortune* list and someone who has specialized in reporting on great workplaces for over 20 years, I have concluded that any organization in any industry — whether privately held, nonprofit or governmental agency — can become an exemplary employer.

We have had almost every imaginable type of organization on this list — from Wall Street investment houses and mass market retailers to small nonprofit hospitals and consulting firms. (In

Written for a professional magazine for prison administrators and staff, this article explains why it is important for the management of any organization to create a great workplace environment. Robert also suggests a few specific ways in which managers can build trust in any workplace.

Denmark, one of two dozen other countries where my Institute conducts similar Best Workplaces surveys, the national Department of Justice was named to the list of the best employers in that country.) The main variable is the attitude and behavior of the management rather than the type of organization. How the management relates to its employees is what makes the difference.

Let me step back a minute and explain why this is an important issue for corrections officials to consider before I talk more specifically about the definition of a Great Place to Work® and discuss how such an environment is created.

The most obvious reason is that everybody, whether senior manager or frontline employee, would prefer to work in a good working environment. Since most of us spend most of our waking hours at work, the quality of the work experience has a big impact on our lives. Everybody wants to look forward to going to work in the morning. And nobody enjoys coming home from work feeling frustrated and discouraged from one's experiences at work.

But there is more than quality of life involved with this issue. The quality of the workplace impacts directly on issues of customer service and productivity. The connection to customer service has been shown in numerous studies. A famous study in the *Harvard Business Review* several years ago showed that an increase in employee satisfaction at a store resulted in an increase in customer satisfaction which in turn resulted in higher profitability for the store. There have been similar studies in the hospital industry, showing that improvements in workplace environments result in better patient satisfaction.

We have seen extremely strong evidence of the same phenomenon from our work in surveying the best workplaces. The companies on our lists both in the U.S. and in the U.K., Brazil, and other countries have far outperformed the stock indices. While this data applies most directly to for-profit enterprises, the conclusions are relevant to the corrections industry as well. As we have seen, the best workplaces tend to have higher productivity and profitability as well as better customer satisfaction. Among the obvious reasons for this result is that the best workplaces typically have much lower staff turnover than their competitors. (In a study we conducted in 2001 that was published in *Fortune*, the "100 Best" companies had an average staff turnover that was 50 percent lower than that of their competitors.) High staff turnover is very costly to any enterprise, whether a for-profit corporation or governmental agency because of the increased costs associated with recruiting and training new staff. Similarly, organizations with reputations as good employers also tend to attract the high quality staff. The better the quality of the staff, the better able the staff will be in performing their duties.

A less tangible, though equally important, reason why organizations with great workplaces deliver better service and products is employee morale. Better morale translates into environments where employees are more likely to provide better service. This, too, has obvious parallels to the corrections industry where employee morale is extremely important in terms of maintaining discipline.

Before going to the subject of how a great workplace is created, we need to be clear about what we are talking about. I define a Great Place to Work® as one where employees trust the people they work for, have pride in what they do, and enjoy the people they work with. This definition is based on the hundreds of interviews

There is more than quality of life involved: the quality of the workplace impacts directly on issues of customer service and productivity.

I conducted in the 1980s for the first edition of my book, *The 100 Best Companies to Work for in America* (coauthored with Milton Moskowitz). From those interviews I observed that employees insisted that the most important factor that distinguished their workplaces was a very high level of trust between the employees and the management.

What do employees of great workplaces mean by "trust"? There are three aspects of trust — credibility, respect and fairness. The first is **CREDIBILITY** — what employees think about the management's believability, competence, and integrity. It all begins with whether you can believe what someone tells you. If management's word cannot be taken to be true, trust is impossible. At great workplaces, management goes out of its way to be believable by doing the following:

Sharing information broadly

The Container Store, a Dallas-based retailer that was Number 1 on the *Fortune* "100 Best" list in 2000 and 2001, makes it a point to share information about such matters as daily sales results from each store with all of the employees.

Accessibility to employees

We have found that even at large companies, like Continental Airlines or Procter and Gamble, the top executives go to great lengths to meet with ordinary employees whenever possible. In smaller companies, this is often done in more informal ways, such as having lunch in the employee cafeterias. At East Alabama Medical Center, a county-run facility, the CEO makes it a point to visit every ward of the hospital every day. Frequently these companies have an open-door policy. The point is that top managers make sure that people within the organization see them as fellow human beings rather than figures living in an ivory tower. To trust someone, you need to feel you have some sense of what kind of person they are—whether they are trustworthy. That can't be done unless you have been able to size them up for yourself.

Willingness to answer hard questions

It is not enough to share information and be personally accessible. Leaders of the best workplaces also realize that they need to face difficult questions from their employees. Thus, we have seen a myriad of mechanisms to insure that employees have regular opportunities to get straight answers to difficult questions. In the past few years, informal breakfasts of randomly selected employees with the CEO have become common. At J.M. Smucker, the jelly and jam maker, Number 1 on our 2004 *Fortune* "100 Best" list, the CEO and president conduct quarterly town hall meetings at each of their sites throughout the country where they answer any question that is asked of them. If they cannot give an answer immediately, they make certain that each of the questions is answered through a company newsletter later. The key point is that management makes itself available for genuine dialogue with employees. Instead of concentrating on one-way, top-down communication, the emphasis on two-way communication is what distinguishes the best employers.

Delivering on promises

Closely related to the question of believability is that of integrity. You don't believe someone, no matter how good they are in their

Instead of concentrating on one-way, top-down communication, the emphasis on two-way communication is what distinguishes the best employers.

communications skills, unless they follow through on what they say they are going to do. Several years ago, our Institute was asked to do a workplace assessment of a large division of a major telecommunications company. A very charismatic leader who was an excellent communicator ran the division. He shared information with everyone, was accessible, and held regular question-and-answer conferences with the staff. But in our assessment we discovered that the staff did not trust him because he was too nice. When people would come in to his office, he would invariably make commitments or implied promises. The employee would leave the office and feel good about the situation and about the executive, in the short run. But the problem was that sometimes he delivered on his promises and sometimes he did not. As a result, people did not know whether his word was any good. They liked him but didn't trust him. We recommended that he follow a simple discipline: After every meeting, to make a list of every promise that he had made. In a matter of weeks, his list became shorter and shorter—and the level of trust within the division began to grow.

The second major aspect of trust relates to what employees think management thinks about them. While the first aspect of trust revolves around how employees perceive the management's credibility, it is equally important that employees feel that the management shows them **RESPECT**. In other words, I can feel that you have a high degree of credibility—you're believable and demonstrate competence and integrity. But I must also feel that you have my best interests at heart for me to genuinely extend my trust to you. This is done in two main ways:

Showing recognition and appreciation

We have found that the best employers make a special effort to say "thank you" in a variety of ways to employees. It becomes part of the fabric of daily existence in these companies. L.L. Bean, a mail-order catalogue retailer in the U.S., has developed a particularly good method for singling out those who deserve special recognition. A committee of employees selects some five workers a year from dozens of employee nominations for an award called "Bean's Best." The committee then organizes special celebrations complete with celebratory horns and champagne at the winners' own work sites.

Demonstrating personal concern. Respect is also a very personal matter

To select companies for our lists, we distribute to several hundred randomly selected employees at each firm an employee survey called the Great Place to Work® Trust Index©. Based on a correlation study of the results of the Trust Index©, we found the following statement to be the most significant: "Management shows a sincere interest in me as a person, not just an employee." In particular, people are especially concerned with how they will be treated when faced with a personal event of significance—an illness, a death in the family, births, and so on. The best employers find ways to show genuine concern in those circumstances.

Becoming a great workplace may not be rocket science. But it does require paying attention to these basic issues.

2005

DEUTSCHLANDS BESTE ARBEITGEBER

By **Frank Hauser**, **Tobias Schmidtner**
Introduction by **Robert Levering**

Germany has the largest Institute affiliates in terms of revenues and has developed a close relationship with the German Ministry of Labour and Social Affairs for whom the Institute conducted a major workplace study involving 314 companies. In 2008 Frank Hauser, CEO of Great Place to Work® Germany and Tobias Schmidtner, Senior Project Manager, wrote a book describing the companies on the list that year. They asked Robert Levering to write the introduction explaining the importance of trust in the workplace.

For more than 20 years, our Institute has surveyed more than a million employees in well over 10,000 different companies throughout the world. We have discovered that three factors are especially relevant in the creation of trust. First, management must develop good two-way communications with employees. They must be accessible and willing to answer questions directly and honestly. Just as nothing erodes trust more quickly than secrecy, nothing builds it more quickly than open communications. Second, management needs to show respect for employees both as professionals (especially by extending good training and development opportunities) and as individuals with personal lives. In particular, it's important for the company to provide employees with unique and special benefits that meet the personal needs of their employees, such as policies that help employees balance their work and family obligations. And finally, management must make sure that the rewards, both financial and nonfinancial forms of recognition, are distributed equitably. Fairness is an important cornerstone of a great workplace.

We have also discovered that being a great workplace has another important benefit: They typically outperform their competitors in terms of profitability and productivity. For instance, a 2005 study by a Wall Street investment service revealed that an investor who had created a portfolio of stocks of the *"100 Best Companies to Work for"* companies in 1997 that we selected when we started the list with *Fortune* magazine would have beaten a comparable stock market index by more than a factor of four. Similar studies have shown comparable results of best workplaces in the UK and Brazil. Indeed, we have seen similar results every time we have produced our lists over the past 20 years.

To understand why this is true we need only recall that the basic ingredient of a great workplace is trust. When a company has a high level of trust, people are more willing to cooperate with the management — and with each other — than in environments with lower levels of trust. At the same time, there is less resistance to change because employees are more willing to accept the leadership of a management in which they have confidence. Innovation also thrives in a high-trust environment because people are more willing to take risks if they trust the people they are working for and with.

At the same time, great workplaces also acquire reputations as good employers in their industries and in their communities. So they usually have many more job applicants than companies without such reputations. As a result, the best workplaces can select the very best workers from a larger pool of applicants than their competitors. Not only do the best workplaces attract the best workers, but they keep them longer because voluntary staff turnover is typically much lower in the best workplaces. (One study our Institute conducted for *Fortune* revealed that the voluntary staff turnover rate was about 50 percent less among the "100 Best."). Lower staff turnover means lower recruitment costs, lower training costs and a more experienced staff—all of which translates into higher productivity and profitability.

Can any company become a great workplace? Our research answers this question with a resounding yes. We have seen examples of world-class workplaces in every country and in every industry. The most important factor is the commitment of the senior management to create a superior workplace environment.

Unfortunately, having a committed senior management is not enough. Running a business is complicated, and the relationship with employees is only one of many competing priorities for senior leadership of any organization. That is where articles and books like *Deutschlands Beste Arbeitgeber* can play an important role. For it is in reading the stories contained in books like this that Germany's corporate leaders can see what is possible. They can see how their peers and others facing similar challenges have created great workplaces—companies that are not only successful businesses but ones that provide a great environment for those who make the business possible the employees.

2003

LEADERSHIP IN A GREAT WORKPLACE

By **Robert Levering**

Q: For the management of a company, how do you think the leadership is important?

A: Leaders obviously make the important business decisions, but they also help determine the quality of the relationships with employees. I define a Great Place to Work® as one where employees trust the management, have pride in their work, and enjoy the people they work with. So, leaders who act in ways that are trustworthy can actually help to create a great workplace.

Q: To intensify the GPTW model within the team or company, what do you think the most important thing is?

A: Improving communications within the company. To create a high level of trust between management and employees, leaders must be sure that employees are fully informed about what is going on in the company and have their questions answered. This implies good two-way

In this interview for a Brazilian magazine, Robert Levering describes the role of a leader in a great workplace and cites several exemplary leaders.

communications. In the best workplaces, this is done in a variety of ways, with large and small meetings where questions are encouraged, through email, with newsletters. The important point is for leaders to remain accessible to employees.

Q: How can you define the Great Place to Work® Leadership?

A. Leadership in a GPTW focuses on increasing the level of trust.

Q: Can you introduce us to some great leaders you've met ?

A: Fred Smith, the founder and CEO of FedEx, who saw combat with the U.S. Marines during the Vietnam War. That experience convinced him that it's crucial for the company to give every employee, especially those with the lowest-level jobs, the opportunity to express their dissatisfactions with management decisions. So FedEx does an annual employee survey called Survey-Feedback-Action where each work group meets to discuss the results of the survey and develops a plan for improvement for the next year.

Luiza Helena Trajano, CEO of Magazine Luiza, a retail chain in Brazil with 250 stores and 7,500 employees, is a charismatic leader with an extraordinary sense of humor. She loves to tell amusing stories that frequently show her sympathy with the ordinary employee. She also feels that it's important for employees to feel like they are special, and she has developed a number of unusual ways of showing appreciation, including using photos of individual employees in advertising billboards.

Franck Riboud, CEO of Danone, the French multinational food, bottled water, and biscuit giant, is a quiet, unassuming man who rides a motor scooter to the office in Paris. He believes that companies have a special responsibility to their local communities. When Danone was forced to close down a factory in Spain, for instance, it worked with government officials to bring in other companies from other industries that hired the former Danone workers.

Kim Soon Taek, CEO of Samsung SDI, places a high value on personal relationships with employees. Despite his extremely busy schedule, he makes time to write personal notes to managers expressing his appreciation for the work they do for the organization.

2006

THE CARE AND NURTURING OF EMPLOYEES

By **Robert Levering**

[PEQUEÑAS EMPRESAS & GRANDES NEGOCIOS]

What role can human resource professionals play in creating a great place to work? In this interview, Robert Levering answers questions commonly asked by HR professionals on this subject.

Q: When a company has an efficient human resource management, what is the influence on business goals?

A: There is considerable evidence that great places to work are more profitable and/or productive than their competitors. One reason for these results is that employees tend to remain in the best workplaces longer than at other firms. In the United States, employee turnover rates were 50 percent less among the *Fortune* "100 Best" companies than their competitors. Staff turnover is expensive because the company needs to hire, train, and orient new employees. At the same time, good management practices toward employees increase productivity in other ways as well. Employees cooperate with each other and with the management better when there is a high level of trust in the working environment.

Q: What has changed in the way of human capital management?

A: Regarding the practical issues of human resources, in the past decade there has been a dramatic improvement in certain areas, such as work-family programs, more flexible work hours, and new benefits to help working mothers. But the biggest change has been in the attitudes of senior executives toward human-resource issues. Senior managers are beginning to see that it is crucial for the success of the business to develop a strategy that incorporates their practices toward people. A good example of this is Accor Brasil. Senior leaders there have developed a business strategy with the slogan "People-Service-Profit." By that they mean that the management's job is to create a great working environment for the people. The employees then will provide better service to their customers. That then will produce better business results. This slogan represents the new attitude among many progressive business leaders who realize that the workplace culture is crucial to the success of the enterprise.

Q: To have an efficient human resource management, is it necessary to offer a lot of benefits? Beyond these, what can a company do to have a good human resource management?

A: No, more benefits do not necessarily make for a better workplace culture. In general, we have discovered that the most crucial issues are related to three other areas—how well management communicates with people, how well they thank people for doing a good job, and how they show that they truly care about people as people, not just employees. None of these factors do involve spending more money.

They require management to spend more time in their relationships with employees. And this is something that must be done throughout the organization, not just at the senior management level nor just at the front-line supervisory level. It is the job of everyone in management to be good communicators with employees. And it is in speaking honestly, listening carefully, and in praising frequently that makes the difference.

Q: If offering greater benefits does not make a big difference in creating a great workplace, what does?

A: With regard to benefits themselves, what is important is how the benefits are given to employees rather than *how* expensive they are. At the best workplaces, the management goes to great lengths to offer benefits that seem to be unique and distinctive as well as fitting the culture. This is something that small companies can do as well as big ones. For instance, two companies can offer a profit-sharing program to employees. At one company, they may offer it in such a way that it appears to employees to be no more than another form of compensation. But at the better workplace, the same amount of profit-sharing can be provided to employees in such a way that it seems like it is a reward for everyone working together cooperatively. In both cases, it is the same amount of money, but in the second case, it will have a much better effect on the workplace culture.

2007

TRUST, NOT **HAPPINESS**, IS KEY TO WORKPLACE **SUCCESS**

By **Robert Levering**

[ÉPOCA]

Happy workers are less productive than unhappy ones. That was the conclusion of a study of workers of a circuit board assembly line by two Canadian social scientists. Such a conclusion may appear to be opposed to common sense. And it certainly is contrary to what many business managers believe. From company presidents to front-line supervisors to human resource professionals, one often hears managers say, "We should try to make our employees satisfied, because happy workers are more productive."

Companies certainly spend a lot of time and effort trying to do things to make their employees feel good about their jobs, usually assuming that this will make a difference in the bottom line. Indeed, we could interpret many articles about *As 100 melhores empresas para trabalhar"* to be illustrations of this assumption. But is this assumption true? And if not, should managers be concerned about what their employees feel about their jobs?

Numerous studies over many years have failed to show a correlation between happiness at work and productivity. Robert Levering offers an explanation and argues that the level of trust in a workplace is a more reliable predictor of productivity.

Let's return to the Canadian study mentioned earlier. As reported in *Scientific American* in 2001, the two researchers from the University of Alberta discovered that sad people were better at assembling circuit boards than happy ones. The scientists suggested that the explanation was that sad people were able to concentrate better because their work took their minds off their problems whereas happy people didn't want to be distracted from their pleasant thoughts.

At first glance these results may sound strange, but the researchers' explanation does make sense when we think about it. I know I have often found work a wonderful refuge when things were not going well in my personal life. And I'm sure others have had the same experience. In fact, this Canadian study is only one of hundreds that have sought to discover whether there is a link between happiness or job satisfaction and productivity starting with the famous Hawthorne experiment in the 1930s. These studies have shown no conclusive evidence that job satisfaction is related positively to productivity. In fact, most studies show no relation at all between the two.

Yet, based on their behaviors, managers continue to believe that there must be some correlation. Since business people are nothing if not practical, there must be some kind of explanation that has eluded academic researchers for decades. One answer to this quandary might be found by looking closely at what is going on inside of the very best workplaces, such as "*As 100 melhores empresas para trabalhar.*"

These best workplaces are very successful if you look at their financial results. For instance, a portfolio of last year's "*As 100 Melhores*" outperformed the *Ibovespa*, the principal index of the "*Bolsa de São Paulo,*" by a margin of greater than four to one over the previous six years in terms of total return on investment. Similar results have been shown in the United States, in the United Kingdom, and in other countries in Europe and Latin America when the financial results of the best workplaces have been compared with the their competitors.

How do we explain why the best workplaces have been shown this consistent result, whereas studies trying to link job satisfaction or happiness with productivity have been so inconclusive? To answer this, we need to look more closely at the how the best workplaces have been selected. We would see that they were selected largely on the basis of the results of a survey that was distributed to their employees by Great Place to Work® Institute, the firm I cofounded that conducts the survey not only for *Época*, but also for *Fortune* magazine in the United States, the *Financial Times* in the UK, and in 28 other countries throughout the world. The employee survey is called the Trust Index© and measures the level of trust in the organization.

In other words, we simply don't know whether "*As 100 Melhores*" have a higher level of job satisfaction than other companies because the employee survey that was used measures trust in the workplace rather than happiness at work. So, based on these results, it looks like companies interested in improving their financial results would do better by focusing on trust rather than on job satisfaction.

Trust in the workplace is extremely important because trust is the primary ingredient for two factors that have a big impact on a company's performance—innovation and cooperation. For innovation to happen, individuals need to be trusted. They need to feel that it is safe for them to suggest new ideas. They especially need to feel that it is OK to experiment and even fail.

Companies interested in improving their financial results might do better to focus on trust rather than on job satisfaction.

For true innovation can only occur if employees are able to make mistakes and learn from those mistakes. This occurs only in environments where there is a high level of trust.

The same is true of cooperation. Today's business organizations are extremely complex, much more complex than in the past. There are few examples these days of the old-style assembly line where individual workers merely repeat the same repetitive task again and again in isolation from others. In the past, it may have made sense to be concerned with an individual's job satisfaction. But in today's workplace, most people work in teams where they need to constantly interact with others. In that context, it is much more important that people work cooperatively than that they be happy.

We all know the example of Brazil's team in 2006 World Cup, which had lots of individual stars who simply did not work well together. Teamwork at work, just as teamwork on the football pitch, requires a high level of trust and cooperation between the various players. For a team to work well, individuals need to be willing to contribute for the success of the whole group. That requires trust. From the employees' viewpoint, trust means that they must feel that the management is credible, that they are respected as individuals, and that they are treated fairly. This is what is true at the very best workplaces.

This distinction between trust and job satisfaction is an important one to keep in mind as you read about "As 100 Melhores". You will see how these companies have created very distinctive workplace cultures. A company like Chemtech, for instance, puts a lot of emphasis on trying to help its new trainees become part of a learning community. In other words, Chemtech's training programs are not just oriented to making employees better individual workers, but they explicitly try to create a kind of community where everyone feels part of something greater than himself or herself.

Similiarly, Serasa, last year's number one company of "As 100 Melhores," places a strong emphasis on providing meaningful jobs for handicapped individuals. In seeing how the company treats those people with respect, other employees see that the company is genuinely concerned about everyone.

Such actions on the part of management build the level of trust in the organization. And trust, as we have seen, is good for the bottom line. But a great level of trust helps create a better world. After all, we all spend most of our time at work. To have a workplace community where we feel respected and treated fairly is something everyone wants. *"As 100 Melhores"* are paving the way for a better future for us all.

2009

VALUES, VIOLATIONS, AND VIABLE WORKPLACES

By **Prasenjit Bhattacharya**

[GREAT PLACE TO WORK®
INSTITUTE INDIA WHITE PAPER]

By detailing several unusual instances where senior managers were held to account for "values violations," Prasenjit Bhattacharya, CEO of Great Place to Work® Institute India, makes a strong case that integrity is crucial to building a great workplace environment.

How many organizations have sacked their highest-paid executive, not for financial impropriety or breaking the law, but for violating core values of the organization?

In a great place to work, senior managers are role models upholding organizational values, so there is no question of sacking anyone from the top team for violation of company values. Right? Wrong!

What sets apart many of these workplaces is not absence of value violations—sometimes even by senior managers—but how such violations are dealt with. The highest-paid executives at Infosys and Mindtree had to leave so that those organizations could be perceived as upholding the values they swear by.

Mindtree even publishes a booklet, *On Integrity*, that documents instances of behavior not in line with their values. Why would an organization try to publicize such stories? Is it not like washing dirty linen in public? Are they not better off dealing with such issues behind closed doors? Will employee morale not suffer if misdemeanors of senior leaders are publicized?

In the past, Mindtree and Infosys have enjoyed their employees' votes as great workplaces. So what do these companies gain by sharing instances of values violation with their employees, and taking prompt exemplary action?

In one word, the answer to all the above questions is Credibility.

Credibility of management is the reason why such workplaces can get away without harming their employer brand, even if they make unpopular decisions. Says an Infosys employee about a recent unpopular decision, " I don't agree with the decision but, heck, even the CEO is not exempt (from being ostracized), I guess they don't have double standards."

Infosys fined its chief executive, S. Gopalakrishnan, for not reporting on time a change in his share ownership. The audit committee of Infosys imposed a fine of 500,000 rupees (about $12,658) for his "inadvertently failing" to notify the company within one business day following the change in his shareholding. Gopalakrishnan had inherited 12,800 shares from his mother.

And guess what, Infosys employees are proud of such instances. As long as these examples remain, employees can be sure that their organization will never be another Satyam—the info tech outsourcer, whose chairman B. Ramalinga Raju resigned in January, 2009, after admitting the firm had falsified accounts and assets and inflated its profits.

So my first lesson is that if you are a value-based organization, you will have examples of

> What sets apart many of these workplaces is not absence of value violations—sometimes even by senior managers—but how such violations are dealt with.

value violations. If you are working in a squeaky-clean organization with no reported instances of value violations, beware!

In great workplaces, values are not posters. Johnson & Johnson's Credo is a living document that guides action. All major decisions in the company have to pass through the "Credo-based decision-making model." Most people know about the Tylenol example back in 1982—when seven people died after taking the pain-relief capsules that had been poisoned, and how the company's quick and exemplary response remains the gold standard for crisis control.

Not many may know how J&J follows the Credo on a day-to-day basis. For example, the group chairman of the company flew down from the U.S. to tell a doctor, one of his most important customers in India, that J&J did not want his business because the doctor's actions were not in line with the Credo. In another instance, a whole consignment of sanitary napkins was withdrawn from the market in India when a corroded earring was found in one package.

J&J has seen decades of double-digit growth and higher and higher returns to shareholders. Similarly, the 20 Basics of Marriott, the Blue Box Values of American Express, or the CLASS (Caring, Learning, Achieving, Sharing and Socially Responsible) values of Mindtree do not just define who these companies are, but also how they do business. Values, when practiced, can be a competitive advantage.

A recent case in point is in the telecom industry in India where a number of major players had to restate their consumer numbers after closer inspection by the regulatory authority. One is reasonably sure that a great workplace, such as the Tata Group Company in the same industry, is unlikely to be on that suspect list. So if you are a long-term investor or a long-term customer, would you make a deal with a company whose numbers are suspect, or would you go with someone who has a reputation for practicing their core values?

However, great workplaces practice core values not because they benefit business. They will do so even if it is a business barrier. Which is why, perhaps, the major part of the Tata Group revenues is from outside India where the Tata Code of Conduct often come in the way of competing with others with lesser scruples.

Newcomers to great workplaces quickly experience the importance of values. Intel trains its hiring managers how to conduct interviews in a manner that assesses values in prospective candidates. As I write this article I am reading the book, *The Qualcomm Equation,* a must read for every new Qualcomm employee. The book not only generates pride by describing how a fledgling telecom company forged a new path to big profits and market dominance, but also reinforces what Qualcomm stands for.

For the first fifty-two weeks, newcomers receive an email story on Qualcomm values–called 52 weeks at Qualcomm. My personal favorite example is from a company called Sasken which has been featured on many best employer lists, including ours. Newcomers would interview existing employees to discover the core values of the company and would present them during their induction, rather than the other way around, where the company presents slides on core values. An interesting discussion always ensues between what the newcomers have "discovered" and what the company says are its core values.

As much as clarifying core values is important,

If you are a value-based organization, you will hear about value violations. If you're working in a squeaky-clean organization with no reported instances of values violations, beware!

unearthing value dilemmas is even more important. The Aditya Birla Group trained hundreds of value facilitators" who would conduct sessions on difficulties in practicing the values and how to deal with them. For example, if integrity is one value, what do you do when the boiler inspector comes to your plant and demands a bribe, or otherwise threatens to close down the factory? Values are important in an organizational context only because they can guide individual action. The best-known case study is that of Texas Instruments, which "invented" the Ethics Test. The quick ethics test of the company includes questions like:

- Is the action legal?
- Does it comply with our values?
- If you do it, will you feel bad?
- How will it look in the newspaper?

Employees are told in no uncertain terms: "If you know it's wrong, don't do it! If you're not sure, ask. Keep asking until you get an answer."

What sets apart great places to work is their willingness to take feedback. The Credo Survey at J&J does not depend on availability of budgets. RMSI is a company that has been number one on our Best Companies to Work For list for the last two years. The values survey of RMSI is extended to not just employees, but also suppliers and customers—people who can observe company values being practiced when faced with market realities. Twenty-four-by-seven ethics hotlines are now an established part of many great workplaces—Qualcomm, Marriott, Freescale, CSC, STMicroelectronics, Sapient, and Godrej Consumer Products Ltd. Many, like Cadbury, provide such hotlines in regional languages to make it easier for their people to access them.

I have sometimes used the term "ethics" interchangeably with "values." Although, I have referred to values in terms of human values, such as respect for people, values need not be only about ethics. Core values can be defined as a set of guiding principles by which a company navigates. They could be in regard to customer orientation, execution, or innovation.

What we have discovered in numerous exercises of creating shared values is that the words are not the most important, but the process of tapping into the collective goodness in any group is—articulating and giving that goodness direction in the form of an inspiring vision. Values make you restless. If you know what you deeply believe in, you are more likely to find a direction that helps you live your values. Organizations with strong values often have an accompanying vision to change the world for the better.

It is perhaps our unique destiny that we are the only species in this world that can change things for the better or worse. The outcome, I believe, depends on whether we are driven by values or instinct.

2009

WHEN THE OWL TAKES FLIGHT

By **Horacio Bolaños**

[*GREAT PLACE TO WORK®* INSTITUTE
ARGENTINA NEWSLETTER]

In this article, Horacio Bolaños places the concepts inherent in the work of the Great Place to Work® Institute into a broader historical context. By doing so, he sees reasons to believe that the future is bright for workplaces that replace "Networks in place of pyramids." Bolaños is a director of Great Place to Work® Institute Argentina, Bolivia, Paraguay, and Uruguay.

Among those who study the matter, there is consensus that we are going through a critical phase of history. It is one of those crepuscular periods in which paradigms taken as truths are dissolved and other certainties emerge to replace them. It is one of those moments when, according to the German philosopher Federico Hegel, "Minerva's owl takes flight." It is worth paying attention to what is debated among thinkers and philosophers.

The question of death and its meaning is no longer the motor of philosophical thinking. Now, the drive lies with life. Rather, what we have done with life and what will living mean as a result of the genetic revolution. The new agenda includes such questions as the right to intervene in the origin or the end of life; the use of the environment and what it implies; the place of minorities; and the cultural migrations—just to mention the main chapters.

However, for those of us who struggle in the labyrinths of organizations and the relationships among the people working there, there is a topic that is a significant qualitative jump. When humanity emerged from it previous great crisis, at the end of the Middles Ages, it did so with the certainty that Descartes had notably established: "I think, therefore, I am." The independent I dictating its own rules, the concept of property as an exclusive right, nature losing its sacredness, and so forth, were assumptions that contributed to creating armies and organizations where roles were more important than people.

Fortunately, the current crepuscule that will dissolve into a new dawn finds humanity with a more ethical perspective, maybe less arrogant but wiser. It is an ethic based on dialogue, the acknowledgment of differences, the need for being able to see in each human being a neighbor that needs us, rather than an "other" that accuses us.

This point of view challenges us to understand companies as communities of people whose feelings, hopes, and frustrations blend with roles and obligations related to specific and verifiable goals. The question is how to conduct decision-making structures that operate with employees who are aware of their rights as citizens and not resigned to leave them outside when they go into the workplace.

Fortunately, thinkers like Russell L. Acoff, Robert Levering, and Marvin T. Brown, among others, have been anticipating the need for re-thinking organizations in order to make them more adequately meet the expectations of citizens who wish to lead, and fitting with the rights to information and privacy, and with the freedom of choice in legitimate environments. Brown, for example, proposes a culture where all of the groups of interest—and the employees in the first place—have access to a dialogue with no pressures, that is egalitarian and with fair-game rules. Through open dialogue, participants have their share of power and autonomy supported, so that they can express their points of view, assured they will be taken into consideration and measured on the basis of their arguments' strength, rather than through hierarchy or threats.

For this author, the development and growth of a productive dialogue is only possible if the participating parties are willing and able to put themselves in the other's shoes, at least to completely understand the other's point of view. This implies flexibility and not necessarily giving up one's own positions. Acknowledging the higher effectiveness, efficiency, or ethicality of another proposal makes one grow as a person and strengthens the debate. Networks in place of pyramids seem to be the dawn of tomorrow's organizations.

Proposals, such as that from Levering or Brown, allow us to glimpse that it is possible to work to build mature, reciprocal relationships with those with whom we live and to whom we know how to transfer the world.

2008

TRUST IS SCARY!

By **Palle Ellemann**

[GREAT PLACE TO WORK®
MAGAZINE EUROPEAN EDITION]

For many managers, the shift toward trust-based management can be intimidating, as it often means letting go of the traditional mechanisms for controlling employees' behavior. For example, you cannot say you trust your people, then insist that they punch a time card at the beginning and end of the work day. Trust is not a verbal commitment; it can only be built on action.

This lesson was reinforced through the 2009 European Best Workplaces study, a survey of more than 250,000 employees conducted by the Great Place to Work® Institute, a global research and consulting firm that conducts similar surveys in forty nations. For European employees, the reliability of management—i.e., when managers do as they say and keep their promises—is the factor most closely tied to whether a company is perceived by employees as a great workplace.

The Best Workplaces study also shows consistently that companies with the highest levels of trust in the workplace are those that grow faster, are more profitable and innovative,

Citing studies that link productivity to higher levels of trust, Palle Ellemann, managing director of Great Place to Work® Institute Europe, offers three lessons gleaned from the study of great workplaces.

Companies with the highest levels of trust in the workplace grow faster, are more profitable and innovative, and have less absenteeism and employee turnover.

have less absenteeism and employee turnover, and receive more unsolicited job applications than other companies. As the graph below indicates, the stock market performance of the Best Companies to Work for in America outperforms the Standard & Poor's and Russell 3000 indices. Similar results have emerged from studies in other parts of the world, including the UK, Brazil, and Denmark.

CUMULATIVE RETURNS 1998- 2008

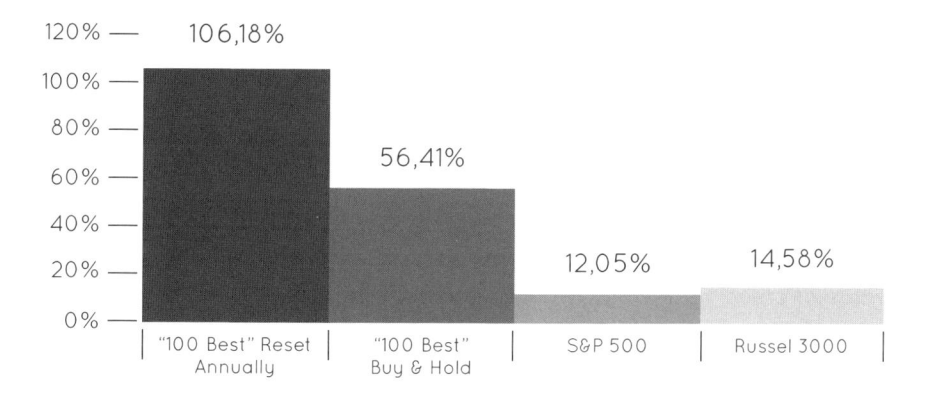

"100 Best" Reset Annually	106,18%
"100 Best" Buy & Hold	56,41%
S&P 500	12,05%
Russel 3000	14,58%

Source *Russell Investment Group. ©2009 Great Place to Work® Institute, Inc. All Rights Reserved*

What should a manager do if he/she wants to reap the benefits of trust-based management practices?

First, realize that there is no such thing as a trust-neutral action. Every time you speak with your people or take some kind of action, it will either build trust or break trust. Thus, managers should use any opportunity available to build trust, for example, by reaching out to employees for input before business-related decisions are made. When people are involved in the decision process, they are more likely to support the final decision, even if the decision does not follow their recommendation.

Second, be available for questions and feedback from people, and respond swiftly to ideas from people in all areas of the organization. You will be amazed how much energy and innovation this can release in the organization. Many of the Best Workplaces have highly effective systems for gathering ideas from employees. Often there is a single point of contact (in some cases the CEO) who commits to responding to employees' ideas within twenty-four hours. The idea is swiftly forwarded to the right person in the organization, and he/she analyzes the feasibility and makes a plan for implementation–or provides a solid response for why the idea cannot work. Such workplaces receive hundreds of great ideas every year, and often the employees are recognized and rewarded with a percentage of the savings generated.

Third, leaders at the Best Workplaces continually reinforce the importance and value of each person's contribution, and they speak frequently about the value of creating a winning culture and setting high goals. It is each manager's role to encourage employees to maintain a positive attitude toward reaching their goals, and to continually recognize and reward people for a job well done.

Although trust-based management may mean abandoning "control mechanisms" and empowering people with more freedom to make decisions, it is very important not to lose control of the culture. The key to building a strong culture is hiring the right people, and also in helping people to understand and behave according to the value system of the organization. Remember that no action (or inaction) is trust-neutral.

To help organizations to move toward trust-based management, the Great Place to Work® Institute provides a wide range of books, magazines, and other materials, including lists of Best People Practices from the world's best workplaces. We encourage you to use these resources and work with your own people to develop a trust-based management approach that is authentic and original within your own organization.

Scary as it may be, you can do it—and your employees—and shareholders—will love you for it.

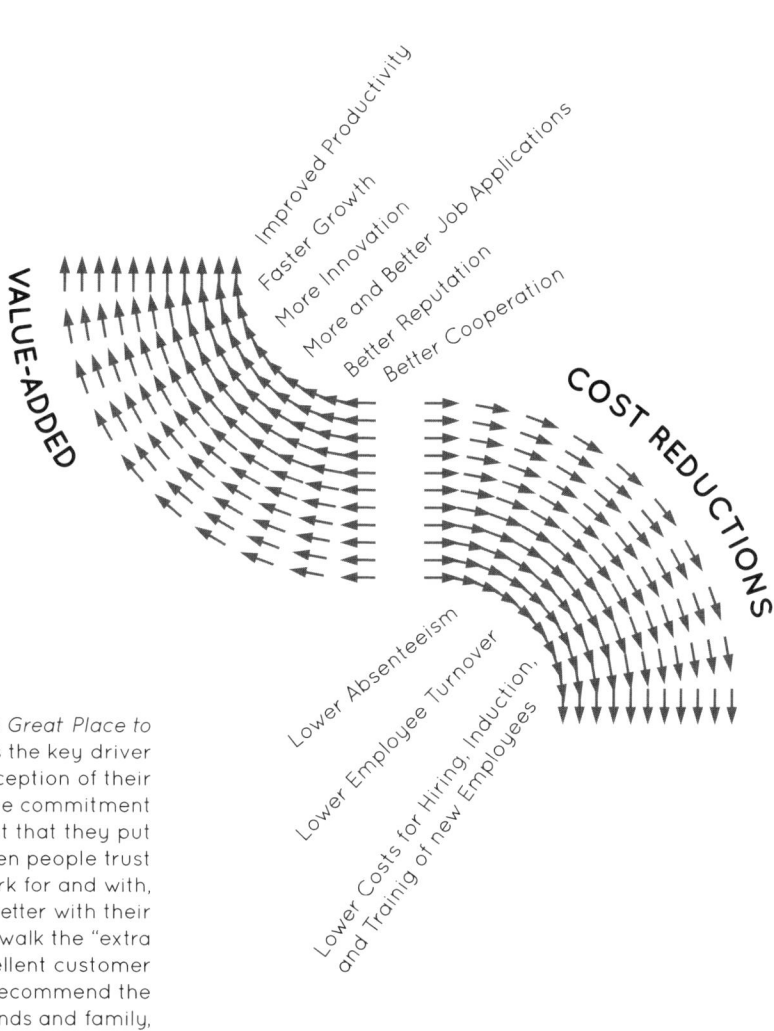

VALUE-ADDED
- Improved Productivity
- Faster Growth
- More Innovation
- More and Better Job Applications
- Better Reputation
- Better Cooperation

COST REDUCTIONS
- Lower Absenteeism
- Lower Employee Turnover
- Lower Costs for Hiring, Induction, and Training of new Employees

According to the *Great Place to Work® Model©*, trust is the key driver for people's perception of their workplace and the commitment and engagement that they put into their work. When people trust the people they work for and with, they cooperate better with their colleagues, they walk the "extra mile" to provide excellent customer service, they recommend the company to their friends and family, and they share their best ideas to improve their company. When people feel pride in what they do and enjoy the people they work with, they are less likely to stay home pretending they are sick, and they stay with the company longer, which saves the company money for hiring and training new employees.

1998

THE ECONOMY OF **EMPOWERMENT**

By **José Tolovi Jr.**

[EXAME]

Henry Ford once asked: "Why, whenever I ask for a pair of arms, does a brain come with them?" This famous question reveals a little about an era when entrepreneurs were only concerned about hiring one type of worker: the manual laborer—not workmen that would reflect on the everyday life in the company. Today, this rationale is met with astonishment. Companies looking for real talents, people who think and are able to reflect on the direction of a business is increasingly common. Yes, we now try to select and recruit more brilliant candidates. But there is a contradiction here: many leaders treat these professionals, once hired, as inferior people who are devoid of intelligence. They do not listen to their suggestions, do not like the hired help disagreeing with their opinions, and they do not grant them appropriate autonomy so that they can work.

Does it sound familiar to you? There it is; in a modern world where the discourse is about

In examining why "empowerment" has become popular in management circles, Great Place to Work® Institute's global CEO José Tolovi Jr. sees that the deeper issue is autonomy with responsibility in order to foster work environments where people thrive.

creativity, entrepreneurialism, and innovation, this situation is quite more common than we think. It is not uncommon to hear young people, hired due to their boldness and personality traits, complain that they are just doing bureaucratic work. Some express regret for never having the opportunity to show everything they know. What happens when we treat adults like children? They will respond like children. They start treating their leaders as inaccessible people and only producing the least required in order to justify their jobs. And, even worse, they will execute their tasks without responsibility or commitment.

That is why the word "empowerment" is on the rise in the market. Actually, it represents the attribution of power and autonomy given to people. Empowerment is not something that emerged as ephemeral fashion, but rather as a need in the current world. It is well known that we have had increasingly fewer people in the organizations. This picture results from the automation and pressure to reduce costs due to the increase of competition and the high speed required by the markets. If, today, there are fewer professionals in the companies, it is expected that they are the brains, as the manual labor is now performed by several forms of automation.

Therefore, we now have more brains and fewer arms, and we have to make good use of all this potential in the performance of tasks that are complex, ambiguous, and carry a high level of uncertainty. Those are tasks for human beings, rather than for machines. What we are supposed to do is to coach, to offer parameters and targets, and to believe that people are apt. We must understand that people make better use of their potential when they feel they are responsible for a mission. Responsibility and autonomy are words that walk side by side.

Responsibility without autonomy stands for a waste of time and talent. Autonomy without responsibility is probably the beginning of a catastrophe. Empowerment is nothing more than having people who know what needs to be done, what their responsibilities are, and who they should look for in case they need guidance. People working with autonomy represent the most economical way to run a business.

2009

BORN TO COMMAND: WHY LESS IS MORE

By **Williams Johnson**

Citing several outstanding examples of leadership, Williams Johnson, commercial director of Great Place to Work® Institute UK, argues for a new style of leader who "shares and derives power from those around him or her."

Marnix Eikenboom, the Dutch-born general manager of Danone Ltd, the UK subsidiary of a world leader in dairy products and bottled water, is one of the new breed of business leaders whose company's performance is far outstripping that of its competitors.

What is exceptional about Eikenboom, who also coaches the local hockey team in Woking, is the way in which he has devolved power to those who work for him. But to assume that he is some utopian idealist or that he has relinquished his role as leader would be a grave misjudgment.

"Marnix is very much the boss," says one of his senior managers." He's approachable and informal. He believes in work-life balance, but you had better know your stuff because he will hold you fully accountable. He's no softie."

It is no accident that Danone Ltd topped our 2009 UK's Best Workplaces ranking. A groundbreaking health program, dedicated employee training, and volunteer program, among many other features, helped secure its edge over other contenders. But what really made Danone stand out was the style and tone of its leadership. Here at Great Place to Work® Institute®, we've been working with some of the world's most successful organizations for the past twenty-five years, helping them to transform their workplaces. We've learned a thing or two along the way, but one thing seems clear: A new style of leader is emerging, and one who is strongly out-performing those who still adhere to old-style imperial forms of authority.

What we are seeing is the type of leadership of Mahatma Gandhi, or even Barrack Obama, where the leader shares and derives power from those around him or her. It is not a soft option, but rather one that imposes stricter accountability on those who work for you.

Despite the recession, Danone has continued to enjoy double-digit growth in the UK, with sales of 281m last year — a performance that far exceeds the returns normally found in fast-moving consumer goods. UK staff enjoy free private medical insurance, health checkups, healthy-living education, and free fruit, yogurt, and mineral water at work. And they get a weekly fifteen-minute head-and-shoulder massage in return for their putting £1 (about 1.14) into the good-cause kitty.

But strong performance isn't just about generous perks. What makes Danone's leadership so exceptional is its underlying acknowledgment that everyone counts and its commitment to employee engagement. Eikenboom and his top team have devolved power to employees who work in small family-like forums, and who are fully accountable for their actions. Danone's

> What we are seeing is the type of leadership of Mahatma Gandhi, or even Barrack Obama, where the leader shares and derives power from those around him or her. It is not a soft option, but rather one that imposes stricter accountability on those who work for you

Leadership for All program, as the name implies, is fun for everyone regardless of rank. Formula One, on the other hand, has been beset by recent high-profile squabbles that nearly split the sport. It is no coincidence that Formula One Australia (F1A) has been dominated by two highly authoritarian figures, Bernie Ecclestone and Max Mosley, both of whom appear to wield power in a highly authoritarian manner, which, far from inspiring, has alienated the majority of its members, who do not trust the leadership.

What we do know at Great Place to Work® Institute is that trust, once lost, is very hard to restore. Consistent winners in our Best Workplaces program enjoy noticeably higher levels of trust. That involves their leaders ensuring that rewards are more evenly distributed than in other companies.

One of the most striking characteristics of the recession (2009) has been the erosion of trust. Edelman's 2009 Trust Barometer reveals that 62 percent of the 4,475 people surveyed globally distrust businesses less than they did a year ago. Yet the companies that are holding up well take trust very seriously.

Take for example, auto insurer Admiral Group Plc, which came in sixth in our 2009 Best Workplace survey, and which has been a consistent winner in our annual survey over a number of years. Founder and chief executive officer Henry Engelhardt has placed trust at the center of everything Admiral does—it is regarded as the single most important determinant of its business success.

As a result of this approach, Admiral has been able to avoid the type of high-profile difficulties and layoffs that plague many competitors. Great emphasis is placed on internal communications. Employees regularly receive business performance updates and reassurances that there are no plans to scale back on jobs. Admiral's senior management has a good track record when it comes to integrity—staff tend to believe what they're being told, which also has a direct impact on their motivation to do their best.

Admiral is a company that has also worked hard to ensure that rewards are more evenly distributed. Staff enjoyed the proceeds of the management buyout in 1999, with mailroom workers netting in some cases £33,000 each (almost $38,000). But Engelhardt does not believe that money is necessarily behind his company's success. "I don't hand out £20 notes. People just keep coming up with great suggestions, because, I believe, we give them the freedom to do so."

The other important aspect about leadership is that the best leadership tends to be rather more long-term than the five years or so that now accounts for the average tenure of the Financial Times Stock Exchange (FTSE) 100 chief executives. In Admiral's case, Engelhardt has been in situ since 1991, which gives him a perspective and accountability to his employees that more short-term bosses lack.

In my own country, Brazil, there is a particularly visionary business leader called Ricardo Semler, the majority owner of Semco in São Paulo, who rejected Taylorism, the theory of industrial-driven processes that has dominated management thinking for most of the twentieth century. Instead, his employees work in family-like units of no more than a dozen people. They are allowed to select their own leaders, set their own goals, and even decide the level of pay that they should award themselves. Far from being the recipe for disaster that some might imagine, Semco, once an unfashionable conglomerate, has grown

"I don't hand out £20 notes," says Admiral's Englehardt. "People just keep coming up with great suggestions, because, I believe, we give them the freedom to do so."

by 900 percent in ten years, moved in industry rankings from fifty-sixth position to number four and number one positions in each of the service activities in which it specializes. It has grown from one hundred employees to 3,000, and has an enviable staff turnover rate of about 1 percent.

Semler regards himself as a type of a coach. His job as leader, he says, is to challenge the decisions of others. The company pretty much runs itself, which is just as well since Semler narrowly escaped death in 2005 after being involved in a horrendous high-speed crash on a Brazilian highway. His company carried on seamlessly during the ensuing months he spent lying in intensive care recovering from the multiple surgeries needed to repair neck and face. Numbers were met, deals closed and business carried. Now that's what I call real leadership.

2008

THE **EMOTIONAL** BOND

By **Ana Maria Gubbins**

[EL COMERCIO]

One of the characteristics distinguishing the best companies to work for in Peru and in the world is the respect they constantly and consistently show for their employees: respect for them as professionals and human beings, for their ideas.

Companies that develop, take care of, and exercise sincere human relationships with their employees have a competitive advantage. They are able to create an emotional bond with their employees, and as a result, they are companies that have an authentic environment of trust, where employees are proud of their work and are united and committed to a common cause.

In the best companies to work for, we find that the work environment is much more human than one could imagine; leaders are genuinely and permanently concerned about their "collaborators"—beyond their roles as employees. In these companies, work is done in a physically,

According to Ana Maria Gubbins, CEO of Great Place to Work® Institute Peru, the key to creating a great working environment is showing respect to employees. She asserts that doing so helps build an emotional bond between employees and the company.

psychologically, and emotionally healthy environment that leads employees to put all their potential at the company's service, with a feeling of loyalty and commitment to it.

Then, where to begin? Begin with showing them that each of them is valuable for the company. Support them in building their careers; listen to them and promote the implementation of their ideas and suggestions; and most importantly, treat them as human beings and, whenever possible, engage their families. It is not a matter of budget; it is a matter of details. Collaborators will thank you; the company will see it reflected in its results. Give it a try.

2001

WHAT DID WE DO WRONG?

By **José Tolovi Jr.**

[EXAME]

Last August, the people in charge of the *Guia Exame*—for the 100 Best Companies to Work for—started to officially communicate the survey results to all of the companies participating in the process. On one hand, we saw the celebration of those organizations that succeeded in appearing on the best 100 list. On the other hand, we watched the sadness and regrets from those not classified. It was exactly then that I remembered a true story that is often repeated.

The story usually begins when the CEO of a large company is informed that it will not be on the best 100 list. Naturally, he feels disappointed and a little upset, because he cannot understand why the company he runs—and believes to be so good to its employees— was not chosen. He immediately summons the HR director to discuss the matter. "Why are we not in the list?" asks the CEO.

"Actually, we do not know for sure," the director answers. "We have taken so many actions, increased benefits, adjusted salaries . . . Nothing seems to satisfy the personnel."

"We have to be on that list next year. It is very important for our company. All in all, IF we have done so much for the employees, then it must not be that difficult. This is now a goal of yours."

The HR director accepts the challenge, starts several programs, changes benefits once again, gives speeches and courses, etc. One year later, a new survey and the same evaluation: not on the list. What is wrong in this story? The HR programs? The salaries? The benefits? A resistance to change? Nothing of the kind.

The mistake is in the approach. Company managers generally believe that "buying the employees" with benefit and salary packages is enough. With that, they are convinced that everybody will become more involved with the company and more motivated—and, indirectly, they will be able to build up an excellent organizational environment. This could not be farther from reality.

We have known for a long time that salaries and benefits are hygienic, rather than motivating, factors. This means that, if these are not good, the personnel will be de-motivated. However, if they are reasonable or excellent, people's motivation will not be changed. Therefore, the organizational environment cannot be changed by just dealing with these variables. What to do, then? How can a company be transformed into an excellent place to work? What really distinguishes the best companies from the others is their attitude.

In fact, revisiting the story of the executives that were discussing the reasons for the company's declassification, there are two mistakes. The first one, on the part of the CEO, is to ask his director to change the company from one day to another. The second one is made by the director when he accepts the task. One cannot order such a change. Every transformation process is started and supported by the organization's leadership, beginning with its main executive. HR cannot change a company on its own.

Companies only change when there, sincere interest from the top management in turning them into an excellent place to work. That is, managers genuinely believe that business results from people. And this must be experienced and demonstrated. Words alonde do not transform companies, but rather attitudes. In order to talk about these actions in a more concrete manner, it is necessary to look at some interesting aspects of the survey carried out with employees for this edition. When analyzing the dimension Credibility (one of the items in the topic Trust), we will see that the major differences between the 100 best and the 100 last classified are found in issues of Communication. It is critical that managers keep their teams informed about important matters and changes in the company. Ethical values are also important. Leaders should fulfill what they promise and do things in accordance with what they say.

In the dimension Respect (another item in the topic Trust), the great difference is in the interest leaders show in their employees. Managers should be interested in the ideas and suggestions given by the team members and should involve people in decisions that impact their activities as well. In the dimension Fairness (the third item in the topic Trust), in turn, the disparity lies in one aspect: petty politics as a way to achieve results, including promotions. People do not forgive it.

Thus, the path to reach an excellent work environment is the reflection about how leaderships are treating their employees. Is there credibility? Do employees feel they are treated as human beings, and therefore, with respect? Is there fairness in the relationships? Is petty politics absent and are the rules of the game clear? If you are the main executive of a company, a division, or even a small area, ask yourself the above questions, and you will know for sure how to start a change process that will lead your organization to appear among the best ones.

MODEL FOR CHANGE AND **GLOBAL PERSPECTIVES**

- GREAT PLACE TO WORK® MODEL
- GIFTWORK®
- GLOBAL PERSPECTIVES

1. GREAT PLACE TO WORK® MODEL

2006

FIVE **CASE** STUDIES

By **Lisa Ratner**

[JMAM HUMAN CAPITAL]

The Great Place to Work® Institute has developed a model of a great workplace based on hundreds of interviews conducted at the world's best workplaces over the past 25 years. The model has five dimensions — credibility, respect, fairness, pride, and camaraderie.

Lisa Ratner, senior business development advisor for Great Place to Work® U.S., explains each of the dimensions with case studies.

• **CREDIBILITY**

Management's credibility with employees is built through three interdependent sets of behaviors and attitudes found in the practice of two-way communication, competence, and integrity. Effective *communication* invites two-way dialogue. Leaders and managers are clear and informative in the information they volunteer; and mechanisms are available to employees that afford them the opportunity to begin conversations about the information they might need or want to hear. *Competence* is seen in the skills and behaviors needed for the effective coordination of people and resources, directing employees' work with the right amount of oversight, and clearly articulating and pursuing a vision for the organization as a whole and for individual departments. Management's *integrity* depends on honest and reliable daily actions.

Managers strive to be consistent in what they say and do, and promises are kept. Additionally, employees have confidence that their managers run the business ethically.

Credibility Case Study: Starbucks' Mission Review Program

The world's N° 1 specialty coffee retailer, Starbucks, operates and licenses more than 8,500 coffee shops in more than 30 countries, including Japan. The shops offer coffee drinks and food items, as well as beans, coffee accessories, teas, and CDs. In addition, Starbucks markets its coffee through grocery stores and licenses its brand for other food and beverage products.

Few companies ask their employees to critique company practices — and employ an entire department to find prompt and honest answers to that criticism. The Starbucks Mission Review program, quite simply, invites every Starbucks employee (called a "partner") to comment on whether company decisions are consistent with the company's Mission Statement and Guiding Principles. Starbucks believes that every partner has a voice, not just in what happens at his or her location, but in how the company operates on a daily basis.

Starbucks Mission Statement is simple: Establish Starbucks as the premier purveyor of the finest coffee in the world while maintaining our uncompromising principles as we grow. Its guiding principles include such items as: "Provide a great work environment and treat each other with respect and dignity; develop enthusiastically satisfied customers all of the time; and contribute positively to our communities and our environment." When the Mission Statement was created in 1990, a group of employees felt that it was important that ordinary employees should

> The Starbucks Mission Review invites every Starbucks employee to comment on whether company decisions are consistent with the company's Mission Statement and Guiding Principles.

be able to challenge actions of the company that they felt did not measure up to those principles. So they proposed that partners have access to an active feedback mechanism. Starbucks leaders accepted their proposal, and the Mission Review program was developed.

Mission Review supports partners' responsibility to hold one another accountable for their actions. It has become "a connection between those who create and generate our policies and those who carry them out," says David Johnson, Mission Review Advisor. "It's self-criticism that's balanced," he continues. "These are people who are passionate about our products and our company. They say, 'I am entitled to ask these questions.'"

From their first day of orientation at Starbucks, partners are introduced to the company's open and accessible lines of communication. From the beginning, they have access to cards which they can submit directly to the Mission Review. Partners with access to the company intranet system, the Starbucks Partner Portal, can submit their concerns electronically.

The program can be seen as an ongoing discussion among partners. "The tone of the conversation is overwhelmingly respectful," adds Johnson. Responses are regularly made by partners at the executive level.

The Mission Review staff conducts the research to identify appropriate responders among the company's decision makers. Since they regard the responders as internal customers no less than those who submit comments, they offer assistance to those whose workloads otherwise might make timely responses difficult, and coordinate among departments when submission topics touch on the work of more than one team.

Adding to the integrity of the Mission Review

program, reports are made available to Starbucks leaders to keep them informed of current concerns, providing one more way for partners to provide input to management.

"Beyond roasting coffee, the Guiding Principles and Mission Review have been the most enduring things we've done here," says Dave Olsen, Senior Vice President of Culture and Leadership Development. And the partners seem to concur. As one partner states, "Starbucks is a company that actually follows their mission statement and guiding principles, they are not just words on paper."

Do Starbucks partners really take advantage of this two-way communication program? The numbers speak for themselves. In a recent six-month period, Mission Review received 1,596 submissions, 1,433 of which asked for and received answers. Comments came from 831 different work sites, including 709 Starbucks stores in 334 retail districts (representing about 70 percent of all retail districts). Responses to those comments came from 261 partners, up and down the Starbucks ladder, working in 61 business units. Turnaround time to receive a response from the appropriate executive or manager relative to the issue averaged 15 business days.

The benefits of this program are two-fold. Starbucks leadership "truly appreciates partners taking time out of their busy day to ask a challenging question," Johnson says. And as another partner describes, "they listen, which is so important. They listen to not only their customers but also the feedback they receive from partners. I also love the fact that partners are allowed the opportunity to be just that—partners in the company."

By encouraging partners to challenge company practices they feel may be inconsistent with Starbucks Mission Statement and Guiding Principles, partners take ownership of the company's values, and ensure that they remain as fresh as the coffee.

• RESPECT

Respect is demonstrated through practices that provide professional support to employees, encourage collaboration, and allow for expressions of care both in the workplace and outside. Professional *support* is shown to employees through the provision of training opportunities and the resources and equipment necessary to get work done, as well as through expressions of appreciation for accomplishments and extra effort. *Collaboration* between employees and management requires that leaders and managers genuinely seek and respond to employees' suggestions and ideas, and involve people in the decisions that affect how they get their work done. Managers demonstrate *caring* by providing a safe and healthy working environment, and by showing an interest in people's personal lives. Caring managers are also aware of the impact that work has on employees' personal lives.

Respect Case Study: Analytical Graphics's training and development programs

Analytical Graphics Inc. (AGI) produces commercial off-the-shelf analysis and visualization software used by more than 30,000 aerospace, defense, and intelligence professionals worldwide. With integrated land, sea, air, and space elements, AGI's software offerings provide technology solutions for all phases of industry programs and initiatives. AGI emphasizes product excellence, customer success, fun, and exceptional stakeholder value and has enjoyed strong growth in its 15-year history. It is privately held and has six sites in the United States with 240 employees.

AGI's Chief Financial Officer is commonly asked how the company can afford the wealth of training and development programs it offers to employees. His standard response is, "We can't afford *not* to."

AGI leaders attribute its recent annual growth rate of more than 33 percent to a philosophy that considers employees' continual development as vital to the health of the organization. "Our employees build who we are," says Lisa Velte, Director of Human Resources. "They are the DNA of AGI, and their knowledge is our single most valuable asset."

AGI recognizes that its financial success depends upon attracting and retaining highly skilled employees—the best of the best—and ensuring they have the support they need to excel. People come to AGI with backgrounds in astrophysics and high-end computer programming. They're highly aware of the cutting-edge and become restless without new challenges. Providing a rich array of training and development opportunities is not merely optional, but essential to AGI's business. Creating opportunities for employees to grow, then, literally is the engine behind the success of the business—the source of AGI's competitive advantage.

Formal training and development programs included a leadership development program through Dale Carnegie® and Institute for Management Development (IMD), over ten formal courses in which 60 percent of the workforce participated, and on-site technical training courses.

> AGI leaders attribute its recent annual growth rate of more than 33 percent to a philosophy that considers employees' development as vital to the health of the organization. "Our employees," says Lisa Velte, "are the DNA of AGI, and their knowledge is our single most valuable asset."

Classroom activities and professional organizations are not the only places AGI employees do their learning. AGI's turnover rates stay low in part because when employees are interested in new opportunities, they have plenty to choose from within the company. AGI's small, informal culture makes it easy to find ways to learn new skills on the job; in 2004, 30 percent of employees took on a new role. Within projects, managers choose their own teams, and as a result, employees gain broader skill sets and the company improves its flexibility to meet business objectives in a highly competitive, rapidly changing field.

More integral to AGI is the myriad of growth opportunities available to employees who request them. At AGI, employees have what amounts to a blank check to seek individual professional development opportunities at local colleges, professional associations, and conferences. "A high percentage of our employees hold PhD's", says Velte. "They love presenting papers—so we give them the support they need to do that." They're encouraged to join the boards of professional organizations and supported in their efforts to publish technical papers.

AGI's training and development programs uniquely fit with its brainiac culture, but other organizations can learn from the principle behind AGI's success. By identifying the personal and professional qualities and traits essential to their business, organizations can create programs that support their employees' efforts to thrive in their industry. "We know we can't afford to lose a single one of our key developers," says Velte, coaching managers to identify what people qualities are essential to their business. "Relentlessly support that quality. It doesn't have to be expensive, but employees need to know you care about their success. If you do, you'll see higher productivity, and your people will stick around."

• FAIRNESS

The three principles that support the practice of Fairness in an organization are equity, impartiality, and justice. A sense of *equity* is conveyed through balanced treatment of all people in the distribution of intangible and tangible rewards. Manager *impartiality* is displayed through an avoidance of favoritism in hiring and promotion practices, and an absence of politicking in the workplace. *Justice* is seen as a lack of discrimination based on people's personal characteristics, and the presence and utilization of a fair process for appeals. Treating employees fairly results in a number of benefits for a company. Work environments that support the fair treatment of employees tend to promote teamwork and in turn, build trust. Freeing people from the distractions of politics and prejudice, employees are better able to focus on their work. Fairly-treated employees are more likely to trust the decisions of managers whom they perceive as consistent, supportive, and impartial. Ultimately, the most valuable benefits of fairness are the ones the companies on our lists reap again and again: enhanced trust, unshakeable team bonds, and unity in moving forward toward a common goal.

Fairness Case Sudy: FedEx's GFT Procedure and RESPECT Program

FedEx provides access to a growing global marketplace through a worldwide network of supply chain, transportation, business, and related-information services. With more than 200,000 employees worldwide, FedEx is comprised of four major operating companies: FedEx Express, FedEx Ground, FedEx Freight, and FedEx Kinko's Office and Print Services. Other specialty companies in the FedEx family include FedEx Trade Networks, FedEx Custom Critical, FedEx Supply Chain Services, and Caribbean Transportation Services. Another company, FedEx Corporate Services, coordinates sales, marketing, and technology support for the global FedEx brand. Each company offers flexible, specialized services that represent the broadest array of supply chain, transportation, business, and related-information services. While each company operates independently, focused on its market segment, they also compete collectively under the powerful FedEx brand.

While customers of FedEx Corporation, the world's largest transportation company, are guaranteed that their packages will arrive safely and on-time to their intended destinations, employees of this thirty-two-year-old organization know they are guaranteed a fair hearing in all matters of justice within the workplace.

At the heart of the FedEx culture lies a strong commitment and dedication to its people who are the driving force behind the success of this $26 billion-company. The company's people-centric culture fosters an environment where people feel appreciated and respected for the work they do, and where fairness and justice pervade the workplace.

Two unique programs in particular, from two different FedEx divisions, evolved from this people-centric culture and bring fairness to life in the workplace—FedEx Express' Guaranteed Fair Treatment (GFT) and FedEx Ground's RESPECT (Resolving Employee Situations and Problems Encourages Company-wide Trust) programs.

GFT Procedure

"Employees have rights, as citizens of this company," says Catherine Banks, Manager of Human Resource Compliance at FedEx Express. The Guaranteed Fair Treatment (GFT) Procedure provides a formal process for handling employee complaints, problems, concerns, and allegations of employment discrimination, and further guarantees an employee's right to participate, within the guidelines of the process.

The GFT Procedure has been in place for over 20 years and is a three-step appeal process available to all FedEx Express employees. Within five days of a disciplinary action or letter, an employee has the option to begin the process by filing a complaint via an online form or hard-copy bubble report. Once the complaint is entered into the system, an electronic message is automatically sent to the employee's managers and Human Resources personnel to begin the process of scheduling a meeting with the employee to review the complaint. After that initial meeting, the employee's managers can make a decision to uphold, overturn, or modify the initial disciplinary action. If the action is upheld, the employee has the option to move on to step two of the process, which takes the complaint to officers and the employee's executive management chain. If the disciplinary action is further upheld after step two, and the employee chooses to initiate step three, the complaint will be submitted to the Appeals Board, comprised of FedEx Express's chief officers and VPs, including President and CEO David Bronczek.

Seventeen to twenty cases are prepared weekly for submission to the Appeals Board. In preparation, the Appeals Board Team gets in touch with employees and their managers to collect the facts associated with each case.

All pending cases are delivered to the Board members each Friday, and "they often take them home over the weekend to review," says Banks. This in and of itself is a strong declaration of senior leaders' commitment and dedication to guaranteeing a high level of fairness within the FedEx Express workplace.

RESPECT Program

While the focus of FedEx Express's GFT Procedure is complaint resolution, FedEx Ground's RESPECT Program spotlights conflict resolution. RESPECT was launched in 2000 by FedEx Ground's Diversity office. The formal program evolved from the zero tolerance hotline for discrimination complaints and is intended to promote and preserve positive working relationships at all levels of the organization and provide a formal process for employee/manager conflict resolution.

The program resolves problems in five main areas: termination decisions, non-selection for an internal position, discipline situations, policy violations, and unfair treatment. To initiate the three-stage process, employees request an HR-mediated conversation with their supervisor by calling the FedEx Ground Alert Line, emailing or calling their Human Resource rep, or downloading an online form. If the conflict remains unresolved after the initial meeting, it escalates to the review stages of the process which includes a review of the case by the Appeal Board of five senior level officers.

"RESPECT is a way to approach conflict in a positive way," says Carolyn Lyle, Senior Manager of Diversity. By encouraging employees and managers alike to have a positive view of conflict resolution, the program provides a safe environment to discuss differences without the fear of reprisal. "They view this as an opportunity to better their relationships in the workplace, and feel valued for their contribution to these efforts," Lyle adds.

FedEx Ground is a place where conflict is viewed positively, and, as Lyle divulges, "we believe it's good news when employees complain. In this business, time is not something that is taken for granted, so when employees take the time to complain, it means they really care."

• **PRIDE**

Employees can feel pride in their personal jobs, in the work that is produced by their own team, and in their organization's corporate reputation, which is made up of its public reputation and standing in the community. Pride marks the level of engagement between every employee and his or her work. When companies develop a culture that fosters pride in individual and team accomplishments and employees feel that they make a difference, increased work quality, enthusiasm, teamwork, and devotion are the results. While helping employees to feel proud of their work, managers and employees also work to enhance the organization's public image. They become ambassadors for the company in their community.

Pride Case Study: Griffin Hospital's Patient Empowerment

Griffin Hospital operates a 160-bed acute care community hospital in Connecticut. With more than one thousand employees, Griffin Hospital has received national recognition and acclaim for creating a facility and approach to patient care responsive to the needs of patients. Many healthcare facilities around the world continue to visit us and incorporate our ideas into their healthcare models. Griffin is also a

Everything about Griffin revolves around a mission to provide personalized, humanistic, consumer-driven healthcare. For employees that means, "taking pride in the organization as if you own it."

teaching hospital and research center and offers outstanding post graduate medical education in internal and preventive medicine. Griffin is a teaching affiliate of the Yale University School of Medicine where many of Griffin's 200 physicians hold teaching positions.

Envision a hospital where nurses and patients mingle without the typical nursing stations, where all rooms are private or semi-private, where artwork covers the walls, saltwater aquariums provide a calm presence, and medical records are available for review by patients and their families. Therapy dogs and musicians roam the halls, and family-like kitchens buzz with activity as patients and staff alike share a meal, enjoy a coffee break, or munch on fresh-baked cookies and muffins prepared by volunteers. There is minimal signage, as staff members are more than willing to guide a patient or lost visitor to their desired destination—a small gesture, yes, but a huge help to the patients, who gratefully remember the experience of a staff member stopping what they were doing to take them where they needed to go.

Griffin subscribes to the philosophy that they can best serve patients and the community by providing the latest in medical technology in a healing, nurturing environment that encourages the patient's involvement and participation. The model is based on providing peaceful, comfortable surroundings, warm and supportive caregivers and access to health information and education to help patients get well faster and stay well longer.

Griffin utilized its philosophy to transform its already competitive spirit to focus fully on putting the patient first. Stories from patients and their families about how the Griffin experience was "different" than other hospitals in the area fueled commitment among employees and helped them embrace the Planetree philosophy (an internationally-recognized method of patient-centered care). Further validation came with returning patients requesting the same room with the same nursing staff over and over again. This, in turn, created close-knit relationships between nurse and patient. Grief counselors are now on call for employees who develop close relationships with patients, to assist them when patients don't recover. This simple practice is an expression of compassion for employees that also confirms management's understanding of the personalized care that employees provide to patients during their time at Griffin.

Visitors are wowed when they learn that everything about Griffin revolves around a mission to provide personalized, humanistic, consumer-driven healthcare. For employees that means, "taking pride in the organization as if you own it." Employees are constantly reminded that their No. 1 priority is catering to patient needs. One employee states, "the philosophy of care at Griffin is to nurture the individual physically, spiritually and emotionally. And the employees exemplify that in their approach to the patients and each other."

"Research shows there is a direct correlation between patient satisfaction and employee satisfaction," says Bill Powanda, Vice President. "We believe the reason we continue to make *Fortune's* 100 Best list is because of this. Griffin is recognized as having industry-leading patient satisfaction. Our staff enjoys working at Griffin because of the care model and the fact that they can practice their profession the way they envisioned it."

Griffin's President Patrick Charmel says: "Healthcare workers enter their fields because of personal motivation to serve people. Griffin's Planetree patient-care model approach to care and a healing environment provides that opportunity. Employees leave each day with a sense of personal satisfaction that they have helped those who are increasingly choosing Griffin Hospital for their care."

Griffin continues to be a model for hospitals nationwide and even in foreign countries. "People would like to think hospitals are different from other organizations," Powanda says. But Griffin is regularly approached by a multitude of other service-focused organizations, such as banks and higher education institutions, seeking information about the value of outstanding customer service. Griffin is an expert in the customer service arena, as the patients are the customers. Griffin understands the value of giving priority to the customer and constantly asks its patients what they need, because providing them just that—what they need—makes all the difference.

With continuous support and encouragement, Griffin employees are committed to constantly improving patient care and satisfaction. As one employee declares, "we really function as a team to give "caring" healthcare to our patients and their families. This gives us an overwhelming sense of accomplishment and pride."

• **CAMARADERIE**

Practices within the Camaraderie dimension encompass three aspects of employees' relationships with their coworkers. Employees experience camaraderie in the workplace through the level of *intimacy* they find, or the ability they have to be themselves. *Hospitable* workplaces are friendly and welcoming to all employees, and encourage people to have fun during the work day. Finally, a strong sense of *community* develops in organizations where people feel that they are part of a team or a family, that they cooperate within and across departments, and that people are connected by common values and purpose. A strong sense of camaraderie among employees can have many benefits. Fostering camaraderie can have a tremendous impact on employees' cooperation, enthusiasm and morale. When employees come to relate to each other not as competitors but as collaborators, it often decreases impediments to work processes and encourages people to work with each other to solve problems.

When company culture fosters pride in individual and team accomplishments, increased work quality, enthusiasm, teamwork, and devotion are the results.

Camaraderie Case Study: Hot Topic's Free To Be program

Hot Topic operates more than 700 specialty clothing retail stores across the United States. Its target customers are young men and women between the ages of 12 and 22 who are passionate about rock music, pop culture, and music-inspired fashion. Walk into a Hot Topic store and you'll immediately feel the energy. The merchandise assortment, store environment, and staff all demonstrate a passion for music. The company has more than 8,000 employees and is headquartered in Southern California.

Upon stepping through the doors of Hot Topic's headquarters, employees are welcomed into a music-driven, fun, and high-energy workplace. The gigantic open floor, filled with creative clusters of desks, seats all employees, including the CEO, and encourages active communication among staff without appointments, formalities or "red tape." Calls and emails from the over 600 in-mall retail stores are handled as top priority. There are no walls to separate levels of employees—no doors, no cubicles, and no barriers of any kind. The love for music is apparent, and televisions hang throughout the office playing music videos all day and night to keep everyone in touch with the music scene. Uniqueness and diversity of thought is celebrated throughout the company, in turn creating a culture dependent on the generation of new ideas, where producing a stimulating work environment for the individual employee is crucial.

There is no doubt that the Hot Topic culture is unique and different—with its roots deep in the rock 'n' roll world, where individualistic style is celebrated. But this music-inspired company truly rises to a class of its own by creating an environment where employees and customers alike are completely free to be themselves. As one employee describes it, "There are a million reasons why Hot Topic is a wonderful place to work, but specifically they allow me to be myself. We can dress however we feel comfortable. We are allowed to wear our hair in any color we want. We can have piercings if we want, no matter how 'strange' anyone looks, everyone is treated well." On the flip side, there are plenty of Hot Topic employees sans colored hair, piercing, or tattoos, who are just as into the music as their tattooed colleagues.

"We've all come together with a love for music," explains Amy Malone, Manager of Office Services, "but if you took away the music, you would see that our people are the priority." People first is as much a part of the fabric of Hot Topic's culture as the music. "When interviewing candidates," adds Lisa Collins, Manager of Staffing, "we don't judge people by the way they look, which allows them to be themselves from the beginning." By taking physical appearances out of the equation, the focus boils down to the individual's talent, enabling employees to showcase their skill set without worrying about their image.

New employees are treated to a full day "culture orientation," communicating to new hires that "people really matter," says Malone. And it doesn't end there. "We go to great strides to keep it alive," she adds. Input from employees about the culture is solicited on a regular basis and everyone is held accountable for upholding and contributing to this culture in which people are the top priority. Employees are treated with respect and they know their opinions matter. "We have over 8,000 employees now and we still feel like a family," Malone describes. "We often visualize our employees as a large flat picture puzzle," she continues, "we all fit together, and with one piece of the puzzle missing, we're an incomplete picture."

Upholding such a creatively unique culture takes serious commitment and dedication. But don't think for a second that these individuals are all work and no play. As a retail employee recalls, "If anything, I don't see it as strictly work. I think it is the best fun in the whole world. For the first time, I look forward to going to work, and when I get there, sometimes I can't stop smiling. You're allowed to be who you are, inside and out."

2007

TODAY'S **EMPLOYEES** EXPECT MORE: A **GOOD WORKPLACE**

[LEARNING REVIEW]

A journalist from a Latin American educational magazine asked Robert Levering about trends he sees in workplaces worldwide, especially in the field of training and development. Among other points, he suggests that to contribute to a great workplace environment, training must go beyond teaching specific skills.

Q: Is there a key element of a great workplace that is common to every country in the world? Or are there different major issues for different regions?

A: The key element is trust, and trust is the most important element throughout the world and in every industry. We have seen this confirmed in all of the countries where we have conducted extensive employee surveys. By trust I am referring to three things: 1) management's credibility — whether employees believe what their leaders tell them, 2) respect toward employees — measured in whether managers demonstrate their concern about employees' professional and personal development, show appreciation for their work, and care about them as people, and 3) fairness in how people are treated in terms of pay, promotions, and recognition.

Q: Multinational companies like FedEx, Microsoft, and McDonald's share spots in the Best Workplaces lists in several countries, but are not even present in others. How is it that corporate culture translates to some places and not others?

A: The multinational companies that have been most successful are ones that have both a coherent people-oriented business philosophy that they have translated into some key behaviors that they expect of their managers and of all their employees. At the same time, they typically give the leaders in various countries the ability to adapt the corporate philosophy to local circumstances. The companies you cite are very successful on both levels.

Q: What are your findings in areas like Human Performance, Knowledge Management, and specific HR issues that employees find to be what makes a good working environment?

A: Based on our research, we have identified nine specific areas where the best companies excel, including their hiring processes, how they communicate with employees, show appreciation, develop people's talents, celebrate successes, and share rewards.

Q: Where do Training and Development methods fit in organizations efforts towards becoming a Great Place to Work®?

A: Training and development is one of the nine areas that can make a big difference. What's important to note, however, is that training for skills is not what makes the difference. We have found that in the Best Workplaces, that programs that help employees to develop their talents and gifts is more important. In other words, the training and development programs must be done in a way that demonstrates respect for employees as people with a variety of abilities, not just individuals who can perform specific tasks.

Q: Innovation is one of today's main assets within company strategies. In companies that always maintained a Best Place status, is there a need for innovation in policies to keep said status?

A: Innovation requires trust. That is, in order for people to be creative, it is important for them to feel comfortable with their work environments. Otherwise they will not be willing to share their best ideas with others. Because the best workplaces are characterized by a high level of trust, they typically are also very innovative. So, if a company wants to be innovative, they need to concentrate on creating a great workplace.

Q: After 20 years of experience in analyzing work environments, would you say there have been changes in the trends of what people expect? What is the main issue nowadays, and has it changed since you started the Institute?

A: The most important change has been in the expectations of employees about having a good workplace. When I started research in this field, employees generally did not expect companies to provide a good work environment. At that time, most of them simply were content to have a job. Today's employees expect more. They expect the companies, for instance, to do more in the area of work-family balance than in the past. They expect the company to make provisions for people with families by offering more flexible scheduling.

Q. What does the Institute do to help organizations improve their workplace?

A: The Institute has various tools that help companies assess the level of trust in the organizations, including an employee survey called the Trust Index©. Using such tools and an extensive database of best practices, the Institute consults with leaders about strategies to help make their companies a Great Place to Work®.

Q: What are the top Best Places to work in Latin America?

A: Our Institute helps produce Best Places to Work lists in the nine largest Latin American countries, including Argentina, Brazil, Chile, Colombia, and Mexico. We also produce a list of the 100 Best in Latin America. You can see the most recent list at *www.greatplacetowork.com/best/list-la.htm.*

Q: Have you learned something specific from Latin-American work cultures that you could apply to organizations across the world?

A: We have seen a number of remarkable workplaces throughout Latin America. We think that the lessons that can be learned are to be found in the specific, world-class practices of individual companies rather than in generalized principles. In other words, I would encourage HR managers to study and do benchmarking of the practices of the companies that appear on our lists, if they are interested in learning how to create a great workplace environment.

2003

MANY OF LATIN AMERICA'S BEST ARE ALSO GOOD CITIZENS

[CLARIN]

In this interview with an Argentine business magazine, Robert Levering was asked to explain the Great Place to Work® Model and how it applies to Latin American companies. He stressed the importance of corporate social responsibility in many of Latin America's Best Workplaces.

Q: Your definition of a "Great Place to Work®" is "one where you trust the people you work for, have pride in what you do, and enjoy the people you work with." What is the specific meaning of each of the terms in this definition?

A. My definition is based on interviews I've conducted at dozens of great workplaces throughout the world. I discovered that employees at these companies invariably talked about three issues. The first was that they had a high level of trust in management. By trust, they meant they believed what management told them; they thought management delivered on promises; they felt management genuinely respected them as people, not just as hired hands; and they thought management treated them fairly. At the same time employees of great workplaces also said they had great pride in their jobs and in the company itself. Finally, they all felt a great sense of camaraderie with the other people they worked with. That is, they said the company was a very friendly environment or, oftentimes, a place where they felt they could have fun.

Q: Could you give me some examples of how credibility, respect, and fairness improve trust?

A. Trust involves the three elements you listed. Credibility involves employees' opinions about management's believability, competence, and integrity. To build credibility, management must be transparent about information so that employees can ask questions and determine whether or not management is telling the truth. This is crucial because we simply don't extend our trust to others unless we can rely on their word. In the workplace, this requires management to share information frequently and widely, but it must also be accessible to respond to questions. At most of the best workplaces, senior managers regularly engage in question-and-answer sessions with employees. Many also extend other opportunities for employees to ask questions, such as through email or the company intranet.

Respect refers to how employees perceive management's attitude toward them. First, this means showing appreciation to employees for doing good work. Respect also is shown by management doing its best to provide employees with the right tools and adequate training opportunities to help them grow. But it's also important that employees feel that management genuinely listens to their ideas and suggestions and involves them in decisions about their jobs as much as possible. A good example is RM Sistemas, a Brazilian computer software firm, which actually conducts on-line voting among all employees to determine which new benefits policies are implemented.

The final trust issue is fairness. This is a bigger issue than pay, though fair pay is important. It also involves whether people feel that they are treated fairly when it comes to promotions or being given opportunities for challenging assignments. Nothing destroys trust more quickly than for management to act in ways that employees feel are unjust.

Q: What kind of work should companies do in order to make themselves great places to work?

A: In every case that I have studied, the transformation of companies into great workplaces began with management improving its communications with employees to bolster its credibility. Typically, top managers initiate new forums with employees where they make themselves more accessible to answering questions than in the past. They also act on issues that are brought up in these sessions, to demonstrate that they do listen and that they follow through on their promises. The second issue that these companies address is making sure that employees feel appreciated for their work. It is always amazing to me to see the importance of saying "thank you." The workplace environment can change dramatically when management makes a concentrated effort to make sure that employees are shown sincere appreciation both informally and through regular programs to recognize the work that employees do. An outstanding example of this is Magazine Luiza, a Brazilian retailer, which shows its appreciation by featuring ordinary employees in its outdoor billboard advertising.

Q: Can any company become a Great Place to Work® in a short period of term?

A: The quick answer is yes. We have seen examples of all kinds of companies that have made dramatic turnarounds in their workplace cultures in as little as a year and certainly within three years. One of the best examples is Continental Airlines, which was not only a terrible workplace but also on the edge of bankruptcy when a new management team took over in 1994. Within three years, the company had made a complete turnaround financially, becoming a leader in the airline industry. Its turn-around was largely a result of changes in its workplace culture in 1999. Continental was named on the *Fortune* list of the "100 Best Companies to Work for" in the US. It did so by concentrating initially on internal communications and showing appreciation to employees. For instance, they rewarded all employees with a $65 bonus each month that Continental ranked among the top three airlines in on-time performance. In a period of only three months, Continental jumped from last to first in the monthly on-time performance ratings among all U.S. airlines.

Q: What is the relationship between a good work environment and profitability of a company?

A: Many recent studies have shown a high correlation between good workplace practices and financial success. For example, a Wall Street investment service recently conducted a study that compared the financial results of a portfolio of stocks of companies that have appeared on *Fortune* "100 Best Companies to Work for" with a portfolio of an established stock market index (Standard & Poor's 500). The results were dramatic. Money invested in the "100 Best" portfolio would have outperformed the S&P 500 by a ratio of almost five-to-one. Studies in Britain and Brazil have shown similar results. It is only common sense that when employees feel well treated, they will provide superior service to the customers, which will mean more financial rewards for the company itself. In fact, FedEx, a company that has been on our *Fortune* "100 Best" list for many years has a slogan—"People-Service-Profit"—that expresses this philosophy.

Q: What do you think Latin America companies could do to become better places to work? Could you mention specifics by region?

A: Our Institute has found that Latin American companies are extremely receptive to the concept of creating great workplaces, as we currently conduct national surveys in all the major Latin American countries. Last year more than 30,000 employees answered our surveys in Argentina and we expect even more to participate this year. We have found that, in general, the results from Latin America are quite comparable to those from North America and Europe. In fact, the survey results of the best workplaces from all three continents are nearly identical, indicating that the best Latin American companies are truly world class. So, themes we discussed earlier about the importance of building trust in the workplace are just as important in Latin America as elsewhere.

The presence of great workplaces in Latin America is true despite the widespread incidence of unemployment and poverty in the region. We have found that the best companies don't feel that it is enough to simply offer jobs. But they offer quality jobs in a good working environment because they see that it benefits both their employees and the company as well as because of higher morale and productivity.

Perhaps because of the difficult economic conditions, we have also found many Latin American companies focus on their corporate social responsibility. A few notable examples include:

- Monsanto Argentina, jointly with the town of Rojas, buys, plants, and takes care of a tree for each and every new-born child in the community. In this way children and their families can participate in the preservation of the environment. Other companies, jointly with the National Forest Commission, organized the tree parenthood initiative, by which "baby trees" are given to employees who take responsibility to plant and care for them.

- Federal Express Argentina's managers use working hours to teach and deliver seminars in schools within their community.

- McDonalds, has its Ronald Mc Donalds house that provides lodging to poor people having to spend weeks living far from their homes, while their relatives (usually children) are being treated in Hospital Italiano,

Such efforts not only assist the communities, but they also help employees feel proud of their companies, an essential ingredient in making a company a Great Place to Work®.

2009

MONEY DOES NOT MAKE PEOPLE, PEOPLE MAKE MONEY

By **Raciel Sosa**

This article sets out the elements of a great workplace according to Great Place to Work® Institute. Those elements are: a human capital well-aligned with the company´s strategy, best practices applied to human capital, and competent leadership. Focusing on these three aspects, companies can come closer to being excellent workplaces. Authentic leadership begins with a process of inner transformation because the true leader "preaches" by example.

HUMAN CAPITAL ALIGNED WITH THE STRATEGY

Only a winning company can generate a great working environment. You would not be motivated to work for a company that has great human resources practices but constantly loses money. At Great Place to Work Institute, our surveys have shown that excellent workplaces are also very productive organizations.

We noticed that there are successful companies that lack a good organizational or optimal work environment but they have the potential to become excellent organizations. These companies have so far based their culture only on immediate and short-term results, though. However, when a company becomes aware of this shortcoming and decides to improve its human-capital practices, that is, to work on forging competent leaders, then, it begins to improve significantly its already strong financial performance.

BEST HUMAN CAPITAL PRACTICES

This element of great workplaces derives/drifts from the conviction that people make the difference. Or, that money does not make people, people make money. Once leaders abandon their former notion, they work to implement strategies that support human capital and working environments which become an investment rather than an expense to people. They then generate great results that increase business productivity.

Best practices focus on welcoming new ideas and inspiring the staff; creating two-way communication channels; acknowledging and recognizing employees; finding means to stimulate personal and professional development; celebrating the company's successes along with the staff; and fostering camaraderie by sharing the fruits of the employees' work in a fair way.

COMPETENT LEADERS

This element of a great workplace is the most exciting and, at the same time, the most complex to develop. The reason is that developing leadership involves human processes that require time to incubate, develop, and mature to full competency. Leadership is an infinite path where people never stop learning. In order to achieve this quality successfully, it is essential to have a solid training base that will allow us to understand that leadership is not a matter of charisma nor good intention.

Authentic leadership begins with a process of inner transformation because the true leader practices what he/she preaches. Leaders are not made overnight just by learning simple techniques which they may not understand or how, why, and when to apply them. A leader

> Money does not make people, people make money. The essence of building leadership is in building and maintaining the confidence of teams.

works first on his/her personal integrity, which is the foundation of true leadership.

Money does not make people, people make money. The essence of building leadership is in building and maintaining the confidence of teams.

Trust allows each of the collaborators who work with the leader to accept with conviction the guidance, support, and feedback offered on a daily basis.

When there is no trust, support rings hollow and fall, and they do not generate the high-level results that organizations expect. Today, most organizations look for means to support their management teams by optimizing the quality of a competent leadership.

Working on these three elements brings to life the goal of Great Place to Work Institute: helping organizations understand and practice the qualities and behaviors that lead to the creation of great workplaces.

2009

OWNER-LED **SMALL** AND MEDIUM-SIZE **COMPANIES**

By **Prasenjit Bhattacharya**

[GREAT PLACE TO WORK®
INSTITUTE INDIA WHITE PAPER]

"This company has been in my family for two generations," comments the CEO of a midsize organization, "however, we have been left behind by many Johnny-come-lately companies. I know I am supposed to focus on long-term strategic issues, like acquisition and growth. But all my time is taken up by firefighting. How can I build a self-sustaining organization so that my day-to-day role comes down?"

The comment is reflective of the predicament that owners of SMEs face all the time. Barring a few who are in a niche that commands high margins, most may not have any significant product, technology, service, or talent differentiators.

So, how can the average SME become a great workplace? This question has intrigued me for some time now. For the purpose of this article, I refer to any organization with fewer than 500 employees as an SME. While any company, big or small, can be a great workplace, our recent study of India's Best Companies to Work For reveals that organizations with more employees

Prasenjit Bhattacharya has long been intrigued by the special challenges faced by smaller companies trying to become great workplaces. In this piece that first appeared in an Indian business magazine, the CEO of Great Place to Work® Institute India describes a number of ways the best SMEs have met these tests.

have a slightly higher chance of making it to the Top 50 Best Workplaces list. If we omit the multinationals, technology companies, and industries like IT and financial services, there are not many SMEs that make it to the Top 50 Best Workplaces list. Is it more difficult for an average SME to be a great workplace?

To understand the factors that might help the owner-led SMEs become great workplaces, we observed a few such organizations. Here are some of the factors that we found were helpful in making them better workplaces for their employees:

- **RELATIVELY SECURE NATURE OF BUSINESS**

A Google or an Apple may have started in a garage with a band of people who believed in the potential of what they were doing, and by many accounts were having fun, even when they were not clear where the next slice of funding was coming from.

An average SME, on the other hand, needs stability to be perceived as a Great Place to Work® by its employees. This stability could come because of many reasons. The owner is often obsessed with quality, and over time the products are able to command a premium, even in a price-sensitive commodity market. We have seen it in organizations with products ranging from coal and coke, pickles and preserves to automobile graphics to textiles. Often, the organization is able to make good use of automation and technical innovation, and in some cases it has strong proximity to key customers, being their sole suppliers.

- **THE OWNER**

Almost without exception, the owner plays the most significant role in making a great workplace. The role of the owner is multifaceted. On one hand, he is often the person most knowledgeable about the organization's products/services or the industry. On the other hand, he plays a key role in building relationships with key customers. The owner knows every employee personally, often because he has recruited all of them. When it comes to work, he leads by example. Most employees are in awe of him. The owner often treats employees like family. He has the image of a benevolent, kind-hearted person, known for his generosity when an employee is in real need. His managers often despair at his enthusiasm to help his people during personal emergencies.

The owner treats people with respect. People willingly work for low salaries in lieu of higher ones because of the "respect" they get from the owner. Indeed, many people do not have formal qualifications or adequate experience for the roles they perform, and are there primarily on account of the trust reposed on them by the owner. "How can I leave the organization, if he trusts me so much? My salary might be low, but I know he will take care of me in time of need," say such employees. (See below, why this situation ultimately has diminishing returns for the company.)

• FREEDOM TO EXPERIMENT, MAKE MISTAKES AT THE OPERATING LEVEL

Many such SMEs provide employees great opportunities to learn. Unlike larger organizations, roles and procedures are not cast in stone. A competent operations head may also look after projects. The challenges provided, and hence the opportunities to learn, are far more than what can be expected in a larger organization. Very often, the organization acquires a new technology or process, say an Enterprise Resource Planning tool (ERP), but

> Focus provides the oxygen to stoke the fire of employee engagement.

doesn't invest in the necessary training for people. Expensive technology or machines may be used but adequate equipment or tools are not provided. All of these are great opportunities for learning to innovate, improvise, or improve. The owner, knowing that adequate support has not been provided, is more tolerant of mistakes made by people.

• FLEXIBILITY

Unlike many large organizations, SMEs provide more flexibility to employees. For example, we heard: "I was relocated to head office because my husband's company transferred him to the city where that office is." And: "During my pregnancy, I was given complete flexibility without loss of pay." Indeed, partly because of this flexibility, and partly because of lower compensation levels, many employees find they have the free time to start their own "side business."

• A STRONG SENSE OF PRIDE

Even if it is a relatively secure business, most SMEs face challenges that are life-threatening to the business. The employees know that their business is a survivor, having survived when the odds were stacked against them. There are many stories of personal and collective heroism that people recall with pride. And as long as threats to their existence do not become a regular feature, they can generate pride in employees. The founder often knows how to narrate these stories so that they become a part of the folklore within the organization.

An SME with the above strengths could be a great workplace. However, the reality may be that the SME still finds it very difficult to be one of the Best Workplaces. Here are some of the reasons:

- **EXCESSIVE DEPENDENCE ON ONE INDIVIDUAL— THE OWNER OR FOUNDER**

The loyalty of most employees is often to the founder, rather than to the company or its articulated vision, mission, or values. Things happen because the founder is involved in a hands-on manner. Most people are keen to impress the founder. They come early if he is there, stay late if he is likely to observe it. Consequently, it is difficult for other managers to command significant authority. If a new manager tries to do so, before long, the owner's ears will be filled by some of his "loyalists."

The founder tries recruiting senior managers from outside, but soon finds them incompetent, little realizing that it is his own style and the culture he has created that is responsible. In frustration, he falls back on the old guard—the trusted loyalists.

"They need to be told everything, but I can trust them," he rationalizes. Realizing that some of the senior managers he recruited from outside have not been able to effectively get the work done by those under them, the owner falls back on the default mode of being a hands-on manager. The employees are happy. They do not want to take orders from anyone except the owner.

Since the owner is all-important, his direct reports are busy taking individual instructions from him and trying to impress him. They do not work in a cohesive team. During absence of the owner, all coordination between his direct reports stops. The owner, therefore, even in his absence, has to review if his team members are giving necessary inputs to each other!

Frustrated with the situation, some of the new managers recruited from outside hand in their papers. This further reinforces the owner's

A clearly articulated business strategy and steps to getting there are also an area of improvement for many SMEs.

belief that a "professional" manager cannot be trusted. Sometimes, he might keep one or two professionals in important positions as "masks" for the external world. However, he is resigned to having to give minute instructions to his people. The old-timers are happy and secure. "You are like a virus, our body will soon reject you," they seem to say to any newcomer. The over-dependence on the owner and the lack of strong second-line leaders has a number of consequences:

Communication is stunted

Since the only communication of relevance, is from the owner, all other managers and all forums where the owner is not present become ineffective as tools of communication. While part of the owner's message still percolates, thanks to his proximity to people across the hierarchy, middle and senior managers are not interested in feeding up his voice from the trenches, lest it impact their own image negatively. As the organization grows, the owner spends less time with frontline employees and none at all unaccompanied by his senior managers. "He will know the truth only if he speaks to us directly— without his senior managers," say many frontline employees.

Impression management becomes the key

If the owner stays away or the company has many sites, each visit by the owner becomes an "event" to be managed. The walls are whitewashed, the roads swept, the guesthouse refurbished, and the entire local management team is at the gate to receive the owner with flowers. "I know all this is being done for my benefit, but at least some good work is getting done this way," rationalizes the owner.

Robust processes for performance management, rewards, and recognition do not get developed

Since the owner is hands-on, formal processes of the above kind do not get developed. While initially the owner knew each individual well enough to assess his or her performance, with time he starts relying on his key executives for assessing people and their performance across the hierarchy, thereby creating power centers, which ultimately results in cliques, factions, and politicking. This takes myriad shapes from caste to community.

Lack of exposure to good practices

Though the owner is relatively well informed by virtue of his association with customers, suppliers, and collaborators, a majority of his managers have seen precious little outside their organization. The owner represents the organization at industry forums. The owner goes abroad to attend industry fairs and conferences. As a result, his key executives do not get adequate opportunities to upgrade their professional expertise. This leads to even more consequences:

Lack of development of second line

The senior executives who have not developed adequate exposure in their professional areas have little incentive to grow their second line. Since their own skills are not always marketable, and many have stuck with the organization due to location or personal constraints, there is little to be gained by developing their potential.

With little growth by way of acquisitions or greenfield projects (remember the owner is too busy with his hands-on involvement), why develop people? There are no roles to grow into. Young professionals who join the company quickly realize the situation and leave. This is a vicious cycle and even if the owner were to acquire a new business or start a greenfield project, he does not have a talent pipeline to help him build his new businesses.

Inability or reluctance to pay market competitive salaries

A key aspect of such SMEs is their ability to keep employee costs low (as noted above). Beyond a point this strategy yields diminishing returns. While the old-timers are willing to work at low salaries, partly because of inadequate qualifications and partly out of loyalty to the owner, new employees will not come at such low salaries. Rather than create huge internal inequity and heartburn among the loyalists, the owner opts to recruit many people who have retired elsewhere as "consultants" or even as full-time employees at senior levels. While these employees bring required skills at an affordable price, they seldom have the ability or inclination to rock the boat. This is a second income for them, an extension of post-retirement tenure. Maintaining peace with the owners and the loyalists becomes more important than crusading for meaningful change. In any case, before long, many of the old-timers themselves graduate into "consultant/advisor" roles and even the owner starts feeling helpless in front of this cabal. Gratitude for past services rendered and their knowledge of many secrets about the business and the owner's family prevents the owner from going beyond this group and try to revitalize the company.

All of these factors start impacting employee morale. Employees are reluctant to give suggestions or contribute because they are concerned that senior managers may take credit for their ideas. In the process, many employees become dead wood, who nevertheless stick with the company due to lack of marketable skills, convenient location, or personal constraints.

- **Why Many SMEs Fall into the Above Trap and what Can Be Done**

In reality, each organization is unique and a cookie-cutter approach may not work for all. However, having observed numerous SMEs, I believe a number of principles apply to most. I have in mind a medium-sized organization with 250-500 employees, which is already a good place to work in many respects with reasonably secure financial performance. Here are some of the steps that an SME can take to be a great workplace:

- **Commitment of the Owner to Creating a Great Workplace**

Commitment to creating a great workplace is not complementary to the goal of creating wealth, but rather a distinct and important goal by itself. It is not a goal that you focus on after achieving the "primary" goal of making money. Just as great products or services do not happen by accident, great workplaces are an outcome of deliberate choice.

Making this choice is not an intellectual decision for the owner. His actions are what help make his organization one of the better places to work. Conversely, he is a key reason why it is not yet a Great Place to Work®. Our research shows that one of the most important drivers in creating a Great Place to Work® is a shared perception by employees that management's actions match its

> **Performance improvements often compensate for any investment made in transforming the company's culture.**

words. But who is to tell the owner that his actions (or inaction) are in the way of creating a great workplace?

Crafting a feedback process for the owner that will help him to understand reality and his contribution to it (without his being defensive) is an essential first step. A more effective way of doing this is by enlisting the help of a competent external coach. If an owner arrives at this stage, he realizes that the most difficult challenge for him is to take feedback from his people. He may feel, "It is easy for them to give feedback, what is their stake? I behave the way I do because I know while my employees can leave me for a 20 percent increase in salary, I will be left holding the baby." It is a Catch 22 situation for the owner, particularly when the feedback is about qualities that are also responsible for his success. It is common for owners to have a lot of drive, which is why they succeed, but which is also why they keep interfering!

This is also the reason why processes like 360-feedback (multisource feedback) often fail—because a strength, when displayed in excess, is an area in need of improvement. A good coach helps the owner navigate through these dilemmas, and ensures that the baby is not thrown out with the bath water.

• Building Credibility for the Change Process

One advantage that many SMEs have in initiating the process of change is that, unlike larger organizations that undergo a plethora of new initiatives every time the CEO changes, there is less baggage from the past. The hands-on SME owner has strong credibility. He has to communicate personally to all employees why there is a need for change and what the objectives are, which often are not adequately clear at this stage. The owner may use phrases like *Great Place to Work®, employer of choice*, or *good to great* to describe what he wants. He need not articulate a the roadmap, only communicate the need for change and his commitment to make it happen. The owner does not pretend to have all the answers, but commits to finding the right answers together with his people as they embark on this journey.

The owner will also have to spell out how change will happen, who will do the initial work, and what will be the roles of the project team. The following steps can help in building credibility for the change process:

Nomination of change agents and creation of a change council: Once the objectives for change have been communicated by the owner, he invites each department or function to nominate change agents who, in the department's opinion, are the right people to lead the process. Anyone below the department head is eligible. The department chooses the agents by consensus, by voting. In the case of larger departments, where more than one person may have to be nominated, care is taken to see that people from across levels are chosen. These change agents have a term of typically one year, and they are a part of the employee council for the organization. The leadership team then nominates up to one-third of members of the change council, taking care to ensure that senior mangers, whose ownership is vital, and technical experts are part of are this council. The owner heads the council, whose role is to finalize the composition of the project team, approve the roadmap for change, review and monitor progress, and remove roadblocks.

The creation of the council is a deliberate way of creating a more inclusive "shadow" structure that tries to involve all stakeholders among employees.

> Communication is a religion at the best SMEs—95 percent of information is communicated 95 percent of the time to 95 percent of the people.

It also serves to highlight the behaviors of senior managers in front of a larger group. If required, norms of behavior for the council are defined and the council is an opportunity for all, particularly the owner and his senior managers, to be role models for the right behaviors.

- **Creating a Great Place to Work®: Change Makers Program for Senior Managers and Change Council Members**

This is a powerful learning experience that is typically as a 2–3-day workshop that delves deeper into all aspects of change required to move toward creating a great workplace. This program is preceded by a diagnostic exercise that ensures that the senior managers and council members are clear about their current reality. The program helps them to understand different aspects of a great workplace, assess the effectiveness of their people practices, and prioritize areas of action. The project team drafts the findings from the above program into a roadmap for change that will be presented to the council at an appropriate time.

- **Study Missions to a Great Place To Work®**

The council members are divided into study groups and are exposed to a set of carefully chosen Best Workplaces—organizations that are relevant to learn from, keeping in mind the roadmap developed by the project team. Each study group prepares a 15–20-minute presentation of key observations and learning from their study tour. The project team now gives the final touches to the draft roadmap and presents it to the council for ratification.

- **Internal Communication**

The project team prepares a 2-hour presentation on the need for change, results of the internal diagnostics (employee feedback), findings from the study missions, and the roadmap for change. Council members present these findings to each and every team, reaching all employees. The owner or one of his senior colleagues from the council is present to answer questions and take note of suggestions from employees. The council meets again after this presentation to freeze the roadmap for change.

- **Implementing Quick Wins**

The council approves implementation of 8–10 quick-win ideas they have adapted from others, which can be implemented immediately with little or no financial or material resources. Many of these ideas relate to improving communication, recognition, and creating an element of fun/enjoyment in the workplace. Many of the subsequent steps will differ depending on the roadmap developed at this stage.

- **Envisioning the Future**

At this point in time, hopefully enough credibility has been established for the company to articulate its core purpose and core values—an inspiring vision of the future and the values they need to build upon to be an organization of substance. These values are critical in cementing the mindset required to bring about desired change. These are values that resonate with the people here. They are not copy-paste values of other organizations finalized by some senior management group in a one-day workshop. For example, "Be honorable" may not be clear to others, but the people of this organization know what it means and why it is so important. For new employees who join in future, the organization may define a few behaviors clearly, perhaps with stories or anecdotes that exemplify given values.

How do we create a core purpose and core values that are owned by most people in the organization? We do it by involving most people in the organization. SMEs can involve all employees in specially designed large-scale interactive processes (LSIP), a technology that is very effective in co-creating change by involving everyone. All employees come together for two days to co-create the vision and values, the behaviors required to demonstrate the values, and the action plans required to cement the vision and values. The exercise of co-creating a core purpose and core values releases enormous amounts of energy and as all decisions within the organization are viewed through the prism of vision and values, the new mindset starts to take root.

The owner and the leadership team soon face the real test of the values. One key senior manager or a set of key executives does something that might have been ignored earlier, but which is a clear violation of one of the core values recently adopted. The owner can choose to ignore the violation, in which case the whole process slowly becomes an exercise in futility. Or the owner can face the situation head on and let this manager go. In the latter case, this incident becomes a part of the folklore and is repeated for years within the organization. Most great places have similar examples.

- **Clarifying the Business Strategy and Stakeholder Value Propositions**

In a Great Place to Work®, leadership has a vision of where the organization is going, and equally importantly, people believe they know how to get there. SMEs struggling to become great workplaces soon realize that you cannot be a great workplace without a business focus. Whether it is career opportunities for top talent, market compensation, or simply the pride of being part of a high-performing team, focus provides the oxygen to stoke the fire of employee engagement.

A clearly articulated business strategy and steps to get there are also an area of improvement for many SMEs, where the owner is bogged down by day-to-day firefighting. The vision and values involved all employees, but formulation of business strategy and stakeholder value propositions involves a small group of carefully chosen people. They work with a structured process to define the business boundaries and answer fundamental questions—What is our business? What products and services do we provide now and in future? Who are our current and future customers? How will we differentiate between us and our competitors? This group also works with the vision, values, and strategy, and translates it into value propositions for stakeholder groups like customers, employees, shareholders, and community. The owner is closely involved in this exercise.

The proof of the pudding is in the eating. There are three sets of action plans, now at different stages of implementation— the roadmap; pilot projects arising out of the vision and values exercise; and pilot projects arising out of the business strategy and stakeholder value propositions. The last category often leads to improvement in business processes, introduction of new techniques like Six Sigma, and a variety of waste-reduction initiatives. Sometimes it also leads to mergers and acquisitions and other high-impact actions.

The pilot projects help incorporate into company culture the change required, and they produce tangible business results. Often, the tangible gains at this stage more than compensate for any investments made in the change process.

Consistent role modeling by the owner and his senior managers is visible at this stage. Processes exist to give feedback to senior managers. Employees can ask questions and the responses are heard by other employees. Values are reflected in actions and in decisions made by the company. Stories of living the values (and value violations) circulate freely. Often the values have been codified and are commonly acknowledged to be the "rules for success." Communication is a religion. Ninety-five percent of information is communicated 95 percent of the time to 95 percent of the people. Employee involvement forums are active and most employees are involved in making and implementing suggestions. Employees volunteer to organize a variety of activities to make the workplace fun. The organization has a credible process for delivering justice. If any employee feels he is unfairly treated, he knows that there is a fair process of appeal. A majority of employees feel "we are unique," and in many cases they say their workplace feels like a family.

We have observed many organizations that have made the leap from being good places to work to being great places to work using the above roadmap.

2. GIFTWORK®

2006

HOW THE **BEST WORKPLACES** CREATE "GIFTWORK® CULTURES"

By **Robert Levering**

[ÉPOCA]

In this article for a major Brazilian newsweekly, Robert Levering identifies the nine occasions when managers can help create what he calls "Giftwork® cultures," the essence of a "great place to work."

How do some companies become Great Places to Work®? Or, we could ask: what is special about what leaders do at companies like Promon, Serasa, Dow, Magazine Luiza, DPaschoal, Accor, Nestlé and the other firms that appear on the list of GPTW® *Melhores Empresas para Trabalhar no Brasil* being published in this issue of *Epoca*.

Those of us who work at Great Place to Work® Institute are frequently asked this question. It's no wonder. We created the Best Workplace competitions more than 20 years ago and currently conduct competitions in 29 countries, including this one in Brazil. In selecting companies for these lists, we survey more than 600,000 employees in some 3,000 companies.

Based on this wealth of data and hundreds of on-site interviews that we have conducted at great workplaces throughout the world, we have come to this conclusion: Great workplaces create workplace cultures that are qualitatively different from others. In particular, we have observed that their business strategy revolves around their workplace culture, they believe that trust is the key to productivity, and they have a common manner of initiating people-related programs. Let us look at each of these three characteristics:

First, leaders of great workplaces see the quality of the workplace culture as central to their strategy for business success. They often state this belief explicitly. Accor Brasil, for instance, expresses it in the form of a slogan: "People-Service-Profit." That is, they insist that management should create a great workplace culture for their employees, who will then deliver superior service for customers which, in turn, will lead to higher profitability for the investors/owners. This "People First" strategy contrasts with the more conventional one of seeing "human resources" as one of many components (like financial assets, marketing, technology, etc.) that can be manipulated independently to achieve business success. The "People First" strategy has been extremely successful. For example, a portfolio of stocks of the *Fortune* "100 Best Companies to Work For" has outperformed the Standard and Poors 500 stock market index by a factor of 5 to 1 over the past nine years.

Second, great workplaces believe that trust is crucial to increasing productivity, fostering innovation, and encouraging teamwork. So, they invariably ask what the impact on the culture as a whole will be of new specific practices or policies. They are especially concerned about whether new practices will help increase the level of trust in their relationship with employees. That is because they believe that employees work harder, smarter, and more cooperatively with management and with each other when

In a "gift-like" culture, companies go beyond the conventional market-like behaviors when it comes to sharing information, giving recognition, celebrating, and other day-to-day interactions: they simply are more generous than required.

they trust management and feel trusted by management. This attitude diverges from more conventional approaches to productivity, which I call Big Carrot (offering incentives to get people to work harder), Big Stick (resorting to coercive measures), Big Daddy (paternalistic practices), or Big Stars (developing systems that focus on the company's high performers). Other methods to achieve productivity may be valid in the short-term, but each has severe limitations as a long-term strategy, especially when compared with the approach of trying to create an environment where there is a high level of trust between employees and managers.

The third major differentiating characteristic is *how* great workplaces create a culture of trust. It starts with their approach to work itself. Most organizations only treat employees' work like a commodity, which often leads to employees feeling alienated, that they are an interchangeable part of a machine. People feel that their work is treated like a pay and benefits in exchange for employees giving an agreed-upon amount of their time and effort. But what happens in the typical workplace over time is that employees feel that the company treats not only their work as a commodity, but they feel as if they are treated as a commodity, too. That's because people consider their own work to be part of their personal identity and sense of self-worth. It's difficult for us to separate our work from ourselves so we feel dehumanized when an employer treats what we do impersonally.

Gift-like versus market-like exchanges

In contrast to what happens in typical workplaces, great employers demonstrate that people are giving part of themselves at work. They respond more generously than may be expected or required. This generosity is typified by the unusual and distinctive policies and practices of the great employers. But it is also characterized by the ways in which the company (through its managers) goes above and beyond what is required in sharing information, giving recognition, celebrating, and a variety of other day-to-day interactions with employees. These practices and behaviors can best be characterized as "gift-like" rather than conventional market-like exchanges. As a result of being more generous, the relationship between the company and employees is strengthened, just as personal relationships are invariably strengthened when gifts are exchanged between friends and relatives. These companies create what I call "Giftwork® Cultures" because they are environments where the management treats employees' work as gifts rather than commodities.

In practice, how do the Best Workplaces create Giftwork® Cultures? The easiest way to explain this is by looking at the specific kinds of policies and practices where we can see Giftwork®-style interactions. But first, it's important to stress that these interactions do not apply to all areas of human-resource policies. For instance, compensation is rarely a differentiating factor. That is, the Best Workplaces generally pay people at or near the market averages. Nor are performance appraisals done differently. In general, these are aspects of the relationship between the employee and the management that are what I referred to earlier as part of the commodity exchange of a job—employee time and effort in exchange for pay and benefits. But there are other areas where companies have the opportunity to engage in gift-like exchanges with employees. Based on our research, there are nine areas where the Best Workplaces typically have unique and distinctive policies and practices. Below is a brief summary of the nine occasions in the workplace where employers can help create a Giftwork® Culture:

OCCASION 1 Hiring

Great workplaces hire people by focusing on the potential and character of a person rather than primarily on his/her skills. They also typically have an arduous hiring process to make sure that the individual fits into the culture of the organization. And when new hires are brought on board, management typically welcomes them into the family/team with extensive orientation programs, small gifts, celebrations, etc. This initiates the gift-giving dynamic by bringing the newcomer into a special relationship as a team/family member rather than merely as an employee.

OCCASION 2 Inspiring

Leaders of great workplaces see that one their most important functions is to help people understand how their job has meaning for the organization and for society, not just a task to earn money for themselves and the business owners.

OCCASION 3 Speaking

Management in great workplaces typically go to great lengths to be open, even transparent, with information. Such behavior leads to a much greater willingness on the part of employees to offer suggestions and creative ideas.

OCCASION 4 Listening

At the best workplaces, they make sure to have special systems for incorporating people's ideas as well as involving people in decision-making.

OCCASION 5 Thanking

Managers in great workplaces recognize and reward good work and extra effort. They try to achieve what one company calls "a climate of approval."

OCCASION 6 Developing

In great workplaces, much emphasis is placed on fostering a learning environment where employees can discover and nurture their talents and interests as well as providing avenues for them to grow professionally and personally.

OCCASION 7 Caring

Our employee survey has consistently shown that whether employees feel cared-about as "individuals, not just employees" is the biggest factor in whether they consider their company a Great Place to Work®. We have found that many employees associate feeling cared-about with how the management responds to a crisis in their personal lives, such as a major illness or a death in the family. On an organizational level, great employers develop a multiplicity of ways (often identified as work-family programs) to create a nurturing environment.

OCCASION 8 Celebrating

Outsiders note that people throw a lot of parties at great workplaces. The celebrations are often for personal events, from birthdays to anniversaries.

But the companies themselves invariably celebrate major and minor corporate successes.

OCCASION 9 Sharing

In great workplaces, companies make sure that employees share in the fruits of their labor through a variety of mechanisms, from profit-sharing to employee ownership to less formal, but equally meaningful methods of rewarding people for their contributions.

By taking advantage of these nine occasions to practice gift-like interactions, we have seen how the Best Workplaces create a workplace culture where employees feel fulfilled and the company can be more successful.

These companies create what I call "Giftwork® Cultures" because they are environments where the management treats employees' work as gifts rather than commodities.

2006

WHAT DISTINGUISHES GREAT WORKPLACES IS GIFTWORK®

By **Robert Levering**

[*MELHOR*]

Several years ago, Robert Levering coined the word "giftwork®" to describe the types of regular interactions that distinguish great workplaces. In this interview with a Brazilian HR magazine, he explains the concept.

Q: What would you say is the basic difference between a Great Place to Work® and others?

A: I have found that the companies with the best workplaces all over the world have what I call a gift-giving environment. The basic idea is very simple. In the more traditional workplace, work itself is considered a commodity, that is, the worker is supposed to do certain tasks for a specified number of hours a day. In return he is given a certain amount of pay and benefits. In a great workplace, people are also paid for doing their jobs, but there is something extra going on. Because the management considers the work that people do as a *gift*, they treat it as one. This is especially evident in the variety of ways most great workplaces show recognition to people for doing a great job.

Q: So companies have to show gratitude. Do you think that companies need formal mechanisms of rewards, or can this gratitude be shown through

the relationship between leaders (or chiefs) and employees in the work routine?

A: Both are important. All of the best workplaces have specific formal methods that typically include both team and personal recognition awards. But they usually have developed an atmosphere where saying "Thank you" is common. In some cases, this requires some training of the managers and supervisors. But often it is done by example, where the top leaders show their gratitude routinely in all their interactions with employees.

Q: What kind of companies and workers' needs should be fulfilled, according to the Giftwork® concept?

A: From the Giftwork® perspective, it is not so much a question of needs as times. That is, there are certain occasions in the relationship with employees when it is important for management to show its generosity. I have already mentioned one: after an employee does work that is more than routine. Other times are: when an employee first joins a company; when the management wishes to communicate a new initiative to employees; when an employee faces a personal crisis unrelated to work (such as illness or death in the family); when an employee needs time to take care of personal or family matters (such as needing a more flexible schedule to take care of children). At all such times, the best workplaces have programs or policies that are perceived by employees as being generous.

Q: How should the employee/employers relationship be in this context?

In Giftwork® framework, employers and employees are constantly exchanging gifts with each other: The employer is more generous in what it offers employees (benefits, time, information, etc.), and employees offer more work than they are required to do. By acting generously, it strengthens the relationship and builds trust, which leads to a stronger company.

Q: What would be the leaders' major contribution in the Giftwork® context?

A: First, their own example is crucial. As I said earlier, it is important that they show gratitude toward employees for their contributions. Second, they need to make sure that all managers and supervisors treat employees in a positive way. For example, top leaders in most great workplaces have mechanisms for making sure that supervisors do not abuse employees verbally or treat them unfairly. This usually requires that they have policies in place to enable lower-level employees to appeal directly to senior leadership. Third, they need to communicate as openly and transparently as possible. It is impossible to develop the trust necessary for good workplace relationships without open communications.

Q: Do HR professionals have any contribution to give in this environment?

A: Yes, in two ways. First, they must continually attempt to find ways of expanding what is given to employees. That is, they must try to find new benefits and develop new policies that are considered to be unique and distinctive. Second, the attitude with which HR professionals deliver benefits or new policies should be one of generosity.

Q: In your opinion, what are the most important challenges faced by the HR professionals in the near future?

A: Oftentimes, HR professionals are considered to be technicians rather than people who contribute to the success of the business. I believe HR professionals must develop a stronger interest and knowledge about productivity.

Q: But almost all HR activities look to improve productivity. Could you give us an example of what a productivity-oriented HR would be?

A: It's true that most HR activities are essential to keep an organization going. But I would distinguish between HR activities that essentially maintain basic HR systems, such as compensation and benefits, and those that help to distinguish one company from its competitors. Consider, for instance, how employees are welcomed into an organization, something that HR has responsibility for in most organizations. Great workplaces typically do something special to welcome new employees, often with the top leaders personally welcoming them to the organization. This makes people feel as if they are part of a team or a family. In many other companies, new employees are simply greeted with a lot of paperwork to fill out and then sent off to the start working on their jobs with the effect that people feel that they are being treated as cogs in a machine. When employees are given a more generous welcome and feel like they are part of a team or family, they are much more likely to be willing to give more back to the organization. That is, they will offer more of their Giftwork® to the organization and the company will be more productive. (If readers are particularly interested in how best workplaces welcome new employees, they can read an online article that was adapted from my book for Fortune's web site. (http://money.cnn.com/2006/01/09/news/companies/bestcos_welcomerituals/)

Q: You visited some Brazilian companies last year. Is there any difference in terms of HR management between these companies and other companies around the world? By the way, did you see the Giftwork® in them?

A: Actually, I have been visiting Brazil regularly since 1997 when we set up Great Place to Work® Institute® Brazil. I have visited many companies during that time in many different Brazilian industries, including manufacturing and telecommunications, retail and financial services. I have also visited numerous companies in the United States, Europe, Asia, and in other countries in Latin America. I have seen many differences in HR management in my travels, but those differences are not related to the country. Rather there are companies in every country that exhibit the phenomenon of Giftwork®. In Brazil, the companies that I have visited, that have appeared high on Great Place to Work® Institute Brazil's list of the Best Workplaces, are good examples.

3. GLOBAL PERSPECTIVES

2004

HOW DO **INDIA'S BEST WORKPLACES** COMPARE WITH THE BEST IN THE U.S.?

By **Robert Levering**

[BUSINESSWORLD]

How do India's Best Workplaces compare with the best in the U.S.? Based on data gathered for *Businessworld's* second annual Best Workplaces survey, we find that India's Best Workplaces rate slightly lower overall than the very best in the U.S. However, on certain key measures, India's Best rate equal to or higher than their American counterparts. What's more, many of India's Best have developed numerous innovative practices that are genuinely world-class.

We can make statistical comparisons with America's best workplaces because the Businessworld list is compiled using the same employee survey (Great Place to Work® Trust Index©) that is used by *Fortune* in preparing its annual "100 Best Companies to Work For" list. In order to compare the workplaces at the top of the lists in both the U.S. and India, we examined Trust Index© scores of the top 10 and the top 25 companies in both countries. Employees of the top 25 companies in the United States rate their companies more highly on almost all survey questions. For instance, where 82 percent of U.S. employees at the top 25 companies feel adequately informed about workplace issues and changes, only 71 percent of employees at India's top 25 agreed. On the survey's key question about whether they consider their company a "Great Place to Work®," 92 percent of the employees at the U.S.'s top 25 answered affirmatively as opposed to 78 percent of their Indian counterparts.

Interestingly this gap shrinks considerably if you compare the top 10 companies for each country. In fact, on the question of whether employees consider their company a "Great Place to Work®," the difference was only 8 percent (94 percent to 86 percent). The top 25 Indian companies are higher than the scores for the average of the scores for the companies rated between 50 and 100 in the U.S. These results indicate that the difference between scores at the top 25 U.S. and Indian companies is not a cultural matter. The scores at these top 10 companies in India deliver a stronger message: any workplace can become a great workplace. Indeed, on a number of survey questions related to whether people feel treated fairly, the top 10 Indian companies rate close to or above the top 10 U.S. companies. On the question of whether people feel that everyone has the opportunity to receive special recognition, India's top 10 rated 11 percent higher than their American counterparts.

That said, we must still raise the question of what are the factors driving the lower scores among the top 25 companies in India? The most dramatic difference between the two countries on the survey was on the question of whether employees consider their workplaces "physically safe." On that question, there is a 43 percent difference, with just over half of Indian employees agreeing with that statement as opposed to a nearly unanimous agreement from U.S. employees that their workplaces are safe. Certainly a sense of safety at the workplace, whether relating to the structure or security of the building or the perceived risks associated with performing work, can influence employees' trust in management. Employee perception of physical safety at India's best is startlingly low when compared with the generally high levels of trust on other issues.

Another area of difference where Indian companies score significantly lower is on the question of whether employees feel the management is "approachable, easy to talk with" (22 percent lower among the top 25 and 15 percent lower among the top 10). This is an area where the U.S. Best Companies have numerous strikingly informal methods of communication. In many companies, the CEO and other business leaders are on a first-name basis with all employees, some reviewing employee directories monthly to ensure they are familiar with the names and faces of new employees. Some of these leaders conduct weekly or monthly breakfasts with employees at all levels, soliciting ideas and feedback about workplace issues. At employee cafeterias, CEOs frequently join employees for lunch, eating with different employees each day . Some companies insist that new employees meet with the CEO after a few weeks or months at the company, in order to ask any lingering questions, give feedback, or make suggestions. These kinds of practices go beyond the open-door policies common in both countries. Since communication is so vital to creating a sense of trust, I would assume that as Indian companies develop more and varied means of promoting management accessibility, their overall scores will improve on this survey.

A final area where the Indian companies score noticeably lower is the realm of work-life balance. Among the top 10 companies, the Indian firms score an average of 20 percent lower than the U.S. top 10 on a question about whether they feel the company encourages them to balance their work lives and personal lives or to take time off of work when they feel it is necessary. This issue has been a major concern among American companies for the past 15 to 20 years, and most have instituted numerous programs and policies for flex-time for instance. We would expect that the Indian company scores would increase in this area as more Indian companies institute such programs.

Looking at the various programs offered by companies in both countries, we can observe that there are both similarities and some striking differences, perhaps cultural in origin, about how companies encourage camaraderie among employees. In both countries, employers celebrate themed "days" (where employees dress up or celebrate anything from Friday to national holidays); design contests across departments; foster activity or hobby groups for employees; and take up collections for employees facing a crisis. "Fun committees" are common at the U.S. companies. Employees comprising "fun committees" plan celebrations, contests, and activities for their colleagues. Likewise, "diversity committees" ensure that workplace diversity across race, age, sex, and sexual orientation is respected and celebrated. Most of the activities promoting camaraderie at the U.S. companies take place during the workday. One exception is a common practice called "Bring your child to work day," where employees bring their children to the office.

Practices at the Indian companies seem to be more diverse. Some of the companies practice regular sports tournaments, monthly picnics, and weekend activities. Many of these activities involve children or families, such as a Saturday morning movie screening for children of employees. In addition, some Indian companies feature cultural celebrations, with employees singing, dancing, and acting. These kinds of activities are much more uncommon at the U.S. firms.

2010

BALANCING WORK AND FAMILY IN MEXICO'S BEST **WORKPLACES**

By **Jennifer Amozorrutia**

[GESTIÓN]

Due to the current conditions in the socioeconomic setting, the professional role has been changing little by little. Not only is work a need, but also a source of personal satisfaction and fulfillment. However, reconciling these two aspects (the personal and the professional) is not an easy task. When this subject is under discussion, some people automatically say that they do not have a personal and professional life balance.

This balance refers to the integration of professional demands with family roles (or roles outside of work). Such balance is essential for people to keep a state of well-being and their quality of life. In Mexico, the Great Place to Work® Institute has evaluated the levels of professional and personal life balance in organizations. Results of the Trust Index© Survey conducted in 2009 reveal that the levels of professional and personal life balance in the organizations has had modifications over time. A growth was observed from 2007 to 2008. In spite of the crisis, the level of personal and professional life balance in The Mexican Best Companies to Work for® has not suffered major mishaps from 2008 to 2009; as shown, they kept their level, despite the economic challenge.

Balancing work and family life has become a significant concern among all companies the Great Place to Work® Institute has surveyed throughout the world. Jennifer Amozorrutia, associate researcher of Great Place to Work® Institute Mexico provides insights from her studies of her country's Best Workplaces.

THE BEST COMPANIES TO WORK FOR® KEEP THEIR LEVELS OF PERSONAL AND PROFESSIONAL BALANCE DURING THE CRISIS

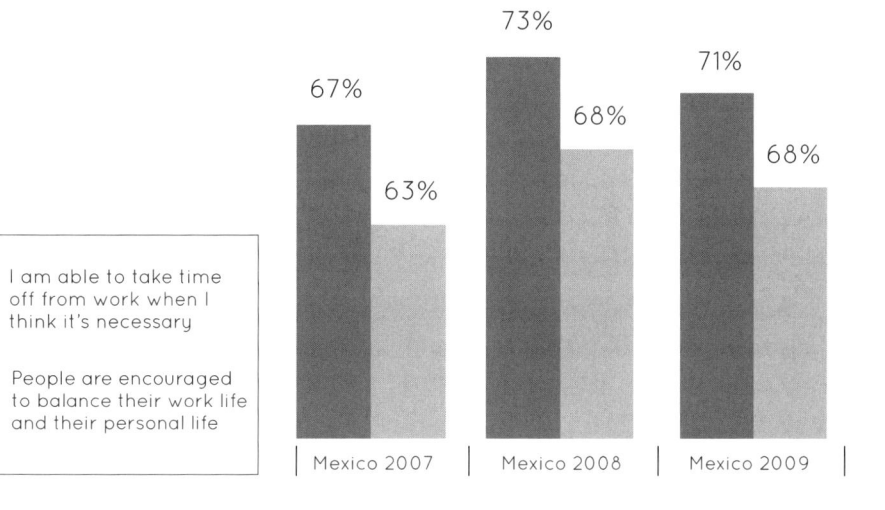

- ■ I am able to take time off from work when I think it's necessary
- ■ People are encouraged to balance their work life and their personal life

	Mexico 2007	Mexico 2008	Mexico 2009
I am able to take time off	67%	73%	71%
People are encouraged to balance	63%	68%	68%

Great Place to Work® Institute Mexico 2009. All rights reserved.

According to a survey conducted by Accenture in 2009, almost 8 of 10 professionals mention wanting a balance between their work and their personal life as a priority. In addition, when identifying their key priorities, they ranked the personal/professional life balance in the second position, followed by salary.

Not being able to find this balance entails many negative consequences for people. Among them, health problems (such as illnesses associated with stress, hypertension, depression, anxiety, tendency for toxic substance and junk-food abuse); but also problems in the family and couple dynamics are found. In addition, according to the International Labour Organization (ILO), on the professional level, it might bring consequences such as lack of motivation, lower professional yield, lower performance levels, less compliance with duties, and less sense of stability. All this results in a waste of the employees' potential.

In 2009, 83 percent of employees in the Top 10 companies included in the GPTW Mexico Ranking considered that, in their organizations, they are encouraged to achieve a personal and professional life balance; and 85 percent say that they can leave their workplaces to solve personal issues. In this graph, a remarkable difference (more than 20 percent) between the companies not qualified in the Ranking and the Top 10 companies that were qualified is also observed.

Another important datum that is worth highlighting is that no significant gender differences were found in their answers (71 percent of positive answers from men and women,

**THE BEST COMPANIES TO WORK FOR ®
IN MEXICO MAKE GREAT EFFORTS TO PROMOTE
A BALANCE BETWEEN THE PROFESSIONAL
AND THE PERSONAL LIFE**

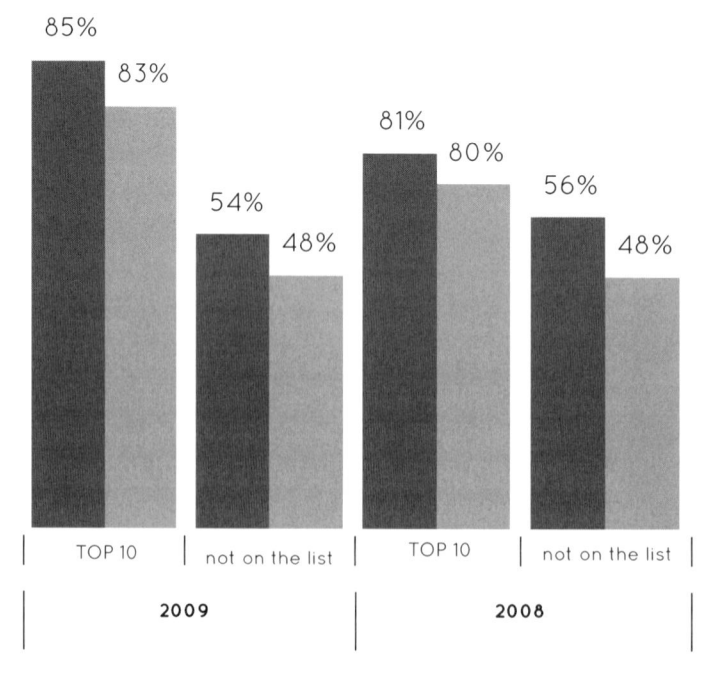

	2009		2008	
	TOP 10	not on the list	TOP 10	not on the list
I am able to take time off from work when I think it's necessary	85%	54%	81%	56%
People are encouraged to balance their work life and their personal life	83%	48%	80%	48%

respectively). However, differences in the personal and professional life balance were found when it comes to hierarchic level, where 88 percent of Directors with 88 Best Companies to Work for® in Mexico answered positively to being allowed to leave the workplace to solve personal issues, against 67 percent of Operative personnel. This indicates that it is necessary that companies focus their efforts on including all hierarchic levels in their practices and initiatives.

In Mexico, it was demonstrated that many organizations are now mindful of this theme, mainly the Best Companies to Work for®. On the other hand, this study revealed that, in spite of the efforts made by the organizations in Mexico, there is still a long way to go. While the professional and personal life balance levels are similar in the United States, Latin America, and Europe, in Mexico they show an important difference of almost 20 percent. This means that it is essential for companies in Mexico to stimulate initiatives and practices designed to create a more flexible work environment, favoring the quality of life.

According to the results of various investigations conducted in the United States, favoring the professional and personal life balance in organizations has an important impact. A study conducted by the consulting company Morgan Redwood states that organizations that promote it have higher profits: 20 percent more a year per employee. In addition, the results of a survey carried out by the consulting company Spherion reveal that 90 percent of the organizations with programs to stimulate the personal and professional life balance improved their levels of professional satisfaction.

Also, and as a result of many years of work and research with organizations in Mexico and

PERSONAL AND PROFESIONAL LIFE BALANCE IN MEXICO AND AROUND THE WORLD

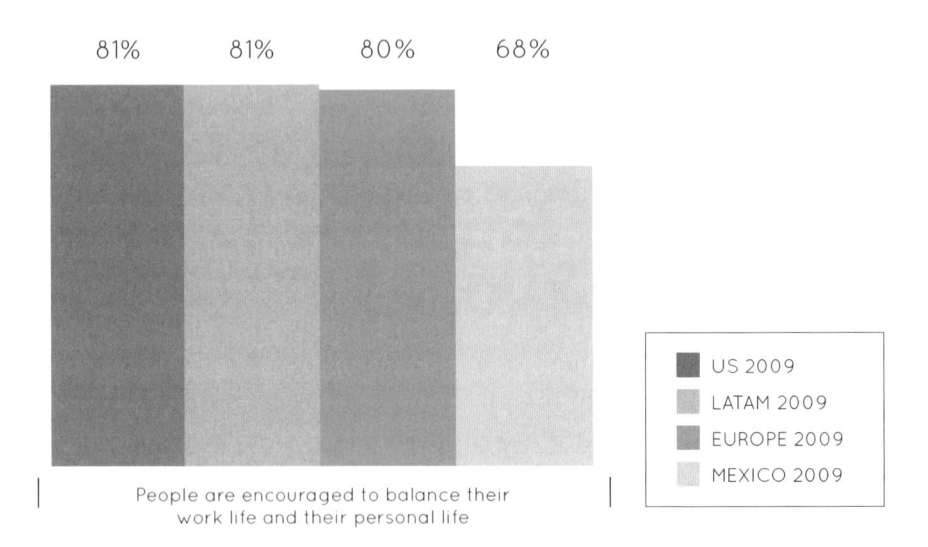

81% **81%** **80%** **68%**

People are encouraged to balance their work life and their personal life

- US 2009
- LATAM 2009
- EUROPE 2009
- MEXICO 2009

around the world, the Great Place to Work® Institute has identified practices that foster and stimulate this balance in employees. Some of the most commonly used practices by the best companies are: flexible hours, partial shifts, home office, programs focused on promoting health, psychological and legal support programs for employees and their families, family integration programs, agreements with sports centers and commercial establishments, day-care service, and personal days.

It is certain that a more balanced life in the family and professional aspects benefits collaborators as well as organizations by increasing creativity, team work, efficiency, productivity, professional satisfaction levels, and a sense of loyalty and commitment to the organization. Additionally, it helps reduce the absenteeism levels and voluntary turnover.

2007

ON TOLSTOY, **BUSINESS** STRATEGY AND CORPORATE **CULTURE**

By **Robert Levering**

[EXAME]

Best workplaces appear to have more differences than commonalities. Yet all have developed cultures that are an extension of their company's business strategy, according to Robert Levering in this article that first appeared in a Brazilian business magazine.

Tolstoy's masterpiece Anna Karenina opens with the memorable line: "Happy families resemble one another, but each unhappy family is unhappy in its own way."

At first glance, Tolstoy's dictum does not appear to apply to workplaces. If you look through this year's list of *As 100 Melhores Empresas para Trabalhar,* you will probably be struck by how these happy workplaces appear to be very different from one another. For one thing, there is a great diversity in the types of companies. There are companies in a wide variety of industries from financial services (BV Financeira, Losango, Banco Itaú Veículos), to manufacturing (Plascar, John Deere, Caterpillar), to software (Microsoft, Sabre Travel Network, Matera Systems), to consulting (Chemtech, Service IT, Kaizen) to consumer products (Kimberly-Clark), to drugs (Mantecorp, Wyeth, Daichii Sankyo). Some are small companies (103 employees at Company G&B Autopeças Alternativas), and some are large (65,637 employees at Bradesco). Some are little-known Brazilian firms (Pormade Portas and Zanzini Móveis), others are well-known multinationals (FedEx and Dell). Some are young (Taií is 4 years old), others are old (Boehringer Ingelheim is 123 years old).

Clearly, it is also difficult to see what these companies have in common in terms of workplace practices. Each has its own unique practices not replicated by other Best Workplaces. Some examples: retailer Magazine Luiza's own internal TV channel, Caterpillar's distinctive performance management process, and Accor Profiles, a database used by the hospitality conglomerate's headquarters to identify skills and interests from their executive leaders all over the world.

However, Tolstoy's statement does apply to workplaces if you scratch the surface and look at the relationship of the company's culture to its business strategy. If you do so, you will see that every great workplace has developed a culture that is an extension of the company's business strategy. In other words, the various practices of the company are intimately related to what the company is trying to accomplish. What's more, the practices are typically well integrated with each other.

We need look no further than this year's number one workplace in Brazil, Chemtech, to see an excellent example of this trait. One of the most notable features of Chemtech's workplace culture is how it does its recruiting of new employees. The company does chemical engineering consulting within the petrochemical industry. To succeed in its field, it believes that it needs to attract the very best new graduates in that field and train them from the earliest stages of their careers. To do this, Chemtech has adopted a number of unique recruiting strategies, including sponsoring internships, to attract the very best candidates.

Caja Madrid, a 300-year-old Spanish banking firm, illustrates another example of how this works. Several years ago, the Spanish government decided to deregulate the banking industry. Before deregulation, Caja Madrid had a savings-bank monopoly in the Madrid area. Deregulation meant that the firm was going to compete with all kinds of financial services institutions, including multinational competitors. The bank's leaders realized that the unique culture was the company's most important asset. The bank gives nearly 25% of its profits annually to various nonprofit groups to help in their communities. It's a company where employees talk openly about a sense of "family" despite the company's large size. So they decided that they would emphasize training everyone in a variety of skills so that people would be capable of the flexibility needed for the new competitive environment. They introduced a remarkable on-line training program with dozens of distinct modules and provided deep discounts for employees to buy their own computers to study at home. The results were remarkable as Caja not only held its own against its new competitors but expanded the number of its branches and opened new lines of business.

Continental Airlines is another company where we can see the interplay of business strategy with workplace culture. In the mid-1990s this airline was struggling and had filed for bankruptcy in the recent past. A new leadership team took over and quickly realized that the company could never survive without creating a new workplace culture. In particular, they realized that the firm could never succeed so long as the different employee groups — pilots, flight attendants, ramp service people, reservations agents, customer service representatives, etc. — kept fighting with each other — a common characteristic among airlines. So the leaders launched a new internal campaign called "Working Together" to herald a new era. Among the various initiatives were a major internal communications effort and a generous profit-sharing plan. The airline also introduced a bonus plan where all employees would receive a bonus of $60 if the company were to rank among the top three airlines in the federal aviation agency's monthly customer satisfaction survey. When the campaign was launched, Continental ranked last among the 10 largest airlines in the monthly survey. Within three months of introducing this campaign, Continental's employees were working together so well that they placed first among all the carriers. This new culture of teamwork also paid off well as the airline became profitable for the first time in years.

A final example of how the best workplaces have cultures that are interlinked with its business strategy is eBay, the world's largest on-line auction community "where practically anyone can sell practically anything at any time." At eBay everything relates to the company's mission of connecting people. Within the company, it has built a culture that asserts three basic values:

• People are basically good

• Everyone has something to contribute

• An open environment brings out the best in people.

This open, trusting internal culture was created to mirror its business model of connecting people in cyberspace through its online auctions. eBay employees are able to experience how their culture impacts their customers and their business at their annual eBay Live convention which brings together more than 10,000 eBay sellers and buyers. The highlight of the convention is a gala event held on one evening where a major music recording star performs. As the attendees enter the convention hall, they are cheered by several hundred eBay employees who form a kind of receiving line. The event demonstrates to both the customers and the employees how both succeed through their internal culture of openness and trust.

2009

THE KEY TO **ORGANIZATIONA**L TRANSFORMATION

By **Adriana de Souza**

It is amazing the power an inspired idea can have. This is exactly what happened with Robert Levering, co-founder of Great Place to Work® Institute, when he undertook extensive research in the U.S.A. to identify the characteristics of a Great Place to Work®. He interviewed managers, middle level people, and all those who were responsible for the hard, daily work of the companies they worked for. What should companies represent to their employees to make their daily activities a rewarding process, that is, more than a "job?"

After analyzing the results of his research, Robert developed a Model©, the Institute's prime element within the 43 countries where it operates.

For more than two decades, over 10,000 companies around the world have taken inspiration from the Model©, including those with characteristics already compatible with it. Numerous other companies have committed to

In reviewing some of the works of leading organizational development thinkers, Adriana de Souza reflects on the importance of understanding organizational culture. She is the CEO of Great Place to Work® Institute Bolivia its transformational process, in order to become a Great Place to Work®.

Up to now, more than 4,500 companies have been recognized as a Great Place to Work®. Furthermore, it is expected that this number will continue to increase, considering the mission of the Institute is to "Build a better society by helping companies to transform their working environments."

A well-known maxim is "What cannot be measured cannot be changed." Thus, the Trust Index® was developed by the Institute as a way to measure the perception of employees with regard to 57 behavior patterns. This tool offers a diagnostic based on 5 dimensions (Credibility, Respect, Fairness, Pride, and Camaraderie) outlined by the Model®, but it also acts at another level. The very process of examining a company's organizational culture, where all change must start, has a transformational effect.

The Model® starts its work among the employees, but the main emphasis becomes the level of trust between the employees and the company leaders. In this light, consider the following observation written by Levering in 2000: "In the same way that love characterizes the attitude between the two sides or elements of a good matrimony, the trust characterizes the attitude between both sides in a fruitful working relationship."

Defining organizational culture

Society has driven organizations to change. Technological, economical, political, and social changes have pushed companies into a completely different entrepreneurial dynamic, which has taken companies across new frontiers. This is evident in the way some companies promote the development of their employees' potential, while others limit them.

To operate in a strategic and efficient manner, it is necessary for a company to understand the importance of its culture. Edgar Schein, in 1984, suggested that the comprehension of organizational culture was key to managing a company. By identifying the culture of the company, leaders begin to act consistently, while effecting lasting changes.

This cultural understanding involves looking at, not only the relationships among the powers, but the non-written rules, or what is *considered* to be truth. Such deep observation can clarify previously inexplicable behaviors and allow the planning of coherent actions, compatible with the reality of the organization.

The first definition of organizational culture appears in a book by Elliot Jacques in 1951, in which he describes the organizational changes within an English steel company. He relates culture to structure and personality, defining culture as the "traditional way of thinking and making things happen, which is shared at high and low levels," and which must be learned by all or at least partially accepted in order for one to be able to work in the company.

Schein said, "Organizational culture is the pattern of basic assumptions which a determined group has invented, found out, or developed in the process of learning how to solve its problems of external adaptation and internal integration, and that work well enough to the point of being considered valid and must be taught to the new members of the group, as being the right manner of perceiving, thinking, and feeling in relation to these problems." In other words, the culture forms upon those premises that appear compatible with the whole group's thinking. The human being needs consistency and order and finds it disturbing to live with contradictory rules.

While Shein says that the culture of a company will always be related to the culture of the country where it is located, Andrea Rodriguez contends that "a national culture is not enough explanation of the differences observed in the entrepreneurial behavior." But Rodriguez has pointed out, in 1993, that the understanding of the organizational culture does provide information that can inform the effectiveness of a company, as well as the quality of life among its members.

James Collins and Jerry Porras (in 2000) identified the different factors within companies that were considered to be visionary and successful. One of their conclusions is that those companies developed a central ideology, group values and goals that went beyond making money. The noble ideals existed in the visionary companies not only during successful times, but also during times when they had to fight to survive. Along those lines, they mention a declaration of values published by SONY in 1947, when that company was only ten months old and operated in an old room amid the ruins of a bombed Japan. Such were the conditions that brought people together, with a strong working team spirit, and helped to develop SONY's "technological capacity from the bottom of the heart."

In line with their challenge, Robert Levering has pointed out that any organization can become a Great Place to Work®, provided its executives are committed to transforming the culture of their companies and share the belief that the success of the business genuinely lies within the people. This is the basis necessary to establish a high level of trust, a determining element in a Great Place to Work®.

2005

CHILE AND GLOBAL WORKPLACES TRENDS

For an interview with a Chilean business magazine, Robert Levering reflects on major workplace trends over the past two decades, particularly with reference to companies in Chile.

Q: In the initial stages, you were very critical of the labor system and the relationhip between companies and their employees. Could you tell us how this influenced the foundation of Great Place To Work® Institute?

A: During the 1970s and early 1980s, I was a labor journalist writing about union disputes and employee grievances for a newspaper in California. What I noticed was the lack of trust in those workplaces. By contrast, when I did research for the 1984 book, The 100 Best *Companies to Work for in America*, I observed that employees in those companies talked about how they trusted the management. That is, they said they believed what management told them, felt respected, and were treated fairly. So, when Dr. Amy Lyman and I founded the Great Place to Work® Institute in 1992, we saw that increasing the level of trust was the key to helping companies become great workplaces. The first tool we created was an employee survey, called the Great Place to Work®

Trust Index©, that measures the perception of trust in the workplace. Our work since then has revolved around this issue of trust.

Q: Since founding the Great Place to Work® Institute®, what are the major changes that you have observed in companies worldwide?

A: First, there is a much greater emphasis on work-family issues than in the early 1990s. Companies all over the world are making a much greater effort to accommodate parents with children, both in terms of flexible scheduling and also with specific programs for new parents. Second, senior executives are much more involved in workplace issues than in the past. That is, more and more top managers see the link between the quality of the workplace and the financial performance of the enterprise. One example of this increased interest can be seen in the great popularity of best workplace lists in the past few years. Our Institute now compiles lists in 29 countries, including eight in Latin America, including Chile.

Q: There is a belief among CEOs in large companies that it is easier for small organizations to develop high levels of trust and therefore have a better labor climate. According to your experience, what is your opinion on this matter?

A: The facts do not support this belief as there are so many counter examples. That is, many very large organizations, like FedEx and Microsoft, have consistently scored high on our Trust Index© survey throughout the world. By the same token, there are hundreds of much smaller organizations, with fewer than 200 employees, that score poorly on the same Trust Index© survey. The difference in all cases can be traced to the quality of the leadership. Great workplaces have leaders who develop strong relationships with their employees by doing such things as being transparent with information and consistently showing appreciation to people for their good work and extra effort. In larger organizations, senior leaders must create good people policies and develop systems of training and accountability to make sure that they are implemented properly by lower-level managers. While this issue is not faced by much smaller organizations, larger companies generally have greater resources to devote to people issues.

Q: In your last visit to Chile, you had the opportunity to visit some companies that have been recognized as great places to work. What aspects were more interesting or innovative about those companies?

A: I visited and interviewed employees and the leaders of three companies, Banco Security, Banchile Corredores de Seguros, and Transbank. All three had remarkable policies. For instance, Banchile Corredores de Seguros has a strong sense of social responsibility, with a strong relationship with a children's hospital. Transbank has a high degree of camaraderie, exhibited by the posters displaying numerous social events. And Banco Security has a variety of programs to insure that mothers in particular are able to return to work and continue contributing to the organization. But the individual policies were not as impressive as the overall culture created at each of the companies I visited. It was clear at each of them that the leaders put the people first, and the employees have responded by providing exceptional service to their clients and healthy returns to the owners.

Q: According to what you experienced in your visit to Chile, what is the level of development of Chilean companies in comparison to the rest of the world?

A: The best Chilean workplaces are definitely world class. My sense is that all Chilean companies can learn much from the excellent examples set by the best workplaces in Chile.

Q: In your recent interviews and presentations, you have mentioned a new concept called "Giftwork®". Briefly, what does this concept mean and how does it relate to the Great Place to Work® Model©?

A: I have observed that the biggest difference between a great workplace and others is the extent to which people feel as if they are treated like a "full person", a "human being" as opposed to a "mere number," a "cog in a wheel," or a "robot." When interviewing employees in great workplaces who have previously worked elsewhere, they often say that the difference has to do with how their work is treated by the management.

In a bad or mediocre workplace, an employee's work is treated like a commodity. That is, employees say that they feel that management essentially takes their contributions for granted, as part of an implied contract where the employee gives their time and effort in exchange for money and benefits.

By contrast, in great workplaces, employees say that an additional dynamic exists, where management is more generous in both attitude and spirit toward employees and their work. So, for instance, in a great workplace, management is especially attentive to expressing appreciation to employees for the efforts. Such companies also celebrate their successes and create policies to equitably share the results of their successes. Employees often say that in response to this more generous managerial approach, they also give more effort, and work more cooperatively with their fellow employees.

In such companies, employees often say that they feel they are part of a "family" or "team" rather than merely an employee. People feel as if interactions with management are more similar to gift-giving exchanges within families or friends rather than the kind of commodity exchanges that characterize most business transactions.

People in great workplaces believe that their contributions are treated more like a gift than a commodity, so I have coined the word "Giftwork®" to describe employee efforts in such organizations. And I use the phrase "Giftwork® culture" to denote the overall environment of great workplaces.

The question most managers/leaders want answered, of course, is "How do I create a Great Place to Work®." My answer is that there are nine specific areas in which leaders of great workplaces can engage in gift-giving interactions, such as in hiring, welcoming newcomers into the organization, showing appreciation, and celebrating successes.

Q: You have said that one of the key elements to having a good labor climate is related to the hiring and welcoming of new employees. Could you further explain this statement?

A: One of the nine steps to creating a great workplace is how new employees are welcomed into the organization. In many companies, new employees are given a brief orientation about their jobs and put to work. This shows that the employee is hired to fill a position, and that the work they perform is like a commodity that can be done by anyone with the required skills. In the best workplaces, there is a great emphasis on welcoming the newcomers as people into the "family" or "team." It is common for the new employee to meet senior executives, often the president, very early on. I wrote about some examples of how this works in practice among the American "100 Best" in an article that is on the Fortune magazine website (http://money.cnn.com/2006/01/09/news/companies/bestcos_welcomerituals/index.htm).

Q: In the last 5 years, GPTW Institute has faced an amazing growth, getting to be present in 29 countries around the world. How do you see the future development of the company?

A: To date, most of our energy has been devoted to helping set a global gold standard for what is a Great Place to Work®. Our Best Workplaces lists, including the one in Chile, do just that. Now that that standard has been established, we feel we can focus more on helping individual companies become great workplaces. We believe that the Giftwork® Culture concept and the Nine Steps provide a framework for us to help companies as they seek to improve the quality of their workplaces. We believe that this can be done both through a variety of workshops and seminars to help leaders develop the needed attitudes and skills, as well as with consulting assignments using our diagnostic tools and extensive database of best practices to give practical advice.

We very much look forward to the future as we think this is very important work that will help create a better society. Since people spend much of their waking hours at work, the quality of that experience is extremely important for all of us. It is for that reason that we believe that great workplaces offer real beacons of hope for the rest of society.

2009

THE CATALYST FOR ORGANIZATIONAL EXCELLENCE

By **Jennifer Amozorrutia**

Internal communication is a complex, interpretative process, through which employees coordinate the essential work processes to function as an organization. Currently, employees are asking for more information about the company they work for, therefore the internal communication is the catalyst for the organizational excellence and effectiveness and should be constant. Collaborators will provide more support to the organization if it keeps the communication channels open and fully operative.

When employees realize the information they are receiving from their supervisors and workmates is accurate, correct, and relevant, they are more likely to feel less vulnerable and more able to trust them. Conversely, when collaborators believe they are receiving irrelevant, inaccurate, or outdated information, they are more likely to become more cautious and distrustful. The average for the 10 Best Companies to Work for® in México 2009 is 89 percent favorable regarding communication, or

How management communicates with employees has profound implications on the development of trust in the workplace, according to Jennifer Amozorrutia, associate researcher of Great Place to Work® Institute Mexico.

being kept informed about the company's projects and activities.

It is necessary that the leaders in the organizations provide employees not only with the appropriate quantity and quality of information, but also opportunities and channels for them to speak out, engage, be listened to, and to actively participate. Employees are more likely to support your organization if it provides appropriate, functional communication channels. When employees consider organization their a safe place to speak out, they are more likely to be engaged in the organizational objectives.

Sharing information with employees helps us develop a clear sense of what the organization actually looks like, and it is also a way to reinforce the sense of belonging. In this respect, the average for the 10 Best Companies to Work for® in México 2009 is 82 percent favorable, employees saying that their leaders keep them informed about issues of importance for the organization.

Furthermore, effective communication is critical for compliance with company objectives, because this is the basis for creating relationships of trust. It is trust that determines the accuracy and volume of information that is exchanged.

Communication has an impact on employees. Communication and trust are important to cultivating a supportive attitude towards the organization. For an organization's employees to consider it trustworthy, it is important that the management be open in its communication of all organizational issues, such as goals, problems, and policies. The management should clearly show its honesty in explaining objectives and be open to problems that might be occurring.

Some studies have demonstrated the core role played by communication in the development and maintenance of the trust. Trust and communication have been shown to bring desirable results such as the improved participation of employees and work performance (Dirks, 1999; Dirks and Ferrin, 2001; Ellis and Shockley-Zalabak, 2001; Kramer, 1996; Pincus, 1986; Ruppel and Harrington, 2000 in Thomas et al, 2009).

Effective communication is created when actions based on strong, reliable relations inside the organization are taken. Trust facilitates sharing information and stimulates employee participation, the process of listening and responding well to daily work, which in turn, makes the organizational commitment stronger.

2000

ARE **MULTINATIONALS** BETTER PLACES **TO WORK**?

By **José Tolovi Jr.**

[EXAME]

Is it easier for a multinational company, with substantial resources, to become a great workplace? José Tolovi Jr. offers an answer in this article that first appeared in a Brazilian business magazine based on Great Place to Work® Institute Brazil's experience in producing annual lists of that country's Best Workplaces.

In these four years of implementing the Great Place to Work® Institute in Brazil, I have received questions about how companies would differ according to their size, area of activity, origin, etc. I usually also receive enthusiastic comments on how it is easier for large companies with a lot of resources to be excellent workplaces. Executives from large companies, in turn, are tireless in claiming how much easier their jobs would be if they worked for small companies owned by only one person. Furthermore, I hear multinationals complain about their national competitors being run locally, thus having an easier task of maintaining a good workplace. The national companies, in their fantasies, dream about how good it would be IF they had head offices abroad that guided them in everything.

Obviously, the path to the truth is self evident: good companies are good independently of the factors mentioned. Let's take a look at the facts:

this year, we have 56 national companies on our list of the 100 best companies to work for. Although tempted, we cannot say that there is national dominance, but rather a real statistical balance, which provides us with good proof that being an excellent company is independent of the origin, or what country holds the working capital. In spite of this evidence, there is a general perception that the multinationals more quickly adopt the new trends in management. This may be true in many domains. But national companies are usually equally represented, and seemingly, even trend toward a dominant presence on the lists.

When we simply associate management trends and workplace, we see a growing concern for the human being. Not that it's news, but organizations are becoming smaller and smaller in terms of people, and the people who remain are more and more intrinsically linked to the business results. Without belaboring this point, already exhausted, automation is reducing the labor force. People— or activities—that are not replaced by devices are those who do the intellectual work. Today's companies are becoming organizations of people who execute functions that are appropriate to the human being, creative, that deal with ambiguity, and demand decisions. Companies of the so-called New Economy are a very clear example of that. If they are the new paradigm, then the new paradigm is to manage intellects rather than labor.

Then, we could say, according to our lists, that the national companies are on the same level in the rush to consider the human being as the key element of the competitiveness. Looking a little deeper, we could inquire if, in the details, both categories of companies are also similar. So, let's talk about approximately 30,000 employees who, in April this year, by completing our questionnaires, evaluated their companies. When analyzing the dimensions in our model—credibility, respect, fairness (these three indicating the trust in the management), pride, and camaraderie, we found the differences between nationals and multinationals did not even reach 1 percentage point. That is just the thing, they are surprisingly identical.

Even in our last question, where we asked whether, taking everything into account, the employee thinks the company is an excellent place to work, the difference was negligible. This last question has a particular characteristic. Our experience shows that employees tend to respond more benevolently toward the company when speaking of it in general terms. That is, they criticize the details, yet they like the company, if it really is an excellent company to work for. The national companies' mean is 88 percent, against 89 percent of the multinationals. This means that nearly 90 percent of employees in all of the companies participating in our survey think that they work in excellent environments—whether they are multinational or national companies.

Now, let's look at the issue from another angle: Are the salaries similar? And the job opportunities? And women's presence? Well, multinationals pay better. At least those that are excellent places to work. Once again, it is proved that salary is not a source of motivation, and even less, a condition of an excellent workplace.

The multinational companies hired, on average, 650 employees in 1999, against 1,000 in the national companies. However, multinationals hired on average 16 directors and managers, while the national ones hired only 5. This might indicate differing concerns among the companies' managements.

In the multinational companies, we find a higher education level rate—about 19 percent of employees have completed the university or post-graduate work, against a little less than 11 percent in the national ones. By associating these data with the hiring of directors and managers, and with the fact that the multinationals have hired 121 interns, on average, against 73 in the nationals, we could alert the national companies about the quality of their managing teams and about their future.

The number of women in management positions is approximately 1.2 percent of the workforce, regardless of the companies being national or not. This gives us a mean of 40 to 55 female directors per company in contingents that have 32 percent of women. That is, there is still about 18 percent missing for the gender gap to be closed.

Therefore, IF you are looking for an excellent place to work, do not use the company's nationality as a criterion. In the best 100 list, there are opportunities in numerous sectors, in companies of various sizes, in several locations. There is no such thing as a perfect company, not even among the multinational ones. Use the criteria that best suit you. Among the 100 best companies, there will certainly be one that will bring you satisfactions, challenges, and rewards.

2008

"DIFFUSE CREATIVITY" AND INNOVATION: LESSONS FROM ITALY'S BEST WORKPLACES

By **Gilberto Dondé**

[L' IMPRESA – IL SOLE 24 ORE]

To get the most creativity from today's workforce, managers must foster a supportive workplace environment rather than focus on the company's most gifted workers. So argues Gilberto Dondé, CEO of Great Place to Work® Institute Italy in an Italian magazine.

When we talk about "innovation," our thoughts might turn to technological innovation.

By the end of the 1980s, industry was fixated on finding the revolutionary product/service, the one that would upset markets and lead a company to beat competitors. This meant huge investments in research and development, a budget that enabled the inventor to highlight his or her almost divine ability of rubbing the "Aladdin's lamp" of success. Shining examples of the efficacy of this business model are abundant: the personal computer, the cell phone, the CD reader, and the finding of more and more potent molecules in the pharmaceutical field.

Obviously, there was a direct, proportional link between the budget spent to invent new products/services and the economic returns for the company. The problem is that this system has not worked. New barriers were raised to finding more and more revolutionary inventions. In addition, the inventor was an asset, but an expensive, unique one. The expenses in research and development in the pharmaceutical sector tripled in the decade 1991–2001 in the United States, while the number of new products compared to the previous period had actually decreased.

If generous R&D budgets don't ensure return—in the form of discoveries and in business results—it is necessary to rely on new approaches. It is necessary to rely on managers who are "creative thinkers," that is non-linear in relation to the past, the written rules, or seeming logic. In a few words, managers should be able to pursue corporate creativity, whether in regard to management techniques; implementing corporate processes that are more agile and efficient and able to reduce time and costs; or in relation to the company's ability to add value to the market through new products and services that are studied and realized—thanks to the manager's creativity.

This "lateral thinking," as opposed to old "vertical thinking," is a distinctive skill sought by managers, and is capable of generating new ideas, new concepts. It is an explorative type thinking, capable of producing creative leaps, unlike vertical or sequential thought, which is strapped by logic and overly selective of ideas.

Creativity is not an innate, or genetic, gift, but rather a skill that can be shaped by creative managers in the labor market. Creativity has become the main target of the personnel searches of many companies, who keep stealing each other's talent.

The idea is not to have only a few "creativity experts" operating, but rather to generate creative thinking among all the organization's population, in any professional position and level.

Every human resource should be recognized as the "raw material of creativity," if the purpose of

The competitiveness of companies favors everybody's participation and constribution for the improvement of products, services, and corporate processes.

each corporate organization is to make use of the best resources available. People are a significant source of creativity, an extensive, diffuse source that, at least in the past, has been under utilized.

The nature of human resources has dramatically changed. A young entrepreneur in a mid-sized company recently told me that the workers in his family business are not like the blue-collar ones who used to work for his father. Today, on the contrary, "experts" work for him, people in white shirts who are able to make machines work through numeric control. And these people have requests and expectations, with respect to the business they work for—quite different from those of their predecessors.

Today's workers are expected to know well the company for which they determine business results. In turn, whether professionals or not, they expect better administration than that of yesterday. They expect to be treated in a manner similar to that of their company leaders. But above all, they want to participate in a more significant way in the decision-making processes, because they are the ones who know the production processes and the technical functions. They are the first ones to notice the occasional malfunctioning, the ones who realize what can be done to make decisive changes to the modus operandi and they bring to the task the "lateral" thinking that they may have done over their tenure.

This "diffuse creativity," this search for ideas, expanded to all the corporate population is what constitutes the approach to innovation. It is not left to the genius of the inventor, not left to a restricted group of gifted managers, but dependent on the organization's ability to stimulate all resources to do "lateral thinking."

It is necessary, therefore, that the company

put into practice a whole set of policies that facilitate the emergence of new ideas, recognizes proposals, not shunning them because they are not in line with routine sequential logic.

There are, among the companies surveyed by the Great Place to Work® Institute Italia in the past years, many significant examples of companies that turned the gifts of innovation among the people in the organization into a corporate value and an essential instrument supporting its own competitiveness.

2007 Contest on "Innovation in organizations"

The 2007 annual survey conducted by the Great Place To Work® Institute Italia, included a contest to identify the company that was most successful in assembling a set of policies that favored the participation of all of the organization's "components" in providing ideas for the improvement of corporate performance.

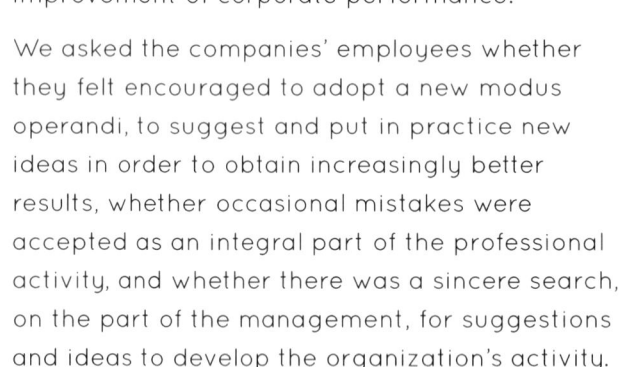

We asked the companies' employees whether they felt encouraged to adopt a new modus operandi, to suggest and put in practice new ideas in order to obtain increasingly better results, whether occasional mistakes were accepted as an integral part of the professional activity, and whether there was a sincere search, on the part of the management, for suggestions and ideas to develop the organization's activity.

With the answers provided by employees, we asked companies how they were structured in order to have all collaborators be part of that ground of ideas that constitutes a better opportunity to make a company vital and competitive.

From the answers provided by the employees and the analysis of the corporate policies regarding Innovation, the Great Place To Work® Institute Italia gathered a pool of six companies to form a technical-scientific committee, consisting of the organizing partners and university professors, who selected the winner of the 2007 Contest on "Innovation in organizations."

The selected companies were Cefriel, Coca Cola HBC, Elica, Google, and W.L. Gore.

THE COMPANY'S APPROACH TO INNOVATION

CEFRIEL	Innovation is the sense of service that the company gives to businesses.

Therefore, this represents the model adopted in each of the internal activities.

The experimentation inside the center is, among other things, the prototype of the organizational innovation and process projects provided in client businesses.

People are encouraged to adopt new modus operandi through the response to the development demands of our reference market. |
| **COCA COLA HBC** | Another company to turn innovation into the constant motor of all organization and management's actions, Coca Cola Italia supports a strong culture of change that permeates the company in all of its departments.

Coca Cola supports pro-activity and willingness to promote new ideas from the employee's first day in the company through numerous programs that invite people to speak up.In addition, its strategy is based on maximum sharing of information and |

	experience among all the population, through all of the communication instruments, whether based on IC&T or in meetings. A **"Box of Ideas"** is available to collect the ideas and suggestions from all employees.
ELICA	Innovation is not a product or manual, but rather it is a way of being in a culture that is spread throughout the company. At Elica, innovation of products is the most visible and the media often highlight it. At Elica innovation is put in practice in many other ways and in many other areas. The company is increasingly opening its doors to the world of education, housing students and providing them with the experience of corporate life. The organization stimulates creativity through the interplay of environments distinct from their own. There is great attention to cordiality and quality in the workplace. Elica is making a CREATIVOGENIC workplace. Much work has been done on a "positive culture of failure" and on the complete gratification and recognition of innovative ideas. When an idea proposed by an employee is not made concrete, the company carefully explains the reasons to the proponent. When, on the other hand, it is accomplished, the person receives a tangible monetary gratification and an intangible recognition for the contribution offered (and often, for people, the intangible part counts more).

GOOGLE	**Some adopted modus operandi to favor the innovative spirit:** • Flat organization: few hierarchic levels make the flow of ideas easier. • Constant sharing of information and ideas with all the population • Work environment— colors, availability of games, break-time areas— that stimulates creativity and innovation **Modus operandi to favor the birth and sharing of ideas:** • Anyone can give birth to ideas • Permission to pursue a dream • Innovation, rather than immediate perfection • In each idea, something good can always be saved
MICROSOFT	Innovation is one of the essential elements upon which Microsoft culture is based, and for this reason, all of the employees are encouraged to use the full potential of all of the tools made available by the company. In addition to hardware (Smartphone, portable computer, etc.), the company encourages the use of IT programs and products such as, the Sharepoint software, used to build Intranet portals that all employees can create and that may be used as repository of documents and information, as well as to carry out Surveys or for any other information sharing purpose. Everybody who works at Microsoft is also encouraged to try out new ideas, implementing new approaches, and giving life to innovative projects applicable to

	their own work. This innovation is a favorite, within a corporate culture that is always directed towards development and progress in the institution, both at a global and local level, for a special award named "Circle of Excellence." Periodically, the award goes to people or work teams, outstanding for having adopted an innovative approach at work, and having obtained excellent results and giving life to new best practices that become part of the corporate expertise asset.
W.L. GORE & ASSOCIATES	The drive to innovation has allowed W.L. Gore & Associates to develop diverse products for various markets, ranging from vascular prosthesis to guitar strings.

The "latex" structure that distinguishes the organization since almost its creation—in the early 1900s—is an example of a significant approach to giving people a clear indication of how much their contribution in terms of ideas is appreciated by the company. Employees are called "associates" and as such they are considered. There are very few formal chiefs: each one plays a leadership role in accordance with skills and experience and the projects and situations they have to face.

Each person in the corporation, not just those directly responsible for the business, is encouraged to present ideas and projects for development.

A policy that distinguishes the company is that there are very few written rules, leaving them for the common sense and ideas.

Each of the "associates" is motivated to feel like a main player of the company's successes. |

TRUST
MAKES COMPANIES **STRONGER** AND MORE **ABLE** TO HANDLE BAD TIMES

THE BOTTOM LINE ▪
MANAGING IN DIFFICULT TIMES ▪

1. THE BOTTOM LINE

2008

CREATING TRUST: IT'S WORTH THE **EFFORT**

By **Amy Lyman**

[GREAT PLACE TO WORK® WHITE PAPER]

In this in-depth analysis, Amy Lyman discusses the variety of ways in which high levels of trust have a positive impact on corporate performance. Dr. Lyman, a former professor at University of California, Davis, is co-founder of Great Place to Work® Institute and director of corporate research.

Creating trust can appear to be a daunting task, especially in the workplace where multiple responsibilities call for significant attention, and leaders have a limited amount of time to devote to each of their activities. However, if one activity successfully accomplished could be proven to make all other tasks significantly easier, then it would be worth the effort to focus on that one. Building trust in relationships with employees is that one task. In this paper, we present strong evidence of the positive long-term success achieved as a direct result of the high levels of trust that have been created in the relationships between employees and management within the 100 Best Companies to Work For in America. Comparisons with a group of companies displaying lower levels of trust affirms the positive contributions that the effort to create a trusting environment makes to the overall financial success of these organizations in which leaders are credible, employees are respected, and policies and practices are characterized by fairness.

Employees in high-trust workplaces show higher levels of cooperation within their teams and across departments and divisions, as well as higher levels of commitment to their own work, the work of the organization, and to the vision of the organization's leaders. The quality of the workplace culture that has been created leads to the creation of highly successful organizations that reap multiple benefits.

For someone looking for work, a great workplace is worth the search. The search is also worthy to an investor looking to find a company that produces positive, sustainable long-term financial success. And for a leader, a great workplace is worth the effort, or the journey, for leaders are the ones who initiate and sustain the creation of great workplaces.

We often hear from employees in the Best Companies that their colleagues and immediate managers are very important to creating the special circumstances in which they find themselves. Yet their leaders are seen as the ones who embody the values and commitment that make the difference in the quality of the workplace experience. Many people can tell stories of other places they've worked where leaders did not pay as much attention to the overall quality of the culture or the unique elements that take a workplace beyond good to truly great. Colleagues and managers help, and camaraderie can be built up among co-workers, yet without the guidance— and leadership—from senior executives, the overall culture never rises to greatness.

For the past 11 years our organization, the Great Place to Work® Institute, Inc. has collaborated with Fortune magazine to produce the 100 Best Companies to Work For list that appears every January; as well as the Best Small and Medium Companies to Work For list produced every June with Society for Human Resource Management (SHRM), and Best Workplaces lists in 31 other countries around the world. Prior to our project with Fortune we produced two books—with Robert Levering and Milton Moskowitz as co-authors—with the same title, in 1984 and again in 1993. So, for almost 25 years now we have been listening to employees in great workplaces as they tell us; "This is a Great Place to Work® because . . . ."

Creating a culture in which employees can say "this place is great" requires that leaders and managers throughout an organization base their relationships with employees on actions that promote and develop trust. Leaders in particular need to reinforce the culture by communicating to people about the long-term benefits of creating an organization culture that is based in trust. Consistency between the communication and actions of leaders develops their credibility in the eyes of employees.

In a great organization, the development of trust also needs to go beyond the leaders at the top and be reinforced in the daily interactions among people throughout the organization. Managers who are treated with respect by senior leaders will in turn be able to share that respect with employees by supporting their professional development, soliciting their ideas, and caring for them as human beings. The practice of fairness—as seen in efforts to promote pay equity, fair hiring practices, and justice, regardless of personal characteristics—is also fundamental to insuring that trust will flourish in an organization's culture. In the Best Companies that make our lists, we are always able to find a deep expression of the workplace culture in the actions of leaders and managers throughout the organization.

The benefits that come from a high level of trust include a spirit of cooperation that is ever-present in great workplaces, along with a deep sense of commitment to the mission, vision, and values of the organization. Cooperation and commitment play out in people's daily actions and their willingness to contribute to the long-term success of the organization. Evidence for this comes not only from the employee survey data that we collect, but also from our analysis of financial performance data.

Great workplaces, with high levels of trust, cooperation, and commitment, outperform their peers and experience as a group. They exhibit:

• stronger long-term financial performance.

• lower turnover relative to their industry peers.

• more job applications than their peers.

• an integrated workforce in which diverse groups of people create and contribute to a common workplace culture of benefit to all.

There is a singular role that leaders play in securing employee commitment to their vision for the future. Leaders in great workplaces are actively involved in communicating their ideas, answering questions, and engaging in discussion to insure that employees are knowledgeable about the direction of the organization and thus able to make a clear, strong commitment to the future. Leaders also serve as role models of cooperation through their own actions. Their visible cooperation with others confirms the strategic importance of cooperative work for the implementation and attainment of the company's vision. These are people strategies at their best, and of course that's what we find and document in the be Best Companies—trust, cooperation, and commitment creating a great workplace at the top of its game.

FORTUNE 100 BEST vs. STOCK MARKET 1998-2007

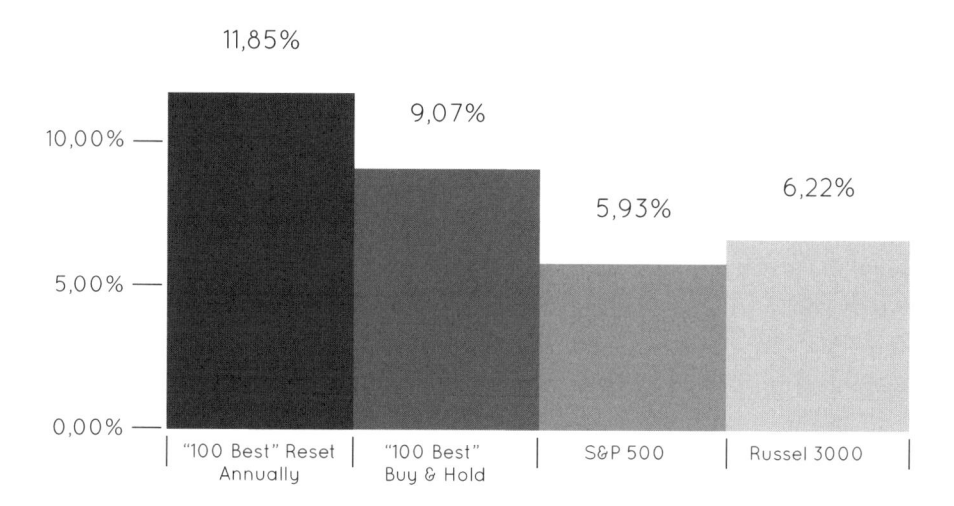

- "100 Best" Reset Annually: 11,85%
- "100 Best" Buy & Hold: 9,07%
- S&P 500: 5,93%
- Russel 3000: 6,22%

Data Source *Russell Investment Group.*

Financial Performance

There are many benefits that come to great workplaces, with one of the most immediately obvious being sustained financial success over time. Over the years we have collected general information, as well as anecdotal stories, academic research, and case studies, that confirm this. Lower voluntary turnover, higher numbers of job applicants, greater collaboration, and confidence in management's leadership abilities all contribute to the creativity, innovation, customer service, and reputation that support the long-term fiancial stability and success of great workplaces.

Compelling evidence of the financial success of great workplaces comes from a number of souces [1]. The longest running study—an annual analysis completed by the Russell Investment Group—documents the financial performance of a hypothetical portfolio of publicly traded 100 Best Companies compared with the S&P 500 and the Russell 3000. The "Fortune 100 Best vs. Stock

[1] Another great study to look at is presented in Alex Edman's recent article titled Does the Stock Markety Fully Value Intangibles? Employee Satisfaction and Equity Prices. An electronic copy of this article is available at: http://ssrn.com/abstract=985735.

Market 1998–2007" compares the performance of two portfolios of 100 Best Companies from 1998 through 2007 with the S&P 500 and Russell 3000.

As you can see from the evidence, over time, the 100 Best as a group have consistently produced higher levels of financial return than the two comparison groups. Why is this? Many theories abound. Ours is quite straightforward. A high level of trust helps people to cooperate more successfully with each other and to commit to the vision and future direction of the overall organization that they belong to.

Trust, Cooperation, and Commitment

Our analysis of the Great Place to Work® Trust Index© survey responses from employees in the 100 Best Companies points to a number of key areas that differentiate their workplace experiences from those of employees in the Best Companies applicant pool. Specifically, among the 100 Best there are higher levels of Trust between employees and management, greater Cooperation across and within teams and stronger Commitment expressed by employees to their work and the organization as a whole. These response patterns point to unique qualities in the workplace culture and relationships that exist within the 100 Best Companies—qualities that are driven by particular strengths within the Trust dimensions of the Great Place to Work® Model© (Credibility, Respect, and Fairness).

The "2004-2008 Average Trust, Cooperation, Commitment and Great Place to Work® graph presents the overall Trust average, and shows the relationships between Trust, Cooperation, Commitment and the response to the final survey statement, for the 100 Best Companies and the applicant pool from 2004-2008 [2] [3].

[2] The two populations of companies represented in this graph represent distinct groups with differences significant at alpha<0.001.

[3] The Trust Average includes all Credibility, Respect, and Fairness survey statements from the Trust Index© a proprietary survey tool of the Great Place to Work® Institute, Inc. The Cooperation Average includes two statements outside of the Trust dimensions: "People here are willing to give extra to get the job done." And "You can count on people to cooperate." The Commitment Average also includes two statements outside of the Trust dimensions: "People look forward to coming to work here." And "We're all in this together." Great Place to Work® Average is for the statement, "Taking every into account I would say this is a great place to work."

2004-2008 AVERAGE TRUST, COOPERATION, COMMITMENT AND GREAT PLACE TO WORK®

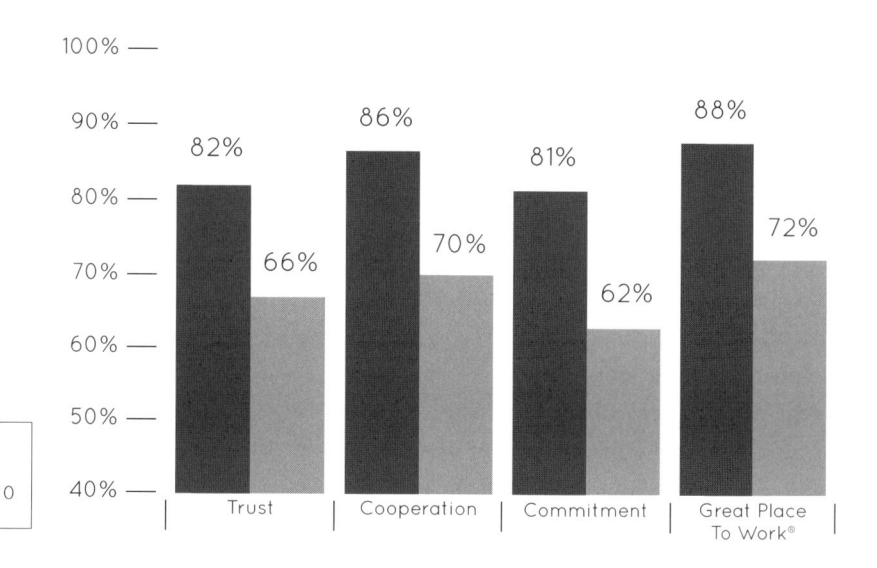

	100 Best	Lower 100
Trust	82%	66%
Cooperation	86%	70%
Commitment	81%	62%
Great Place To Work®	88%	72%

©2008 Great Place to Work® Institute, Inc. All Rights Reserved

When talking about the impact that higher levels of Trust, Cooperation, and Commitment can have on the success of a business, we often ask managers and leaders to consider the numbers in this graph (or their own custom graph) to be a representation of groups of 100 employees in their organizations. The questions we pose for people to consider include:

• Imagine what you could do if you had 80 out of 100 employees in your organization who often or almost always look forward to coming to work every day.

• How much more effective would your workforce be if 86 out of 100 employees knew that often or almost always people were willing to give extra to get the job done?

• What could you do as a manager if 86 out of 100 people in your department believed that they could count on each other to cooperate?

• How much more successful would you be as a leader if you knew that 80 out of 100 of your employees experienced a strong sense of togetherness on a regular basis?

• How much stronger would your organization be if 82 out of 100 of your employees experienced a high level of Trust with their managers on a daily basis?

The discussions that result from these questions are often insightful, covering both the dilemmas companies face when Trust, Cooperation, and Commitment are low, and the incredible opportunities awaiting companies that are able to develop high levels of trust and the cooperation and commitment that follow.

The graph in the following section stirs things up even more as it is the financial results that go along with the differences in Trust, Cooperation, and Commitment that open the eyes of even the most skeptical.

Financial Impact of Trust, Cooperation and Commitment

High-trust organizations are better financial performers. We've been saying this for the past 25 years, and numerous other researchers and consultants have been saying this as well. High trust eases the way to collaboration and idea-sharing, a confidence in management's vision for the future, and a belief in the fundamental fairness with which people will be treated, all of which contribute to the successful coordination of activities and output that make an enterprise successful.

The "Financial Results 2004-2008 100 Best and Lower" graph compares the financial performance

FINANCIAL RESULTS 2004-2008
100 BEST AND LOWER 100

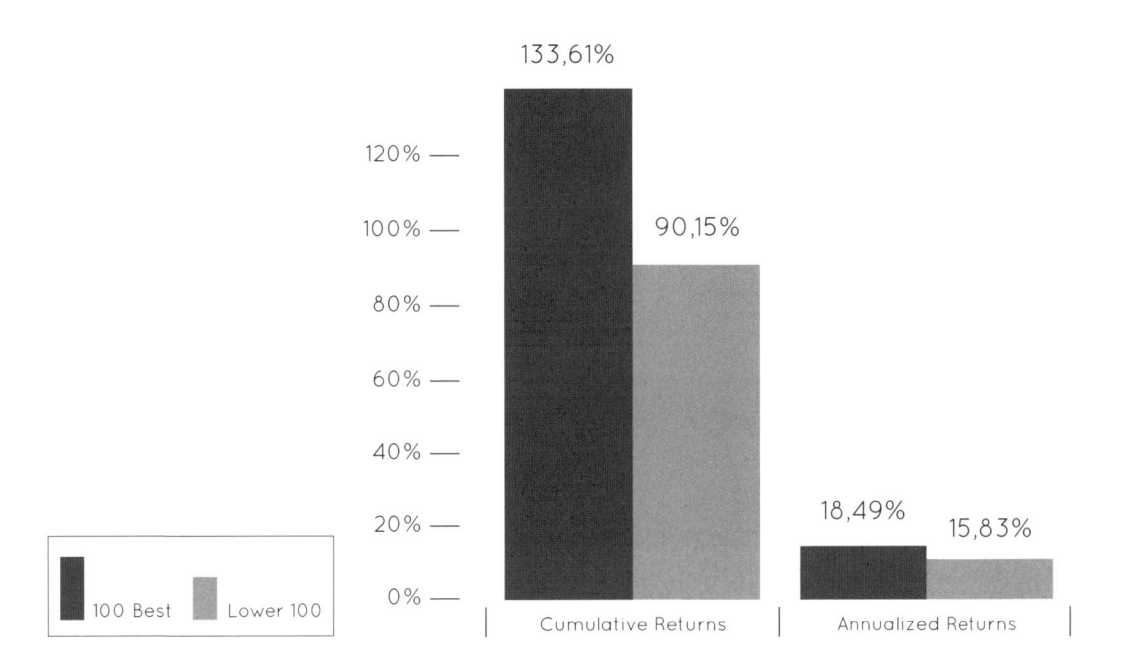

- 100 Best
- Lower 100

Cumulative Returns: 133,61% (100 Best), 90,15% (Lower 100)
Annualized Returns: 18,49% (100 Best), 15,83% (Lower 100)

©2008 Great Place to Work® Institute, Inc.
All Rights Reserved

[4] This analysis was conducted internally at the Great Place to Work® Institute using the methodology used by the Russell Investment Group, which conducts annual studies of the performance of the 100 Best Companies referred to above. The results affirm that the financial performance of the 100 Best companies, both cumulative and annualized, is notably stronger than that of the companies in the Lower 100 group of list applicants, for 2004–2008, with a significant difference in performance confirmed at the .05 level.

of the 100 Best Companies relative to the performance of the 100 Lower Trust Companies in the Best Companies applicant pool from 2004-2008. The applicant pool does represent a self-selected group of companies that are interested in the 100 Best list selection process, and presumably are also interested in creating a great workplace in which high levels of trust exist between employees and management. Our analysis of the survey results of the two groups confirms that they represent two distinct populations of companies with distinct levels of trust5. Our analysis of the financial results affirms that over the long-term, a high-trust culture provides a significant competitive advantage to an organization [4].

Components of Trust

We have always believed that high levels of trust will lead to levels of cooperation among employees and across work groups, and to high levels of commitment to an individual's work and the organization as a whole. The evidence presented in the previous section affirms that higher levels of trust come with higher levels of cooperation and commitment, which in turn bring with them a higher level of long-term financial success. All around it is a powerful story!

The 100 Lower Trust Companies are all good workplaces. They represent successful organizations in which leaders have made a commitment to creating a great workplace, yet they haven't reached "100 Best" status. The positive response from employees indicating that often or almost always they experience their workplace as great (71 percent of them indicating this) is far above the responses received in other national surveys of employers in which we are lucky to see 35-40 percent of employees saying that their workplace is great.

So what is it that is happening at the Best Companies that provides them with such a critical boost in Trust, Cooperation, and Commitment?

In the 100 Best Companies, employees are more likely to experience effective two-way communication, see management as competent and believe that managers and leaders are reliable and act with integrity. In particular, management's ability to deliver on promises and act in ways that are consistent with what they have said shows a 34 percent boost in positive response from employees at the 100 Best Companies relative to those in the 100 Lower Trust group.

High levels of trust lead to greater cooperation.

Best Company employees also indicate that they are involved in collaborative decision-making activities to a much greater degree than are employees in the applicant pool companies. Employees often are invited in to decision-making activities or have their ideas solicited by manager—and responded to sincerely.

What's the evidence? A 33 percent higher level of positive response to statements indicating that employees feel they are involved in decisions that affect how they get their work done and that their ideas are genuinely sought out. What's the benefit? Employees become engaged in their work, share their bright ideas, collaborate with each other, and invest themselves in their work. All because they are invited in to the decision making process, rather than told to just "do your job."

Applicant-pool companies are no slouches in terms of seeking collaboration as their employees do provide evidence that managers and leaders in these companies are making the effort to be open to questions and provide clear answers. Among the 100 Lower Trust Companies just under two-thirds of employees believe their ideas are genuinely solicited and responded to, while slightly over half of the employees find themselves involved in collaborative decision making. Relative to employees at the Best Companies—where close to three-quarters of employees have these experiences—there is clearly room for improvement though.

At Best Companies, employees also develop a deeply-rooted set of beliefs that they will be treated fairly during critical decision-making times involving pay, promotions, job assignments, and the handling of grievances. These Fairness markers provide tremendous benefits to companies looking for employees to make long term commitments to their organizations, as it is through a sense that one can be successful over the long-term within a group that one's personal investment in and commitment to the group deepens.

One of the greatest differences between employees in the 100 Best Companies relative to those in the applicant pool emerged on one of the statements assessing employees' sense of the equity with which they are treated. Over two-thirds of employees at the Best Companies believe that they receive a fair share of the profits made by their organizations, compared with fewer than half of the employees among the 100 Lower Trust Companies of the applicant pool. Nearly every company that applies for the list offers some form of profit-sharing—whether it's through contributions to the 401k, stock purchase plans, profit-sharing checks, gain-sharing programs, or other mechanisms. So the issue isn't whether there is a plan to share profits or not. The issue that makes a difference for employees is their sense that they are receiving a fair share of the profits.

Another area of notable difference between the 100 Best and the applicants concerns employees' views on the fairness of the promotion process. Among the Best, 71 percent of employees believe that promotions go to those who best deserve them while 52 percent hold that same belief among the 100 Lower Trust Companies of the applicant pool.

What is interesting to note here is that the item of interest to employees—based on our years of research and employee interviews—is a concern with the overall fairness of the promotion process, not their particular promotion history. Employees have often explained that if people believe the system is fair for everyone—it they can see that and hear stories about it—then they know that when their turn comes, they have a pretty good shot at being treated fairly. Employees can enter the promotion "competition" with more confidence and less anxiety about the outcome— knowing that the best likelihood is that they'll be treated fairly.

Using the analogy shared earlier, and thinking in terms of groups of 100 employees, we can understand the magnitude of the difference here. At a 100 Best Company, 71 out of 100 employees believe that often, or almost always, promotions go to those who best deserve them. At a company in the 100 Lower Trust group, 52 out of 100 employees hold that belief. So there are 19 more employees out of 100 at a Best Company who are having an experience that gives them a sense that the playing field is level—and that they will be treated fairly. And, if the total employee population at the two hypothetical companies in this comparison is 5,000—then the 100 Best Company actually has 950 more employees who believe they are likely to be treated fairly during the promotion process than does the company in the lower third of the applicant pool. Where will you find the more highly committed employees?

Benefits Galore

No, not the perks kind of benefits, or HR benefits. Benefits galore here refers to the additional benefits that come to great workplaces that have developed high levels of trust and strong reputations as premier employers. These benefits, that come back to the organization in the form of lower costs for basic business functions, or a higher return on an item like training and development, contribute to the overall quality of the workplace and the competitiveness of the company.

Voluntary Turnovers

Employee turnover is expensive. There are the hard costs of hiring a temp worker to fill the empty slot, advertising, interviewing, and training. And then, there are the harder-to-calculate costs of lost knowledge that the person who left takes with her, the workflow costs associated with the network of relationships and information sources that are broken when someone departs, and the reputation questions that may arise if a key employee decides to leave. If you can create a culture that reduces employee turnover then both the hard and harder-to-calculate costs can be minimized, leaving more money to spend on value-added services and projects, and more knowledge and expertise in your own business rather than in someone else's. We have often calculated the employee turnover of the 100 Best and compared those results with industry average data provided by the Bureau of Labor Statistics (BLS). And the 100 Best always show that as a group and within their industries they have lower levels of turnover than companies in their industries.

But what's the case when the 100 best are compared with the 100 Lower Trust Companies in the applicant pool? Our hypothesis was that the turnover figures would be much closer to each other as the 100 Lower Trust Companies are all good companies that have indicated to some degree their interest in creating a strong trust-based culture for their employees, simply by the fact that they have applied for the 100 Best list. Many of them have applied for a number of years, and some of them have been on the list in the past and are working their way back to a spot on the list.

We found in general that the 100 Best as a group do experience lower voluntary turnover than the 100 Lower Trust Companies—for all companies across all industries. And the 100 Lower Trust Companies do show a distinct advantage compared to the general population of companies as represented by the BLS "Quit" data for 2006 and 2007.

VOLUNTARY TUNOVER AMONG FULL TIME EMPLOYEES IN THE 100 BEST AND 100 LOWER TRUST GROUPS

	100 BEST	100 LOWER	BLS DATA
2007 LIST (2006 DATA)	12,06%	13,97%	23,4%
2008 LIST (2007 DATA)	11,21%	13,68%	22,6%

Job Applications

Another area in which we have seen that Best Companies often exceed their peers is in the volume of job applications received by these companies once they are recognized as a great workplace. We have heard numerous times from companies that show up on the 100 Best list that they can be inundated in the weeks following the list announcement with unsolicited resumes from people wanting to work at a great place. This seems to be a clear marker of the interest of many employees in the overall quality of the workplace culture, and of their willingness to consider switching employers if they can find a position at a great workplace.

Many of the Best Companies have developed unique recruiting operations to handle the abundance of resumes that flow their way, especially once the 100 Best List has been made public in Fortune magazine.

Recruiters pay particular attention to finding new employees who show an interest in learning about

RATIO OF NUMBER OF JOB APPLICATION TO POSITIONS FILLED - ALL INDUSTRIES

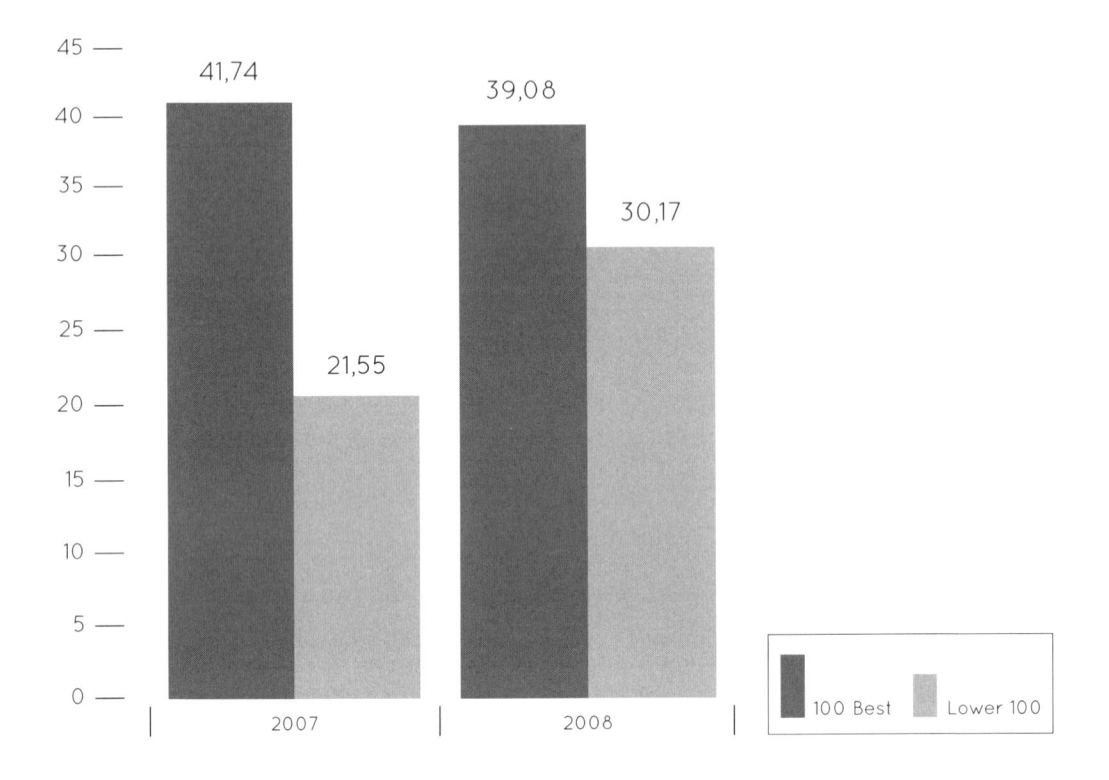

Year	100 Best	Lower 100
2007	41,74	21,55
2008	39,08	30,17

©2008 Great Place to Work® Institute, Inc. All Rights Reserved

the company's history and its values as this is seen as one way to insure a continuation of the strong culture that has already been built. Also, numerous companies involve current employees in the process of determining whether a potential employee will be a good cultural fit by including him/her in the interview process.

At Google, hiring is an art form that is consistent with company culture and the approach they take to many of their employee-focused practices [5].

[5] Taken from the 2007 100 Best List Culture Audit© part 2 submission materials

Hiring at GOOGLE: Philosophy, Principles and Practice Guidelines

We hire people who are great at what they do and interesting to work with. For such a lofty goal, our strategy is pretty down-to-earth. We believe that the best ideas surface when people who think differently from each other start talking together. Diverse backgrounds help us understand problems from a different perspective and discover unique solutions.

Google's hiring principles, written by our co-founders and referred to by our recruiters, are simple but very effective:

Hire individual candidates consistent with our Hiring Do's and Don'ts:

- Hire individual candidates who have interests and activities that "jump off the page" and make you want to talk to them.

- Hire leaders and potential leaders who have a proven willingness to "roll up their sleeves" and get things done.

- Avoid hiring specialists with narrow capabilities; instead hire generalists with relevant experience and capacity to learn.

- Hire people into roles that they have a clear potential to outgrow.

- Don't hire people with urgency. Good hires take time.

GOOGLE'S HIRING DO'S AND DON'TS

Hire people who are smarter and more knowledgeable than you are;

Don't hire people you can't learn from or be challenged by;

Hire people who will add value to the product AND our culture;

Don't hire people who won't contribute well to both;

Hire people who will get things done;

Don't hire people who just think about problems.

Hire people who are enthusiastic, self-motivated, and passionate;

Don't hire people who just want a job;

Hire people who inspire and work well with others;

Don't hire people who prefer to work alone;

Hire people who will grow with your team and with the company;

Don't hire people with narrow skill sets or interests;

Hire people who are well-rounded with unique interests and talents

Don't hire people who only live to work;

Hire people who are ethical and who communicate openly;

Don't hire people who are political or manipulative;

Hire only when you've found a great candidate;

Don't settle for anything less.

Creating an Inclusive Culture

A number of studies during the past few years have looked at societal responses to diversity, the creation of an inclusive culture, and the most successful ways of approaching inclusion in the workplace and in communities. One study, authored by Robert Putnam10, received a great deal of attention in the press for one of its "halfway" conclusions. I say halfway, as the conclusion reflected the ways in which people can initially respond to increased ethnic diversity by "hunkering down," as Putnam put it. That is, when people are initially exposed to demographic shifts that bring them into more frequent contact with people who they believe to be ethnically different from them, they can do a number of things that look like they are closing ranks, seeking easy similarity in their friends or associates, or simply shutting themselves inside with a small group of family, friends, and neighbors with whom they are familiar and comfortable.

Yet in the study itself, Putnam provided the other "half" of this conclusion in which he firmly states his belief that diversity is inevitable, desirable, and beneficial. He states, "Ethnic diversity is, on balance, an important social asset, as the history of my country demonstrates."

Among Best Companies, diversity has often been approached from the perspective of seeking to engage all employees in the work of the organization, whatever the characteristics are that they bring to the table that might be seen as "different." A culture is created in which people from distinct backgrounds can work well together. People's various talents are uncovered and exploited. And, a great workplace is created that is financially successful, able to attract and train the best people, and able to provide products and services that attract and retain customers.

After reading through the Putnam study, another recent work, The Difference, by Scott Page , and conducting our own research on differences and similarities among employee survey responses for the list applicant pool, we are convinced that one of the greatest strengths of Best Companies is their ability to create inclusive environments in which all employees are invited to participate and most are able to do so.

One of the reasons that more employees are fully engaged—with their hearts and minds—at great companies is that formal and informal support networks are in place that create strong internal ties among people who may be seen as "different" or who hold positions traditionally seen as having different status or value. This can create a sense of belonging for people who may not usually feel a part of the group, and provide and openness for

2004-2008 OVERALL TRUST AVERAGE BY AGE

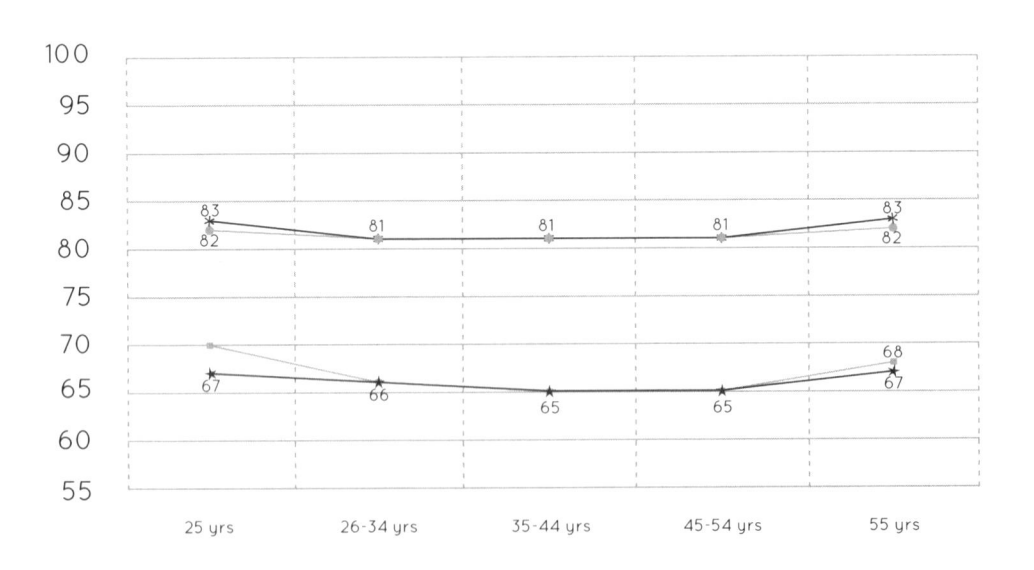

Age	25 yrs	26-34 yrs	35-44 yrs	45-54 yrs	55 yrs
100 Best	83	81	81	81	83
100 Best Overall Avg	82				82
100 Lower	67	66	65	65	68
100 BLower Overall Avg	67				67

* 100 Best
- 100 Best Overall Avg
- 100 Lower
★ 100 BLower Overall Avg

2004-2008 TRUST AVERAGE BY RACE

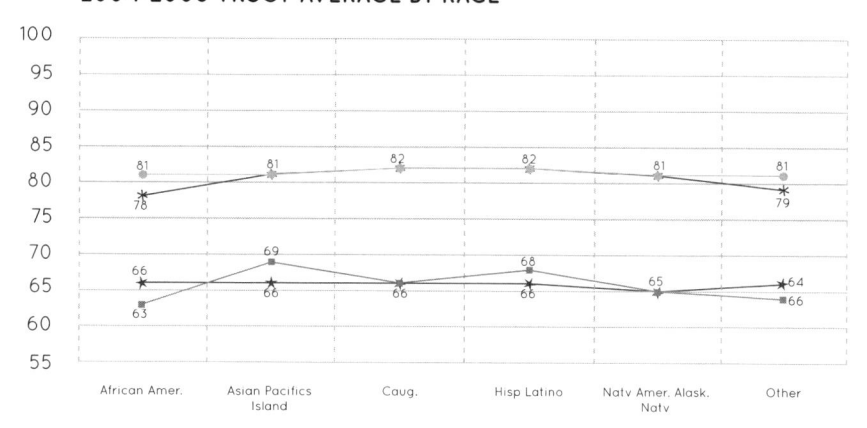

	African Amer.	Asian Pacifics Island	Caug.	Hisp Latino	Natv Amer. Alask. Natv	Other
100 Best	78	81	82	82	81	79
100 Best Overall Trust Avg	81	81	82	82	81	81
100 Lower	63	66	66	66	65	66
100 BLower Overall Trust Avg	66	69	66	68	65	64

people to share their ideas when they may not initially have confidence to speak up. Diversity networks and collaborative groups can also serve as resource networks that expose executives or senior managers (who may be similar to each other) to people, sources of information, and ideas that are different from their own. They can also help those same executives to understand the difficulty that people who are "different" have in feeling comfortable in some business settings.

Thus a strong culture of inclusion created by leaders helps people who might be seen as "different to feel like full members of the group, and enables them to participate without losing their valuable different way of looking at things. While some companies may try to create a culture of inclusion by asking everyone to be the same and by trying to help "different" people be more "similar"— like the majority group or the leaders—this can diminish any value that could be gleaned from the varying approaches and experiences that different types of people bring to a situation. In general, Best Companies create strong cultures that include people and their differences, and support the development of cross group ties that help people to share their distinct approaches and ideas.

Our evidence for this comes through in the survey results that show that in Best Companies more people across all demographic categories experience a high level of trust than is the case for employees in the 100 Lower Trust Companies.

For example, when we look at the data for the 2004-2008 100 Best and 100 Lower Trust Companies, by race and age, it is clear that many more employees in Best Companies are sharing a consistent high-trust experience with each other—regardless their age or race differences—than are employees in the 100 Lower Trust Companies.

The benefits that come from inclusive cultures are often recognized by employees, who provide strong anecdotal support for the value of diversity in their comments:

"Goldman Sachs values diversity and has zero tolerance for unequal treatment of any group of people. It holds weeks of events celebrating various ethnic identities, accomplishments of women, and gay/lesbian/transgender contributions to society. I think it is the most fair and principled of any company for which I could work."

"I always feel like a part of the team and that my part is recognized in the midst of the group's work product. We do a great job of hiring different types of people, all of whom mesh well together. The firm has made it incredibly easy to be a working mom, with flex-time and an on-site day care and incredible health coverage. As a young female attorney, I know the firm is trying to keep me here before and after I decide to have children."

"A unique quality that Wegman's has is their diversity. I enjoy that so many cultures work together in one place, and with it I feel right at home. For this being my first job, I feel very proud of what I do and for the people I work for."

"I can honestly say that from day one, AstraZeneca has treated me not only as an intelligent and self-motivated individual but also with the utmost respect. It is with great conviction that I can say, Astrazeneca seeks individuals from diversified backgrounds in order to not only represent the world at large but also to assure the continued evolution of the company with new and fresh ideas. Employees are respected and cherished."

"One thing that makes our company a Great Place to Work® is diversity. Employees from different nationalities work so well together. The Principal understands that to be successful globally, we have to have diversity at work. In promoting diversity, several clubs within the company are sponsored such as Asian Resource Group, African-American Resource Group, Muslim Resource Group, etc. These groups make employees feel like they belong in this organization and the management care about who they are personally."

"The diversity of co-workers at all levels of the company is significant—racially, ethnically, gender, sexual orientation, beliefs, etc. Best of all, this group of people gather and support each other in appreciation of all the value our differences bring to drive the business. I believe this generates great connection and communication, understanding and opportunity."

"Our diversity initiatives consistently work to improve awareness, increase productivity and celebrate the differences that result in a competitive advantage for TI . . . There are groups representing various religions, race, sex, and sexual orientation whose activities are supported and encourage . . . People are proud of TI's work force and its diversity."

"The most unique thing about this company is that it makes you into a unique person. I was raised in small town Idaho and when I got a job at Starbucks in Boise, I was fairly narrow-minded and specifically didn't have a love for diversity. As I learned Starbucks' mission and actually saw my managers utilize it in their everyday stores and hiring decisions, I realized the importance of it. This is a value now that I am very passionate about. Diversity opens you up as a person and expands who you are, just as much as it can expand a company."

"The diversity in the people of our company makes it great—at any location we have people from many different countries, races, religious preferences, sexual orientations, size and shapes. We all just naturally coalesce into one very unique and effective team. I wish it would be this way outside the company."

"These employee comments present a powerful message about the power of diversity and

2004-2008 INTEREST IN STAYING

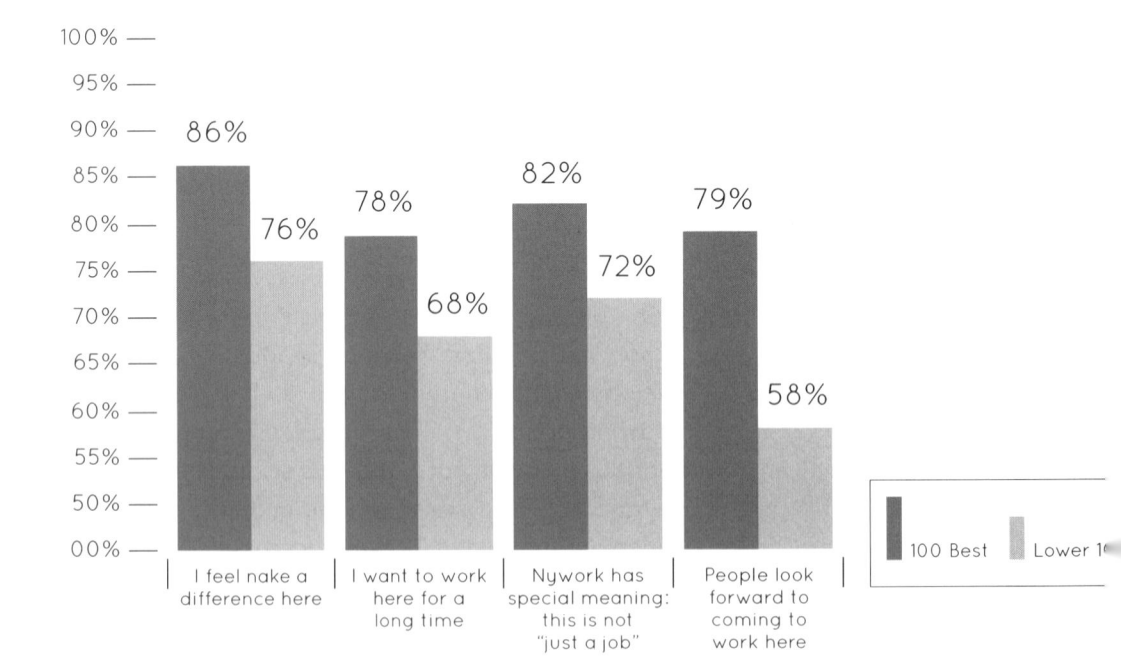

Statement	100 Best	Lower 1
I feel nake a difference here	86%	76%
I want to work here for a long time	78%	68%
Nywork has special meaning: this is not "just a job"	82%	72%
People look forward to coming to work here	79%	58%

©2008 Great Place to Work® Institute, Inc. All Rights Reserved

> "I've been here almost six years and I can't imagine finding a better place to work."

the vaule in bringing people together from different backgrounds. In a culture of respect and collaboration there is the possibility of creating a world in which people do finally all just get along."

Interest in Staying

Much attention has been paid recently to the link between employees' commitment to their work and their intention to stay with their employer—the "retention" question. In our research we have focused on an employees' expressed interest in staying—what a person says about what he or she wants to do—and have considered this in relation to a person's sense that work has special meaning and that coming to work is something one looks forward to.

Employee comments about their work experience at several of the Best Companies confirm the relationship between a person's desire to stay, the special quality of the work people get to do, and that they look forward to going to work—for both the camaraderie they experience and the challenges of the work they do.

"Staff tends to stay and relationships develop and continuity improves care and becomes a social benefit."

"There is no better place to be in our industry. The cooperative culture is unique in this industry. The people are the best and the most challenging."

The following survey results presented here affirm with numbers what employees' comments express in sentiment.

"In high tech, it's unusual to find people who stay at one company for a long time. At Intuit, it's not uncommon to see people who have worked here for 5, 10, or more years. I've been here almost 6 years and I can't imagine finding a better place to work."

"Kimley-Horn is the ideal company that I have been looking for my entire career. I'm glad to be here and hope to stay until I retire."

"The strong emphasis on information, education, and training offered to managers is a great tool for helping people move up in their careers. It is a great way of encouraging people to grow and yet stay with Marriott."

"This was my first job and when it came time to choose my career field, I decided to stay with Wegman's based on their strong core values. They give you an opportunity to explore all avenues they have to offer."

At times the sheer volume of data affirming the good qualities and strong benefits that come to great workplaces can be a bit overwhelming. Are these workplaces really that great? It may be that we simply need to keep telling their stories over and over again to ultimately change people's understanding of what corporations can actually become.

The Best Companies

Every Best Company has its own story of the ways in which their great workplace culture has been created through the words and actions of leaders, managers, and employees. These stories are the best illustration of what it means to create a great workplace, where employees trust managers and leaders, and tell others,"My company is one of the best."

Baptist Health Care (Pensacola, Florida)

Baptist Healthcare has a vision to be the best health care system in America. The CEO and Senior Vice President have pursued this vision, to reinvent in their hospital and the employee management relationship, so that it would also be a role model for the U.S. healthcare industry. The challenges they faced when first pursuing this vision were many. Patient satisfaction was weak—they were in the 18th percentile. Employee satisfaction was weak—just 44 percent of the employees were satisfied. And the competitors were placing significant pressure on Baptist's viability as a hospital. Baptist's leaders knew that they could not outspend, out-equip, or out-program their competitors. Their choice was to build their competitive edge on service. Making this choice, to use service as the competitive advantage for their healthcare services, brought with it a natural focus on the internal service provided between and among people who work at Baptist. Thus the strategic choice, how to compete, required much introspection about what was happening inside of Baptist that had created the culture that led to its current state, and about the changes that would be needed to truly create the best healthcare system in America.

One area that received significant attention was an effort to improve the leadership training programs offered to support people's professional growth. In order to fully change the culture, employees would need to be supported in new ways. Training and education programs were developed to help people understand the Baptist Vision and how they could participate in achieving it. Other programs were developed to teach staff new ways of interacting with each other, the goal being that supervisors would be just as accountable to their staff, as their staff had to be the supervisors.

Employee involvement and idea-sharing programs also received a great amount of attention with one program in particular, the Bright Ideas program, providing a wonderful example of a way to solicit employee ideas.

The Bright Ideas program solicits innovative ideas from all people throughout the organization, giving employees an opportunity to share thoughts, suggestions for improvement and cost-savings ideas. Any idea that helps a department operate more efficiently or makes life easier for the customer is a Bright Idea. Employees submit their ideas directly into the Bright Ideas database. Their leader is responsible for implementing the idea, forwarding the idea to the most appropriate leader to implement, or providing feedback on why the idea won't or can't be implemented.

Besides being the repository of initial submissions, the database also serves as a warehouse of ideas that all leaders can access to see if a solution to a problem they are experiencing was solved in another area. Leaders can also simply review ideas in the database to look for great suggestions for ways of doing things better.

Employees are recognized for submitting their ideas with "Food for Thought" (free meal) certificates and receive 10 points for ideas that are implemented. The points are redeemable for prizes, from a small light-bulb pin (10 points) to a director's chair (150 points). All employees are encouraged to implement at least 2 Bright Ideas each year.

The program has been a tremendous success, generating positive changes in organizational processes and stimulating millions of dollars in cost-savings initiatives since its inception in 1998. Monthly celebrations, hosted by a senior leader, are held to honor all implemented ideas, and a drawing for $50 gift certificates are held. The program stimulates employees' sense of empowerment and motivation, and also some creative ways to celebrate the implementation of ideas. At one hospital (Atmore Hospital) the celebration of Bright Ideas involved a special employee and family picnic at which people, who

We need to keep telling these great-workplace stories over and over to change people's understanding of what corporations can actually become.

had submitted a Bright Idea, earned the chance to dunk a leader in the dunk-tank!

Granite Construction

Granite Construction is a heavy civil construction company and a construction materials provider with over 140 plants in various US locations. From its founding, leaders at this construction company placed a premium on insuring that its primary purpose was to provide an employees with the opportunity to make a decent and safe living while doing the work they could enjoy and be proud of.

One of the unique qualities of Granite's culture is an emphasis on looking back to the qualities that made the company successful in its early years, and projecting forward to see how those qualities can be adapted and built upon to insure future success. Company leaders present the organization as one that is comprised of reliable, hardworking and pragmatic professionals, craftsmen and engineers who also aspire to be Master Builder's. They express a commitment to the long-term success of their projects in terms of both the physical product or result and the social and environmental impact of their work. Granite's leaders proudly point to their leadership in Project Enduring Legacy, an industry-wide effort to shift the entire construction industry into a leadership position in sustainable construction, their social responsibility record, and their just drop missing words and for from the "word record" toonto the Domini 400 Social Fund investment index as proof of their positive reputation and impact. And this is a construction company! Not the first place that most people would turn for examples of how to create a workplace in which people say "I trust the people I work for."

What is it that has happened at Granite Construction over its more than 100-year history that led to its current culture and commitment to employees, safety, quality, and an enduring legacy? There are a few fundamental beliefs that seem to fuel much of Granite's culture, and a number of basic decent practices that help to reinforce that culture on a daily basis.

In their 2006 Culture Audit, Granite writes:

"... [we] believe [that] all people want to do a good job, and they will, if you trust them. This means allowing them to make the decisions in regards to their jobs and operations without oppressive oversight from Division or Corporate management. It means minimal intrusion of standardized policies and programs to avoid smothering their creativity and initiative; in most cases, a guideline rather than an inflexible policy will suffice. It means no excessive monitors and controls that convey distrust and disrespect.
It means making expectations clear, jointly arrived at whenever possible. It means providing resources, information, feedback, and recognition that support and encourage your people.

Getting the most from your people is not the job for efficiency experts. People are not units of production. They are living breathing imperfect divine creations that will thrive on learning and challenges. They are self-organizing creative, and ingenious when they believe they are working for a noble purpose and they will collaborate with synergistic results when they respect their coworkers, their leaders, and their company."

This would be a powerful statement in any company, yet for a 100-plus-year construction company it seems extraordinary. There are other construction and manufacturing firms on the 100 Best Companies list with similar unique, people-focused philosophies. There are also law firms, high-tech companies, and production service firms— and all have found truly special ways of structuring

"We believe that all people want to do a good job, and they will, if you trust them."

themselves and creating a culture that works for them. They are almost all atypical for their industries. Yet the practices of senior leaders and managers are in many ways ordinary.

At Granite Construction, leaders and managers excel at sharing information and listening to employees. Most of Granite's employees work at isolated worksites spread across the country. This could pose some problems for effective communication, yet with a clear commitment to sharing information and hearing from people, the senior leaders at Granite have incorporated responsibility for communicating and listening into their core work responsibilities. Granite has been able to retain much of the personal connection between senior management and employees in the field because leaders and managers visit construction sites frequently. President and CEO Bill Dorey and COO Mark Boitano personally visit all field locations nationwide at least once each year to participate in employee dialogues. These visits give the two most senior leaders a chance to hear people's thoughts and share their own vision for the future of the organization.

One special practice that is incorporated into all of these visits involves CEO Bill Dorey conducting a one or two hour walkabout to check in with every employee at the site. This practice is special for another reason as well— it's not just something done by the CEO. Division and assistant division managers also visit everyone working in the field offices and at job sites. There are also more formal quarterly or semi-annual employee dialogues that occur, to insure that no matter where a person's work location is, a live, face-to-face discussion with senior management will happen every year. It is this personal human contact that best exemplifies why Granite Construction is seen as such a special and unique workplace by its employees.

In response to the question, What makes this company a Great Place to Work®? one employee wrote:

"It is a very nice feeling when the president and CEO of the company comes to your workplace and he knows your name and is genuinely interested in what you are doing. Granite gives you as much responsibility as you want and they trust that you will make it happen and help you make it happen."

Principal Financial Group

The Principal Financial Group provides a variety of financial services (401K retirement plans, health and life insurance, asset management, etc.) to small- to medium-sized businesses, individuals, and institutions. These financial services are provided by many competitors as well, with some providing a similar mix of services and others specializing in just one or two. What does The Principal do to stay ahead of the competition and retain their employees? They have chosen to make tremendous investments in their people through personal and professional development offerings. Their goal is to create an environment in which people's ability to learn and grow is seen as a core part of the culture that contributes to the company's financial success.

A number of the professional development offerings are similar to those available in many organizations—coursework, development plans, mentors, and coaching sessions, for example. There are some twists to the approach as well, with on-the-job experience and informal learning built into the process along with a strong emphasis on the involvement of leaders as teachers in the training and development programs.

The development framework that is used to

The ability to learn and grow is a core part of Principal's culture that contributes to the company's financial success.

guide their efforts emphasizes the outcome of the development instead of the activity of the development. This is a valuable distinction that we see in many great companies— and reflects an understanding that development is a process that occurs over time, and should result in more than the tracking of a set of classes or participation in a set of experiences.

Two of the more unique elements of the Principal's approach to professional development underscore the small gestures that have helped to make this company great. A Listen In program, gives employees the opportunity to hear customer service representatives take live customer calls. Hearing service reps put "customer service" into practice helps all employees develop better customer service skills. It's also an honor for the call center representative whose calls are featured in this program and helps them to feel part of the broader set of activities occurring throughout the organization.

The Big Map of Initiatives is a visual depiction of the key role that employees play in the success of the company. It was designed to give employees a snapshot of both what the company is doing and how it is being done. The map shows the flow of the major initiatives employees hear about throughout the year and covers the organization's purpose and mission, the success measures used for different initiatives, and how each employee contributes to success through their work and upholding of the company's values. The Big Map of Initiatives is used during new employee orientation to help people understand their role in the firm's success from their first day on the job, and is also provided to leaders for use with their teams. This provides leaders and managers with a tool for reinforcing the message about each employee's importance in creating and sustaining the organization's business and culture.

Genentech

Genentech is a biotechnology company, a simple statement that belies the fact that they often are credited with having created an industry. There are not many companies with that claim to fame. In existence for 30 years, they have recently experienced remarkable success due to the acceptance of numerous specialized drugs that they have produced. One of the most significant challenges currently facing the company is that of maintaining their unique culture and creative research-based work environment in the face of this tremendous success and growth.

Leaders at Genentech have identified three cultural hallmarks as the ones that employees value the most and that they believe have created the company's singular success in the biotechnology industry over the past 30 years. These hallmarks are a commitment to science, dedication to patients, and respect for the individual. These three hallmarks are a reflection of commitments that leaders at Genentech have made to support the basic work of the organization, serve customers, and take care of employees. We hear about commitments of this type from leaders in many organizations, yet we rarely see results similar to those that have been achieved by people at Genentech. What's the difference? A consistent set of actions throughout the organization, practiced by leaders and managers, which continually builds and reinforces the culture of the organization.

Genentech's commitment to science is well reflected in its practice of allowing research scientists to take time away from their job-specific tasks to pursue their own research interests in the form of individual projects that may not necessarily lead to the development of a new product or service. This practice expands the horizons of scientists at the same time that it contributes to

Leaders in great workplaces are known by the companies they create.

the professional success of the company. A number of new products or new research techniques have resulted from scientists' pursuit of their own ideas. Genentech leaders identify this practice as one that shows respect for the individual, yet it is also inseparable from the commitment to science and dedication to patients. This is as it should be. The practice is part of the culture, which supports the business.

The logic for this practice is unassailable. Genentech needs good, smart, dedicated people in its organization to produce the products that will generate revenue. Research scientists, who will create these products, are curious people. Groups of people are needed to complete all of the research— not just the scientist, but the technician and support staff as well. And if an idea goes beyond the research lab, then project managers, in order to assist with clinical trials, will need to be involved, as will marketing and sales people. The cycle begins with the freedom to explore ideas and is supported in a culture of openness and curiosity. Funds are provided to research scientists to pursue their own work—this is to help attract and retain top scientists who want to do research rather than chase grant money. Yet the ability of Genentech to be so successful in the biotechnology industry is dependent on more than the ability of scientists to do their research, as every competitor of Genentech also has practices that seek to promote and take advantage of the creative scientific process.

Genentech has created a culture that supports intense curiosity. This is fueled by many programs and practices built into the structure of people's work lives yet the cultural practices of open questioning, honest conversations, no hierarchy, and no buzzwords are reflected in the small practices that have helped to elevate the success of their efforts above those of their competitors. They have created an environment in which more people can participate fully in the work of the organization.

Take the practice of open questioning as an example. How is this promoted at Genentech? Managers and leaders share information broadly with employees through online and email channels, yet informal, in-person discussions between management and all levels of employees are frequent and encourage. Senior leaders get up from their desks and walk around. They share a commitment to talking directly with employees—and because they do this, others do so as well.

Genentech was founded on academic roots, and scholastic traditions are still present. One example provides and illustration of the open dialogue between employees and management in the Corporate Information Technology (CIT) department: Office hours! Office hours give employees in the CIT group, in addition to employees throughout the department, the opportunity for valuable informal one-on-one discussions on any topic.

Margaret Pometta, associate director of CIT, says, "It's a great opportunity to hear from employees who might not set up an official meeting, but want to get your input on a project, voice a concern or briefly get advice about managing an issue. It gives me the chance to hear what's on people's minds, which is valuable to hear as our department grows and matures." Every member of the CIT Leadership Team is available for office hours once a month.

Additionally, CIT Leadership Team office hours are part of the department's Dialogue Day's Program—a kind of "lunch and learn" at the department level, where employees have the chance to have lunch (or sometimes breakfast) and converse in small groups with leaders of the organization. Dialogue Days are held every Wednesday and are always well attended.

Genentech CEO Art Levinson understands the importance of paying attention to product, quality, and culture of the organization to create a company that is one of the Best. In a Wall Street Journal article (June 5th, 2007), Levinson is quoted as saying that creating a great workplace environment is one of the three critical factors that contribute to Genentech's success in the marketplace, with the other two being a commitment to great science and a clear market focus on producing anti-cancer drugs.

Levinson says: "The third thing is we place a huge emphasis on making Genentech a Great Place to Work®. Eight or nine years ago, we didn't appear on many lists of the best places. We started doing employee surveys, asking people "What do you like; and more importantly, what do you not like about the company? What bothers you?" We've been pleased by the validation. We made it to Fortune's list fours in a row. Last year we were No. 1. This year, Genentech slipped slightly, to the No. 2 spot, behind Google Inc." [6].

Each of the companies cited above has created its own unique culture and set of practices that reinforce that culture. Yet beyond the practices, each group of leaders and managers has developed a way of behaving, a way of interacting with employees that clearly let's employees know that they are valuable to the organization for their work and valued by people in the organization for their contributions as human beings. While people are often said to be known by the company they keep, leaders in great workplaces are known by the companies they create.

[6] Wall Street Journal June 5th, 2007 "How Genentech Wins at Blockbuster Drugs" by Marilyn Chase

2009

CONSUMERS, EMPLOYEES AND THE TRUST BAROMETER

By **Amy Lyman**

[GREAT PLACE TO WORK® WHITE PAPER]

At the Great Place to Work® Institute we've been tracking levels of employee trust in management for over 25 years and have always believed that higher levels of trust bring greater rewards. The evidence that fuels this belief comes in the form of employee comments about their loyalty and commitment to the organization, and in the cooperative spirit with which all people in great organizations work together and support each other. The financial returns (see www.greatplacetowork.com/great/graphs.php) of the 100 Best Companies as a group have also affirmed that over time, high-trust organizations are more successful that their lower trust peers–even when those lower-trust companies are known to provide good products and services to consumers.

Further evidence, collected through the administration of our Trust Index© employee

The benefits that come to companies in which leaders, managers, and employees experience high levels of mutual trust are significant, and have just received further confirmation of their value from the recently released 2009 Edelman Trust Barometer report, according to Institute Co-Founder Amy Lyman.

survey and Culture Audit© assessment of an organization's policies, practices, and values, affirms that employees who trust their leaders also look forward to going to work, are willing to help each other out, and are proud to tell people about where they work.

Employees trust their leaders when they act in ways that convey their credibility, show respect, and insure fairness in the implementation of policies and practices. The behaviors of leaders create trust. These same behaviors are visible to the public through leaders' public appearances, and also become well known to people through employees' word of mouth interactions with customers, colleagues, friends, and family.

The impact of trustworthy behavior

2009 – 100 BEST COMPANIES

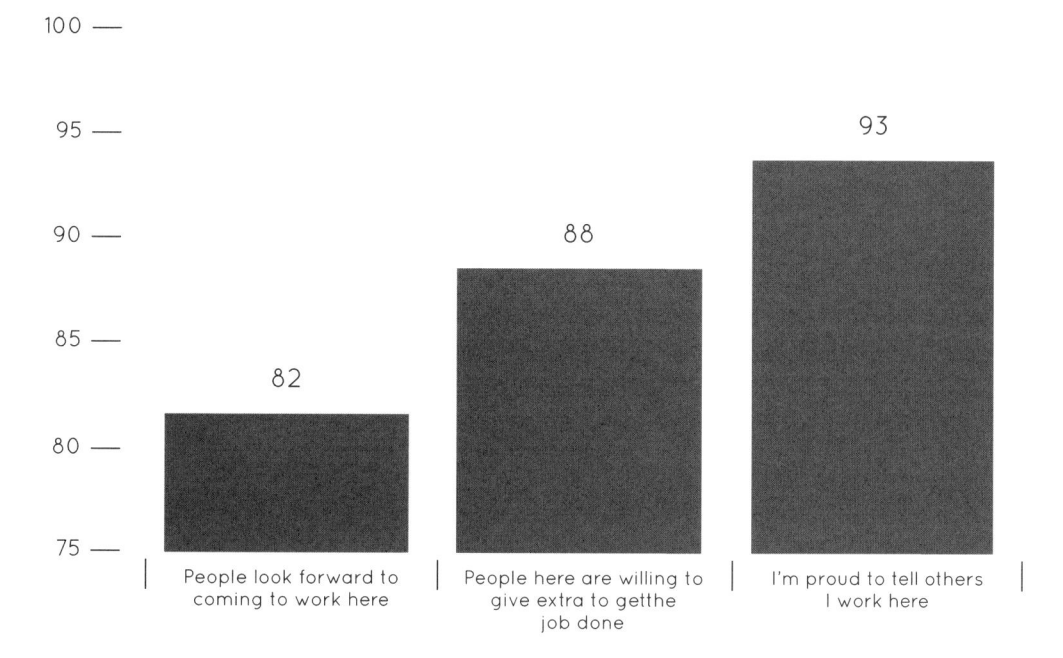

Statement	%
People look forward to coming to work here	82
People here are willing to give extra to get the job done	88
I'm proud to tell others I work here	93

Numbers represent % of employees responding positively to each statement

According to the 2009 Edelman Trust Barometer, consumers' behavior is significantly affected by their perceptions of the trustworthiness of a business. In their most recent survey, Edelman reports that, "In the past year, 91 percent of 25-to-64-year-olds around the world indicated they bought a product or service from a company they trusted, and 77 percent refused to buy a product or service from a distrusted company."

And, one of the most significant ways in which consumers determine whether or not a company is trustworthy is by how the company treats its employees. Consumers were asked: "When you think of good and responsible companies, how important is each of the following factors to the overall reputation of the company?" The option receiving the second-highest acknowledgment of importance was "a company that treats its employees well," with 93 percent of respondents indicating that this is important to them. This is a stunning affirmation of the impact that creating a great workplace culture can have on the reputation of a company.

In further response to the question about actions taken relative to the level of trust one has in a company, 67 percent of Edelman survey respondents indicated that they have recommended a company they trust to a friend or colleague, and 72 percent indicated that they have criticized a company they distrust to a friend or colleague. Word-of-mouth recommendations are often cited as one of the most powerful referral sources used by customers and potential customers for determining whether or not to patronize a particular organization.

Financial performance of the 100 Best Companies

The publicly traded 100 Best Companies

have consistently shown that as a group of organizations, their long-term financial performance is superior to that of comparable groups of companies–whether it is the Dow Jones, the S&P 500, the Russell 3000, or our own internal comparison index of the Lower 100 group of companies. The 100 Best perform better in strong economic times, lose less in weak economic times, and recover faster to pursue new opportunities during times of renewal.

Why is this? In these Best Companies, employees believe their leaders, leaders respect their employees, and the workplaces are set up to insure that fairness is in practice every day. This creates a culture in which the natural instinct of people to cooperate with each other is broadened beyond an immediate small group of close friends and kin to include the wider group of employees, managers, and leaders throughout the organization. Trust makes broader levels of cooperation possible.

1998 - 2008 RETURNS

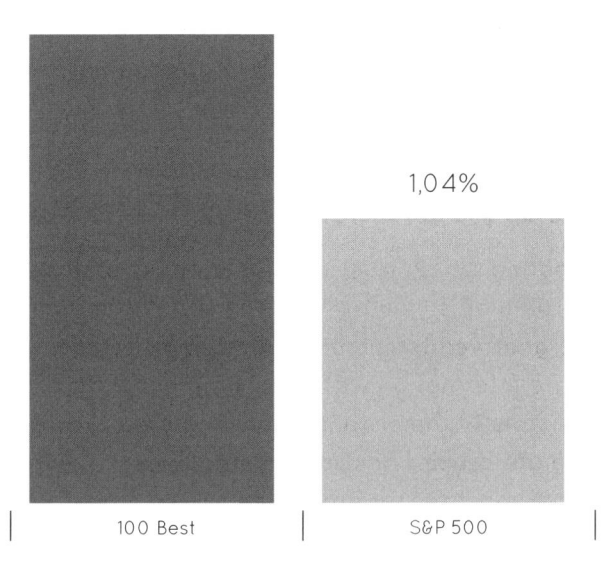

100 Best	S&P 500
6,80%	1,04%

Employees are also more committed to leaders whom they trust. They are more likely to contribute their ideas, experiment with new ways of resolving dilemmas, address customer concerns, and follow leaders into uncharted territory–because they trust their leaders and find them to be credible.

One surveyed respondent writes:

"The most impressive thing I find about the company is the open door culture. I can approach any other engineer with technical issues, product marketing with new ideas and anyone in management with any questions. This company is unique in my experience for avoiding the politics and empire building, typical in growing companies this size, and fostering an environment where cooperation is the expected and actual norm."

Trust thus gives leaders the ability to focus more on leading rather than spending time trying to control people, put out fires, or respond to a crisis brought about by unethical behavior. Leaders set the direction for the organization in a collaborative environment permeated with mutual trust, and employees, who have often been involved in the process of developing implementation strategies, are willing to follow. This is the virtuous circle that some people say is beyond reach. Yet the 100 Best Companies have been living in this virtuous circle for years.

Trust starts the virtuous circle that some people say is beyond reach. Yet the 100 Best Companies have been living in this virtuous circle for years.

How do you get there?

Creating a high trust organization is not easy, yet neither is it so difficult to justify abandoning the goal. Leaders in Best Companies regularly share information with their employees about the state of the organization, and they provide straightforward answers to employees' questions. In our most recent employee survey (the data used for the 2009 Best Companies list selection process) 82 percent of the more than 26,000 employees from the 100 Best Companies who responded to the survey said that often or almost always management keeps them informed of the important issues affecting the organization, and 82 percent said they can get straight answers to their questions. This is compelling evidence that a great place to start on the journey to becoming a great company with a high-trust culture is by sharing information and answering questions.

Employees at the Best Companies also believe that their managers and leaders are competent at running the business—89 percent of them indicated that this is true in their organizations. How do they know that their leaders are so competent? It could be because they have a chance to interact with them, to hear from them about the state of the business, and they get straight answers to their questions–the start of the virtuous circle.

Another respondent writes:

"Throughout the organization, people are incredibly hard working and professional. No one person takes credit for things; it truly is a team effort. This creates a tremendous amount of pride in our organization, which makes us all excited and proud to work for the firm."

Honesty and integrity are also right up there as qualities that employees are able to assess in their leaders. Among the Best, 90 percent of employees indicate that managers and leaders are honest and ethical in their business practices. Ninety percent! This is far different from the perception registered by the respondents to the Edelman Trust Barometer in which only 17 percent of respondents aged 35-64 believed that information was credible when it came from the CEO of a company.

The way to "get there," to create a great workplace, is to be honest with your employees, treat them with respect, and insure fairness throughout the organization. No company is perfect and there are ups and downs among the Best Companies just the same as with any other organization. Yet the 100 Best Companies provide a wonderful positive marker for what can be accomplished when leaders focus on leading in the truest sense of the word.

2005

WHY **GREAT** WORKPLACES OUTPERFORM **COMPETITORS**

By **Robert Levering**

[EXAME PORTUGAL]

Comparative studies have invariably shown that the financial performance of the Best Workplaces outdistances those of their competitors. Robert Levering offers three reasons to explain this result.

Soon after the publication 20 years ago of the first edition of The 100 Best Companies to Work for in America, a Wall Street researcher contacted me to report that he had discovered that the companies my coauthor Milton Moskowitz and I had selected for our book had significantly outperformed other companies on the stock market by a wide margin. We were surprised at the result largely because we had picked companies on the basis of their workplace practices rather than any financial criteria.

This result has been repeated every time someone has analyzed the financial performance of the lists. Last year, for instance, an investment firm saw that if an investor had created a portfolio of stocks using the companies we had selected for the Fortune "100 Best" companies, that portfolio would have beat a comparable stock market average portfolio by more than a factor of five over the period between 1997 and 2004.

We have seen similar results with lists selected by the Great Place to Work®

 Institute in Europe and in Latin America. For instance, in the United Kingdom, a study of the firms selected for the Best Workplaces in the UK list published by the Financial Times showed those companies outperforming the FTSE all-share index by a margin of almost two-to-one for the period between 1999 and 2004. And in Brazil, a 2001 study from the University of São Paulo revealed that over the previous four years, the companies selected for Exame's "100 Melhores Empresas para Voce Trabalhar" had seen a significantly greater return on investment when compared annually with the magazine's list of the 500 largest companies.

How can we explain this consistent finding? I think there are three obvious explanations and one that is less obvious, but equally compelling. First, companies that have good workplaces have lower costs related to staff turnover. Three years ago, for instance, we conducted a study for Fortune magazine and discovered that when we compared the staff turnover for specific jobs between companies on the "100 Best" list vs. their competitors, that the overall rate among the "100 Best" companies was 50 percent lower. Staff turnover is costly because companies must spend money every time they hire new staff in recruiting costs and training costs.

Second, better workplaces tend to recruit a higher-quality employee for the simple reason that companies with a good reputation as a workplace attract more applicants. Again, we have strong data from studies in the United States. Microsoft, for instance, had more than 100,000 applicants last year for slightly more than 1,000 job openings. Because they have such a large group of applicants, they can pick the very best. That is,

We must not underestimate the impact higher morale in the workplace has on productivity. The most important element of a great workplace is the high level of trust between the employees and the management.

they can pick people who are likely to be the most productive and creative people, which also helps the company's productivity.

A third factor is that the best workplaces tend to have a number of lower costs related to employee absenteeism, health care, and on-the-job injuries. Lowering these expenses helps improve a company's profitability.

Finally, we must not underestimate the impact higher morale in the workplace has on productivity. The most important element of a great workplace is the high level of trust between the employees and the management. Indeed, the employee survey instrument (Great Place to Work® Trust Index©) used to select the companies measures the level of trust in the workplace. Having a high level of trust within the workplace means that people cooperate with one another better than when there is a lower level of trust. In today's complex organizations, cooperation is crucial— and it can make the difference between business success and failure.

2008

GERMAN STUDY: CULTURE COUNTS

By **Frank Hauser**

[REPORT TO THE MINISTRY OF LABOUR AND SOCIAL AFFAIRS]

What is the value of being a great workplace for a company's success?

In 2006, the Great Place to Work® Institute Germany partnered with the German Federal Ministry of Labor and with YouGovPsychonomics, a research and consulting firm, to conduct research on the value of culture for employees satisfaction—and for a company's financial performance. The project was one of the largest of its kind ever conducted.

The project had three main goals:

1) to analyze the state of corporate culture, quality of work, and employees' commitment in a range of companies in Germany;

2) to assess the impact of organizational culture on corporate success;

3) to develop concepts to support the development of a high-performing culture.

A major study sponsored by the German government in 2006 demonstrates the business benefits of being a great workplace, according to one of the authors of the study, Frank Hauser, CEO of Great Place to Work® Institute Germany.

Through this research, 314 companies and organizations from 12 of the largest industrial sectors were randomly chosen, with companies grouped into three sized categories. Employees at the participating companies completed a quantitative questionnaire mainly including the Great Place to Work® Trust Index© Survey to describe their work experience, while a management representative was interviewed about each company's human-resource (HR) and leadership policies and practices as well as indicators of financial success. In total, 37,151 employees participated in the survey.

The results from the sample companies were then compared with those from the 50 Best Companies to Work For in Germany 2007. Key findings:

• Among German companies on the whole, only about half of employees regard the various dimensions of employee-orientation in their organizations—including leadership skills, support of individual development, fairness, and team-orientation—in a positive light. These figures are considerably higher for companies on the list of the 50 Best Companies to Work For in Germany.

• The researchers first looked at how an employee's commitment can be positively influenced. The results showed that the corporate culture experienced by the employees has an exceptionally high impact on their overall engagement ($r=0.86$; $p<0.01$). Such aspects of culture as team spirit, camaraderie, and showing appreciation for and personal interest in employees had the highest impact.

• The researchers also created a "success index" to define companies' financial success, based on the EBIT margin (quantitative criteria) and a rating of profits in the last three years in intra-industry comparison by the management (qualitative criteria). Based on this index, corporate culture and employee commitment were shown to have a strong correlation to a company's financial success, based on a statistically significant correlation ($r=0.32$ ($p<0.01$)).

- A regression analysis showed that the combined aspects of corporate culture— including employee orientation and engagement— can account for up to 31 percent of the difference between the financially successful and the not successful companies ($R2 = 0.31$). Key drivers here include employees' identification with the company, team-orientation, support of professional careers, and fair co-operation, as well as the organization's capacity to change. Among these areas, engagement has a particularly important mediating function.

- When asked to rate the importance of employee commitment for their company's overall competitiveness, 95 percent of surveyed managers said they consider it to be "very important" or "exceptionally important." But when asked what the most important factor is for competitiveness, those companies classified as "very successful" most frequently ranked employees' commitment as the most important competitive factor, while less successful companies attached less importance to employees' commitment, instead focusing on the price of their products as the primary driver of competitiveness.

- When asked to cite which methods of developing a positive/high-performing culture are most helpful, surveyed managers listed: adoption of best practices (84 percent indicated "rather helpful" or "very helpful"); company networking (74 percent); research studies (73 percent) and seminars (71 percent). Overall, the data from this study overwhelmingly showed that developing a more

These results apply to companies of all sizes and industries---and most likely apply to companies in other countries.

employee-oriented corporate culture constitutes a very important opportunity for increasing the competitiveness of a German company. This applies to companies of all sizes and industries— and most likely also applies to companies in other countries. Great Place to Work® Institute's CEO Frank Hauser states: "the question is no longer if it is reasonable to develop a Great Place to Work® culture but how to do it within a specific company."

2007

BUSINESS **BENEFITS**: AN **INDIAN** PERSPECTIVE

By **Prasenjit Bhattacharya**

[GREAT PLACE TO WORK®
INSTITUTE INDIA WHITE PAPER]

A company does not have to be a great workplace to be financially successful. But Prasenjit Bhattacharaya, CEO of Great Place to Work® Institute India, argues that the reverse is not true. He contends that great workplaces invariably succeed.

Ever since The Great Place to Work® Institute was set up as a separate entity in India, I get to spend a lot of time addressing in-house conferences and meetings of senior management of organizations. One common question I face in many of these meetings is, "What is the business benefit of being a great workplace?" Examples are given of organizations that are doing significantly well financially, but who are known to be, well, not great places to work. Recently, a senior marketing manager gave the example of his previous employer in the white goods FMCG market. This organization, according to him, pays great incentives to its sales team, and has one of the highest growth rates in the industry. However, according to this gentleman, no one lasts in the sales function for more than 3 years due to the high pressure to perform.

"Can you disagree that a great workplace and financial results have no correlation?" he

> Softer aspects like employee engagement and morale impact hard results such as turnover, productivity, profits, and market cap. So much so, that Jack Welch, the former CEO of GE says, "The soft stuff is the hard stuff."

challenged me. I decided to pose this challenge to participants in a workshop on employee engagement that I was facilitating.

As I had anticipated, we discovered that there were many more examples of "successful" organizations that are apparently not great places to work at all, based on the collective experience of the group. We debated the possible reasons. In the case of a few organizations we found that their compensation was a huge attraction, talented employees joined them even though as an employer they were not perceived to be great. In some cases, the organization operated in a monopoly or oligopoly kind of market, and in yet other cases scale, price, or technology were the key success factors in their market rather than talent.

We discussed how it required only one competitor to change the rules of the game like Southwest airlines did in the U.S. in the low-budget airlines business where most low-budget carriers had assumed that low prices alone are sufficient to be successful. As a result, Southwest is consistently successful in an industry where most competitors have burned their fingers. How much more successful will these companies be, we argued, if only they could engage their employees better?

Try as we might to find reasons for financial success of organizations with poor employee experience, and speculate on how things can change, the stark fact before us is clear—there is enough experiential and anecdotal evidence that tells us it is possible to be financially successful and yet have low levels of employee engagement/morale.

How about the other way round? Would there be examples of organizations who are great in employee engagement, but do not do well financially. Many people again gave examples of working in organizations where employees are respected and co-workers care about each other, yet the organization lags behind its competitors.

The trick is in the definition of the term "employee engagement." It turns out that all major studies have defined the term differently leading to different key drivers and implications. A random search in the free dictionary in Google gives the following definition:

"Employee engagement is a concept that is generally viewed as managing discretionary effort, that is, when employees have choices, they will act in a way that furthers their organization's interests. An engaged employee is a person who is fully involved in, and enthusiastic about, his or her work."

There is an ever-growing body of evidence to show that softer aspects like employee engagement and employee morale do impact hard results such as turnover, productivity, profits, and market cap. So much so, that Jack Welch, the former CEO of GE says, "The soft stuff is the hard stuff."

In the book, *The Enthusiastic Employee: How Companies Profit by Giving Workers What They Want*, author David Sirota and colleagues draw on 30 years of research to conclude that enthusiastic employees consistently out-produce and outperform their less satisfied counterparts.

David Maister, author of Practice What You Preach, has done comparable research with very analogous findings. One of Maister's primary takeaways was that employee attitudes clearly cause financial results, rather than the other way around.

The Gallup organization in its research has found a correlation between the 12 items of its

Great Place to Work® offers one framework that looks at the organization from an employee's eyes, rather than looking at employees from an organization's (read management's) eyes.

framework and hard outputs like productivity, turnover, profits, and customer satisfaction.

The Great Place to Work® Institute does not define employee engagement. Instead, it defines a Great Place to Work® as an organization where you trust the people you work for, take pride in what you do, and enjoy the company of people you work with. This is one framework that looks at the organization from an employee's eyes, rather than looking at employees from an organization's (read Management's) eyes.

While on the surface the definition may give the impression that there could be a number of organizations with high trust, pride and camaraderie that yet lag financially and in other hard measures when compared with competitors. In reality, this is almost never true. To find the reason we will have to study the details of the framework. Can you have trust in your management if you do not perceive it to be competent? Unlikely. At a personal level, perhaps you will trust a friend who is professionally not competent. You would not trust him to manage your business. Trust in management is directly proportional to the kind of credibility that the Management of an organization has.

Over 90 per cent of employees of the Top 25 Great Places to Work in India agree that management is competent at running the business. If an overwhelming number of employees agree that management has a clear view about where the organization is going and how to get there, and management does a good job of assigning and coordinating people (all statements from the Great Place to Work® survey), it is unlikely that the organization is an industry laggard.

In fact, our experience shows that organizations whose employees say that it is a great workplace are likely to be subsequently recognized by others as evidenced by their inclusion on other lists like Most Respected Companies List (which are based on industry perception and hard data). This is the difference between a lead indicator and lag indicator. What your employees think today, your industry and market will think tomorrow.

Sometimes we equate terms like employee engagement and Great Place to Work® with being a caring organization and a fun place to work. In reality, these are but two elements—necessary but by no means sufficient. To put it simply, great places to work care for people and care for results.

To revert to the original question, "Can you disagree that a great workplace and financial results have no correlation?" my answer would be unambiguous. It is possible to get financial results without being a Great Place to Work®, but it is almost impossible to be a Great Place to Work® and be a financial laggard.

If financial results are our only goals, we have more than one way of achieving the same. The choice and consequences are ours.

The author can be reached at pbhattacharya@greatplacetowork.in.

2. MANAGING IN **DIFFICULT** TIMES

2008

MAINTAINING **TRUST** IN **DIFFICULT** TIMES

By **Amy Lyman**

[GREAT PLACE TO WORK® NEWSLETTER]

How should leaders of great workplaces handle tough economic times. Institute co-founder Amy Lyman offers five pointers.

There are a few specific actions that leaders **and** managers can take to insure that their peers, and the larger group of employees in the organization, all work together to get through the difficult times ahead.

1) Involve People

First, it is important to remember that everyone is aware of what's going on, everyone is vulnerable, and some people will be harmed significantly by a job loss or decrease in hours. To mitigate the impact of job changes, involve employees in developing the strategies you seek to implement.

Employees may come up with creative ideas for staffing changes–rotating unpaid days off, taking unpaid leave, reducing hours–or may be open to early retirement packages that could prevent layoffs. When people are involved in addressing difficult situations, not only are you able to gain from their creative ideas, but you also give people a portion of control over what is happening to them.

A sense of losing control is one of the most harmful aspects of difficult situations—harmful to people's health and harmful to the camaraderie and commitment of the group.

2) Share information broadly and consistently

Everyone in your organization is already talking about what's happening. The grapevine and rumor mill are in high gear. People will create their own answers to questions, if they do not receive enough information, or if they receive inconsistent information from leaders. Therefore, it is of great importance to let people know on a regular basis what is happening in your business and industry.

As a leader or manager, it is singularly important that you be seen as a source of information about what steps are being taken to address the current situation. Even when full answers to questions can't be given—many of us don't know right now exactly what will happen next week or next month—letting people know what you are doing to stay on top of the situation is very important.

3) Show up, be available, say thank you

Leaders and managers can help to convey a sense of confidence that the difficult times facing the organization are being addressed by simply making themselves available and being visible. This is definitely a time to visit people at their desks, in the factory or in the call center or sales room.

Listen to what people are saying and answer with the information that you have. Let people know what you are doing, how you are keeping yourself informed. And let people know that you appreciate their contributions and hard work. "Thank you" is one of the most powerful ways of showing appreciation.

4) Start with yourself

If cuts need to be made, leaders and managers need to be the first ones to make changes in their own pay. Generally hours do not get reduced for leaders during difficult times, yet reduced salaries can have a tremendous impact on the perception among employees that "we are all in this together." And the salary savings from reductions for the highest paid employees can have a more significant impact than cuts made among the lowest paid employees.

The benefit that leaders and managers will receive back from this act of going first will more than make up for any economic hardship that might be experienced. Leading by example is truly worth its weight in gold.

5) Layoffs as a last resort

Decisions about layoffs are some of the most painful ones to make for caring leaders. Yet after everything else has been tried, sometimes layoffs are necessary. Many of the 100 Best Companies have, during difficult times, had to resort to layoffs to serve the best interests of the organization.

If that is the situation facing your organization, challenge yourself first to see if there is anything else that can be done before layoffs. Have people's hours been reduced, has unpaid leave been offered, have some people taken early retirement? If all of this has been tried, then layoffs may simply need to happen. Let people know everything that has been done to avoid this situation, let people know the strategy considerations, and then proceed with layoffs with humanity and justice. Share with people as much information as you can about how those being laid off will be supported, what the severance packages are, what kind of career or other assistance will be provided.

Remember, as well, to pay attention to the employees who stay. Much has been written about "survivor guilt" for those who make it through a layoff. Keep people engaged and remind everyone that the sooner the economy recovers and businesses are on solid financial ground, the sooner everyone will be able to return to work.

Difficult financial times are a challenge for everyone. When people trust their leaders and work together to find a solution, the choices available will be greater, and the cooperation and commitment that come from high levels of trust will fuel a collective effort to succeed.

2009

KEEPING EMPLOYEE LOYALTY DURING TOUGH TIMES IN AUSTRALIA

By **Trish Dagg** and **Chris Taylor**

[CORPORATE WELLNESS MAGAZINE]

Directors of Great Place to Work™ Institute Australia offer brief examples from each of that country's 2009 top 10 Best companies to Work for list.

Difficult financial times pose a challenge for employers and employees. However, as Amy Lyman, co-founder of the Great Place to Work® Institute, says, "When people trust their leaders, work together to find solutions, and enjoy spending time with each other, the cooperation and commitment that follow help to fuel a collective effort to succeed."

Indeed in Australia we have seen that this is certainly the case for the companies on the Great Place to Work™ 2009 Best Companies list. At all of these organizations we find leaders who have made a long-term commitment to creating trust and making employees feel valued. Our research has consistently found that leaders build trust with employees through walking the talk; valuing employees and their contributions to the organization; respecting their work-life balance; having policies and practices in place that take into account the needs and desires of their employees; and communicating in a way that is honest and transparent even in tough times.

> **TOP 10 COMPANIES TO WORK IN AUSTRALIA IN 2009:**
>
> 1. Google
> 2. NetApp
> 3. Russell Investments
> 4. Diageo
> 5. Dynamic Property Services
> 6. ETM Group
> 7. BMD Group
> 8. MRWED Training and Assessment
> 9. Red Ballon
> 10. OBS
>
> (To view the full list of 50 Best Companies please visit our website at www.greatplacetowork.com.au)

Organizations on the 2009 list of Best Companies in Australia were all assessed using our employee opinion survey, the Trust Index© which has been developed by the Great Place to Work® Institute and is used in more than 40 countries to examine workplace culture. The survey consists of 5 multiple-choice questions. Each question measures one of the 5 dimensions of the Great Place to Work® Institute's trust-based model: Credibility, Respect, Fairness, (these 3 dimensions combine to make up the Trust factor) Pride, and Camaraderie. In addition 2 open-ended questions contribute to providing an accurate and employee-based perspective on what it is like to work in the organization.

The companies on the 2009 list of best workplaces in Australia come in a variety of shapes and sizes. They represent many industries and range in size from 20 employees to more than 4,400. And while all exhibit cultures of high trust, we do know that what works in one organization may not work in another. It is therefore important for organizations to consider the needs and desires of employees when planning programs and policies that will help foster positive relationships among staff and high-trust relationships between them and management. Such considerations help sustain a great work environment and ensure that employees want to stay with the organization a long time.

The #1 company on this year's list is Google, which is very well known for its high-trust work culture, flat organizational structure, open communication, and employee involvement in decision making. Googlers recognize that they are valued and have a real sense of purpose in their contribution to Google's mission. Google also has a culture of risk-taking, which not only empowers employees to try new things, but also celebrates both successes and failures. Learning is important to Googlers, and they recognize that there is no better way to learn than to take risks, be creative, and make mistakes.

At NetApp, they make it a priority to keep everyone informed about all the important things that go on within the organization. NetApp believes in the strength of a shared vision regarding direction and objectives. This is achieved, in part, by utilizing a variety of tools to communicate openly and transparently with employees about events—good or bad—that affect the company. NetApp's senior management communicates frequently with employees because these managers recognize that sharing information with employees is crucial to the success of both the employees and the business. NetApp CEO Dan Warmenhoven constantly reinforces this concept regular visits to the Australian office where he spends time with staff and customers.

Russell Investments, also near the top of this year's list, is dedicated to caring about the health and well-being of all its employees. In fact the company reports, "At Russell Investments, each associate is valued first as an individual—one with a life outside the company—and then as an associate." Russell Investments is wholeheartedly dedicated to ensuring that its associates lead balanced lives. The company offers an array of benefits to promote work-life balance, good health, and well-being. Programs include boxing, pilates, healthy-cooking classes, massages, and health checkups.

Diageo is another company whose human-resource practices and strong employee feedback landed it near the top of the Best Companies to Work For in Australia. Included in its practices is a policy of regularly thanking employees. Diageo feels it does not need a specific reason to thank employees and often does so as a spontaneous surprise. Recent examples include three-minute massages for all staff and boxes of Krispy Kreme Donuts delivered to each department across Australia.

At Dynamic Property Services, the term "on the bus" is used extensively in a variety of contexts. It represents the collective view that if you have committed, talented people on the bus, then you can take the bus anywhere. It also reinforces that anyone at Dynamic can influence the direction the company takes and the way things are done. Dynamic knows that when people are inspired new ideas and better ways of doing things can and do come from anyone in the company.

If you have committed talented people on the bus, then you can take the bus anywhere.

Professional and personal development is so important to the etm Group that it has established its own "etm University," which includes a program of scheduled internal training. This was developed following one-on-one sessions with each and every staff member, finding out what they wanted to develop or learn more about. Some of the programs are job related, but many are of a personal nature, such as a series of sessions on well-being, personal finance, and communication. This has been very well received with more than 60 percent of staff attending each session.

The BMD Group seek employees who can stay and grow with the business. For this reason, they do not hire contractors for the duration of specific projects. This is a somewhat unique approach in the construction industry, where many companies employ staff on contract for a project, enabling them to then terminate that employment at the completion of the project. In addition, in 2008, BMD launched a Good Health & Well-being program to encourage everyone to take a more active role in maintaining overall health. To make sure the program offers something for everyone, BMD provides a wide range of opportunities for staff, including general fitness, discounted gym memberships, boot camps, group or personal training, competitive and social sports, corporate and charity events, educational seminars, and health assessments.

MRWED Training and Assessment recognizes the value of team-based rewards. MRWED has an incentive program, Go for Gold! Once employees hit certain performance milestones, all staff members are rewarded with gifts of increasing value. MRWED recognizes that everyone makes a contribution in unique ways. However, if all are working towards the same vision and they strive to be "ReMARCable," this eponymous award of excellence and other rewards, say a trip to Las Vegas, will come.

RedBalloon takes an interest in its employees' well-being and development. The company holds fortnightly "lunch 'n' learn" sessions where successful entrepreneurs come and share their trade and their experience in starting their own businesses. Recent guests included the CEO of the Sydney Swans, Tim Pethic from Nudie Juice, Seth Godin, Peter Sheahan, and many more. This enables RedBallooners to learn from the best across a range of different industries how other businesses are run.

OBS believes that new employees' first impressions of an organization are crucial. Once new hires have signed their employment contract, OBS sends a big blue box to their homes, with OBS shirts, a Hitchhikers Guide to OBS, lollipops, and items relating to their specific role. On their first day, employees participate in a thorough induction, getting orientation on a 3-month plan, which they discuss with their managers. OBS keeps employees happy and on track with 30-, 60-, and 90-day reviews.

The above examples are just a few of the many practices we see that help to lay the foundation of a great workplace in Australia. The current economic challenges provide a wonderful opportunity for leaders to revisit the quality of their leadership brand with those that matter most—their employees. While many perks come and go through time, our research tells us that Trust, Pride, and Camaraderie are not transients, and it is important for management to realize that *how* they handle these factors will have the greatest impact on their staff.

2008

HOW **BEST** WORKPLACES IN U.S. HANDLE LAYOFF

By **Leslie Caccamese**

[GREAT PLACE TO WORK®
WHITE PAPER]

In this article, the marketing manager of Great Place to Work® Institute US reviews strategies used by leaders and managers of great workplaces in that country when faced with serious economic difficulties that require drastic actions including layoffs.

The Best Companies to Work For are not immune to stressful circumstances, however, as the following stories and practices illustrate, leaders in great workplaces are skilled at addressing staff reductions in a manner that maintains and even builds trust with employees.

What sets great workplaces apart in managing staff reductions is not the "benefits" offered to employees who are let go–though the Best Companies to Work For generally offer generous severance packages and out-placement services. Rather, it is how leaders approach these difficult situations and how information about the process of staff reductions is communicated throughout the organization that makes a difference. When great workplaces cannot avoid layoffs, the reductions are managed in a way that maintains the trust that managers have built with their employees. A review of information we have collected over the years about how leaders in Best

Companies approach layoffs points to a number of themes of how they make it through:

Employees in Best Companies trust that layoffs are only being pursued as a last resort.

Employees are kept informed about the business conditions that necessitate the reductions.

Reductions are communicated in a way that is appropriate to the culture or circumstances of that particular workplace.

Details regarding the reductions are communicated to all employees, even those not directly affected.

Layoffs Pursued as a Last Resort

The Best Companies to Work For frequently make an explicit commitment to employees that layoffs will only be considered as a last-resort option. Saying this regularly and directly helps employees to feel that they are valuable and essential to the success of the organization. Moreover, leaders in great workplaces regularly communicate with employees about what the organization is doing strategically to avert layoffs. For instance, at TDIndustries, a construction and real estate company in Texas, and #35 on the 2008 100 Best list, leaders assess workforce needs, capacity, and workflow to avoid a situation that might necessitate layoffs when an economic slowdown is anticipated. A Production Oversight Committee evaluates upcoming projects and may recommend taking on temporary labor instead of hiring for positions that could later need to be eliminated. Additionally, during difficult times TDIndustries considers taking projects at little or no margin in order to make an extra effort to avoid layoffs.

Similarly, leaders at American Fidelity Assurance, a financial services and insurance firm in Oklahoma, and #24 on the 2008 100 Best list, use careful business planning to anticipate difficult times. They allow the natural attrition of their workforce to offset mandatory job eliminations. Layoffs are clearly a last resort for these companies who instead rely on strategic planning and forward thinking to anticipate ways to survive tough situations with minimal impact to employees. A commitment to work strategically to avoid layoffs and, more importantly, clearly *communicating* this commitment, help employees at great workplaces to trust that they are valued and that layoffs will be used only as a last resort.

Understanding Business Conditions

Especially in difficult times, it is important to address the business conditions and forces at play that may threaten an organization's success. "Maintaining Trust in Difficult Times" (see page 281) by Great Place to Work® Institute Director of Corporate Research Amy Lyman offers tips on trust-building behaviors that are particularly relevant during challenging business conditions. Among those recommendations is "share information broadly and consistently." Minimizing the potential for gossip and speculation at this time is critically important. Organizations use a variety of mechanisms to communicate business conditions to their employees. At town hall meetings or in internal memos, a strong, clear commitment to publicly address any and all questions about the health of the business and any staff-reduction plans is vital.

Herman Miller, a Michigan-based manufacturer of office furniture, experienced a 40 percent staff reduction a few years ago as a result of an industry-wide downturn. Herman Miller, number ninety-six on the 2008 Fortune 100 Best list, has emerged from the crisis not only financially successful but is also experiencing greater employee commitment to the organization. Herman Miller, an employee-owned company, consistently conveys to employees that they share both the "risks and rewards" of the business. Generously sharing the rewards of business's success through employee ownership and an innovative profit-sharing program demonstrates that employees are full stakeholders in the business. As owner-employees, everyone is kept abreast of the business climate and made aware of how variances might affect them. Though layoffs may sometimes be unavoidable, an ownership culture has contributed to Herman Miller's ability to weather a severe downturn while maintaining positive employee morale.

It is not enough to simply state the company's intention to only pursue layoffs as a last resort. Leaders in the organization must remain committed to openly and honestly communicate the state of the business in a timely manner, and must assure employees of steps being taken to avoid layoffs.

Culturally Appropriate Communications

When last-resort layoffs are pursued, the Best Companies to Work For understand the importance of communicating with employees in a way that is consistent with the company's culture and values. Camden Property Trust, a Texas-based real estate management firm and #50 on the 2008 100 Best list, boasts a company-wide value of Have Fun that over the years has morphed into a pattern of using skits and role-playing to communicate both positive and negative information. A few years ago, addressing some challenging market conditions at the

> **Herman Miller tells employees that they share both the "risks and rewards" of the business.**

company's annual conference, the CEO appeared before employees in full-costume as Captain Kirk of Star Trek fame. Patterning his speech after the 1982 trekkie film *Wrath of the Khan*, the CEO discussed the "attacks" the company was suffering and laid out a plan for how the Enterprise-ing crew would help Camden survive. Since the Have Fun value pervades all behaviors at Camden, this mode of communication was effective and appropriate. Bad news and challenging situations need to be relayed to employees in a manner that is consistent with the organization's culture.

At American Fidelity Assurance, when staff reductions occur, they are first announced to the affected division by the division president. This occurs before any company-wide announcements are made. This gives affected employees an opportunity to react, respond, and have their questions directly addressed by their immediate leaders. Having a "corporate" communication come down to employees when they are accustomed to receiving communications from their division could cause discomfort and doubt, and leaders at AFA are very sensitive to the impact that news about staff reductions can have on people. The office of the chairman has also made a commitment to be responsive before, during, and after any mandatory staff reductions. Each and every question submitted by employees to the chairman's office is addressed head-on. Almost a year after experiencing staff reductions, the office was still responding to inquiries submitted anonymously via the company's intranet.

At R. W. Baird, a financial services and insurance firm and #39 on the 2008 100 Best list, associates directly affected by any changes in staffing are the first to receive news of the changes. The person affected is told in an individual meeting held with his/her department head and in the presence of human-resources representatives and other individuals best able to offer support. This approach fits with Baird's culture and is consistent with other communication practices used in the firm.

Sharing Details about the Layoffs

Communicating details about the benefits made available to employees who are being let go ensures that employees who are remaining know that their colleagues are being well cared for. This gesture helps to maintain the trust that exists between management and employees. At R. W. Baird, managers and leaders understand the emotional reaction that a workplace change, such as a layoff, can create. They use town hall meetings and memos to reinforce that the organization is handling the reductions in a respectful and compassionate manner.

In a unique situation a few years ago brought on by the change in a significant business relationship, R. W. Baird went above and beyond the call of duty to accommodate displaced employees by offering outsourcing services prior to termination; offering a 50 percent COBRA reimbursement; fully vesting the 401k of employees with fewer than 5 years of service; offering the full 401k match for the year (even if the persons were terminated in the beginning of the calendar year); and contacting local businesses in similar industries to see if they had positions for displaced Baird employees. These actions contributed to creating an environment where even those directly impacted by the layoffs worked diligently and in their clients' best interests until they left the firm. Even more notable is that morale at Baird and the company's standing as one of the 100 Best Companies to

> **Communicating details about employees who are being let go ensures that employees who remain know their colleagues are being well cared for.**

Work For remained intact, despite this challenge.

When a bank acquisition resulted in the need to eliminate 2 positions at Umpqua Bank, #3 on the 2008 100 Best list, executives remained committed to showing compassion, understanding, and support for affected associates. Immediately after receiving the news, those who were directly affected by the layoffs were invited to the career center to search for jobs, both other positions within the bank and at local companies, and were given a chance to practice their interviewing skills. Sharing with all staff the news of the 99 percent success rate in placing affected associates in new jobs, including the 33 percent who found other positions at Umpqua, conveyed to all employees the commitment of leaders and managers to respecting and caring for people at Umpqua.

Difficult times and challenging situations present every organization an opportunity to do right by continuing to build and foster trust with employees. Moreover, companies that already experience high levels of trust between employees and management are better situated to survive challenging times with employee morale intact. While mandatory staff reductions are certainly one of the more stressful situations an organization may undergo, layoffs certainly do not preclude an organization's being a great workplace. For companies that already sport strong workplace cultures or are Best Companies to Work For, staying focused on employees during these times may be key to continued success.

For those working to build a great workplace, difficult times should not be a deterrent to pursuing measures to enhance the relationship between management and employees. Focusing on your people throughout challenging times may indeed be the key to current and future success.

2002

HOW **BRAZIL'S** **BEST** HANDLE **CRISES**

By José Tolovi Jr.

[EXAME]

Recently, I talked about the concept of excellent workplaces with a group of human resource directors. On that occasion, a curious question was brought up: How to keep a good workplace in difficult situations? One of the directors said that her company was not on the list of the Guia EXAME's The 100 Best Companies to Work for because she had dismissed several people. Before I could respond, three other directors intercepted, saying that their companies had also promoted layoffs, but they still succeeded to continue on the list of the best companies.

All in all, to what extent can events like layoffs, mergers, market crises, loss of sales, etc. impact the quality of the workplace? Of course, an impact exists. However, I have observed in our studies over the years that it is exactly in the worst moments that the efforts to maintain an excellent quality in the relationships with employees are really worth it.

How have Brazil's Best Workplaces dealt with severe economic challenges? José Tolovi Jr. describes strategies they have used to enhance their workplace cultures despite tough times.

Thus, how to observe the good environment when one is facing a situation of crisis? A good answer would be to recall the old popular saying that goes: "It's useless to lock the stable door after the horse is stolen." If you say something like "I cannot have satisfied employees in a critical situation," then you will be indirectly saying that you cannot keep your people satisfied in positive moments. Good companies to work for are always concerned about their employees—not only in situations of crisis.

A good workplace does not deteriorate due to a crisis or because of the hard times faced. The really good environment is built and maintained continuously, over the years. When a company falls into crisis, it does not have time to change. However, if an environment of trust (credibility, respect, and fairness) existed previously, then it is more likely to prevail.

Currently, when we speak of crisis in companies, we are almost always referring to dismissals. When we asked employees in the best organizations whether they believed that managers laid off hundreds only as the last possible resort, 87 percent on average in the last six years agreed. This is not surprising. Almost all the companies ranked in the best 100 lists in the last years did not dismiss people in significant numbers.

There are, nevertheless, exceptions. A company on the list dismissed over 25 percent of its employees in the last years due to the strategic decision of outsourcing some of the services. What did the human resources management, responsible for carrying out the layoff do? They carefully planned the operation. Once the benefit packages to be offered to the employees being dismissed were defined, they trained the people in charge of giving the news about the layoff and made an extremely important decision: special cases received special treatment. The extensive layoffs are usually treated as a bulk, not allowing for exceptions or reconsiderations. And that was the point where the company turned the game in its favor.

In addition to prior warning, the company announced that those remaining in the organization would be informed about the reasons for the cut and how the operation was being performed—also revealing the benefits offered and the care taken regarding the dismissed ones. Among the measures taken, a book with all of the names of professionals available was printed and presented to a number of companies that could potentially hire those talents. The company also offered training to help the laid-off employees develop their résumés in a correct manner and tutored them how to behave during a job interview, among other things. The former employees also participated in a number of sessions aiming to preserve self-esteem. Another detail: because the layoffs had to be kept confidential for reasons of operational risk, the company apologized personally and publicly for this to those dismissed and those remaining on the team for this breach of trust.

The truth is that it is possible to keep a good workplace even when there is the need for a cut involving a large number of people. There will be no problems if the environment is truly consistent and coherent and the managers are aware that a good relationship with their employees is critical to obtain good business results.

Therefore, we can come up with a series of general recommendations to those who ask what to do in a situation like this:

Before making the decision, review all of your cost.

Would it not be cheaper and more productive to keep the people? If your conclusion is that there is no other way, prepare yourself for each step to take next.

Carefully plan your actions.

There is always time to prepare actions around decisions with negative side effects that the company is forced to make.

Communicate extensively and overtly.

In a crisis, communication has an even more importance than it normally has. Make sure that the communication is not affected by distortions of facts and that the same content reaches all levels.

Communicate the bad facts.

Transparency and openness are essential. Remember that you are dealing with an adult public. Never try to convey a positive image of the situation when in fact it is really critical.

Communicate the good facts.

In every crisis, no matter how bad it is, there will always be good things or positive facts that might soften the impact of the actions. Show it to your people. Just be careful to not emphasize too much these data and thereby seem hypocritical, because employees would perceive that.

Disclose your concern with people.

In all of the actions, show the care you are taking of the dismissed people and with those remaining in the company.

Make all the actions with respect.

Remember that you are dealing with people who have families, commitments, and a personal life. Never try to hide behind the numbers.

Therefore, always cultivate an environment of trust in your organization. It is worth investing in it. The fruits will be harvested in a regular, continuous manner during the good times. But the best ones will be harvested in the moments of crisis.

BUILDING A BETTER SOCIETY

2005

RATING CORPORATE SOCIAL **RESPONSIBILITY**: MINIMUM STANDARDS VS. **COMPETITION**

By **Robert Levering**

[EXAME]

Corporate responsibility standards aim to improve the behavior of companies. Most standards do this by prescribing the minimum levels of behavior that are required either to avoid legal sanctions or to achieve membership in or certification/recognition by a standard-setting body.

For the past two decades, I have been involved in efforts to improve corporate behavior with a slightly different approach. Instead of prescribing a minimum standard, we have challenged companies to compete in contests to determine which ones provide the best workplaces. This approach, I will argue, has much to recommend it as we consider Corporate Social Responsibility standards in the future because it appeals directly to the natural competitive instincts of companies. By contrast, the minimum standards approach relies heavily on an appeal to a sense of responsibility to the wider community—something that is unfortunately deemed optional or low priority in most corporate suites.

Let me first briefly describe our experience to date with the various Best Workplaces (Best

Most efforts to improve corporate social behavior have prescribed minimum standards, often involving imposing legal sanctions. Robert Levering argues for encouraging companies to compete to be the best – the approach used by Great Place to Work® Institute in producing its Best Workplaces lists.

Companies to Work for) lists. In 1984 my coauthor Milton Moskowitz and I published the first such list as a book entitled *The 100 Best Companies to Work for in America*. It was an immediate national bestseller. We published a revised and updated edition in 1993. Since 1997 we have produced the list annually for *Fortune* magazine. The list also went international that same year when *Exame*, Brazil's largest business magazine, approached my organization (Great Place to Work® Institute) to help produce a list of that country's best workplaces. Now the Institute and its affiliates sponsor contests in 25 countries, including all major countries of Europe and Latin America as well as Korea and India with several other

countries soon to join the ranks. More than 2,500 companies worldwide, ranging from well-known multinationals with more than 100,000 employees to small, nonprofits with fewer than 100 workers, participated in these contests.

These lists are extremely well-known throughout the business community as they are published in prestigious business publications like *Fortune*, *Financial Times*, *Capital* (Germany), *Korea Economic Daily, and Businessworld* (India). Earning a spot on a Best Workplaces list is a highly coveted honor within corporate circles. A large number of those firms named to these lists publicize their selection widely to their customers/clients, shareholders, and prospective employees.

We have seen the popularity of these lists grow steadily, not only geographically, but also within the countries where the competitions take place. In the United States, for instance, the number of candidates for the *Fortune* list has jumped 32 percent in the past two years. And this year in Brazil, where there has also been a significant increase in the number of applicants, *Exame* will publish the "150 Best Workplaces" instead of 100.

Much more important from the standpoint of the issues discussed here, the expansion of the Brazilian list reflects that the Best Workplaces lists are also having a positive impact on the workplace. The decision to go to a list of 150 was also made because the quality of the candidates has increased so dramatically since the initial list in 1997. In other words, the Brazilians responsible for this competition believe that more companies deserve this recognition.

The improved quality of the workplace is also true in the United States. Over the past seven years, we have seen a significant improvement in the quality of the candidates—both firms that have participated for many years and those who are new to the competition. And we have numbers that bolster this contention. Not only have we seen improvements in the benefits offered to employees, but the average scores on the employee survey (the Great Place to Work® Trust Index©) that we use to select the companies have risen. We would not claim that these lists are the only reason why there have been improvements in the corporate workplace in the past few years, But we do think that it has been a factor. We know of numerous companies that make an explicit corporate goal of being selected to one of these lists and make immediate improvements as well as develop long-term strategic plans to improve their workplace practices, specifically to garner a position on these lists. As I mentioned earlier, we have plenty of evidence from looking at the employee survey scores from these companies that these efforts do pay off.

Let me give some background about our methodology as that also bears on the issue of standards. In all countries, we use the Great Place to Work® Trust Index© employee survey

Competition between companies should be encouraged. The Best Workplaces lists appeal to the competitive urge so natural to corporate life. Quality awards competitions can play an important role in encouraging positive change in corporate behavior.

with the same identical questions. We also use a management questionnaire, the Great Place to Work® Culture Audit©, to gather data about each company's policies and practices. Ten open-ended questions on this questionnaire are also identical across countries. Our evaluators use the same process worldwide to assess companies. As a result, we have established a global standard for evaluating corporate workplace practices that combines both employee input and an appraisal of workplace cultures.

As we look toward 2010, what do we see as some of the lessons from our experience in running these workplace competitions? I would suggest that there are at least three implications:

1. Competition between companies should be encouraged

As we have seen, the Best Workplaces lists appeal to the competitive urge so natural to corporate life. Businesses are used to competing with one another for market share, investors' funds, etc. The Best Workplaces contests—like the various quality awards competitions (like the European Quality Award and the Baldrige National Quality Award in the U.S.)—can play an important role in encouraging positive change in corporate behavior.

2. Attention should be paid to maximizing publicity

Our experience shows how lists are popular within the business world and also with the public at large. It seems every business publication has several standard lists that are part of its identity. Most of the lists relate to the biggest (*Fortune* 500, *Business Week* 1000) or richest (*Forbes* 400) based on some other objectively quantifiable standard. But magazines of all sorts frequently have lists that are considerably more subjective, like the Best Dressed or Most Powerful. While many of these lists are based on dubious methodologies, publications find that they sell magazines or papers because of their appeal to human curiosity.

3. Benchmarking is important

We have found that the ability to benchmark results is an important reason why companies participate in the Best Workplaces lists. We provide companies with the ability to obtain customized benchmark reports that show them how their company's workplace environments compare with other companies.

These are three implications that others seeking to spread the role of standards in changing corporate behavior can learn from.

2008

HOW BEST **WORKPLACE** **LISTS** BENEFIT SOCIETY

By **Robert Levering**

[ESTRATÉGIA & CARREIRA]

In recounting the background and history of the Best Workplaces lists, Robert Levering points to evidence that wherever the lists have been introduced, they have had an impact in raising the quality of the workplace.

I never imagined 25 years ago that there would be a list of the best workplaces in Central America and the Caribbean. For it was in 1982 that I began working on the first such list, The 100 Best Companies to Work for in America. Today there are comparable lists of the best workplaces in 30 other countries all over the world from North and South America to Europe, Asia, and Australia. The upcoming list in Central America and the Caribbean will add more than a half-dozen countries to the total.

There are several reasons why these lists of best workplaces were unimaginable a quarter century ago. The media, including the business press, virtually ignored the workplace as a topic at that time. Most stories about the workplace focused on what was wrong. I should know because I worked as a labor reporter in San Francisco during the 1970s. So I wrote many articles about bad workplaces — about labor strikes, union organizing drives, and lawsuits filed by employees who were unhappy with their employers.

My own personal experience as an employee, and those of my friends and family, confirmed my perception that most workplaces were unpleasant. Although some people enjoyed their jobs, they did not generally like the companies they worked for and/or their own bosses. I could not imagine that there was such a thing as a Great Place to Work®. So, when a book editor, called me in 1981 and asked if I'd be interested in writing a book entitled *The 100 Best Companies to Work for in America*, I thought she was joking. I did not think there were 10 good workplaces in the country, let alone 100. So I suggested a book I felt more qualified to write *"The 100 **Worst** Companies to Work for in America"*. She laughed and said that her company did not have enough lawyers to defend a book like that and urged me to consider writing the other book. I agreed, though I was skeptical about what I would find.

For the next three years my coauthor, Milton Moskowitz, and I crisscrossed the country in search of great workplaces. We visited 150 companies that had been recommended to us by various journalists, business school professors, and others. These companies were in all major industries from investment banks on Wall Street to software makers in Silicon Valley, from forest products companies in the Pacific Northwest to supermarket chains in Florida, from oil companies in Texas to car manufacturers in the Midwest, from retailers to insurance companies. At each of the candidate companies, we interviewed groups of employees as well as senior managers, including the CEO when available. Much to our delight we found dozens of companies where the employees praised the management of their

The best workplace lists do it possible for companies to benchmark their own best practices.

companies and described very distinctive and unusual workplace practices. Soon after our book was published in 1984, it hit the national bestseller lists.

Because of the intense interest in the book, many people asked me what these companies had in common. So I decided to write a book that would answer that question. To do it, I looked carefully at the 20 companies of the "100 Best" that I considered to be the very best examples. Originally I thought that they shared certain progressive human-resource (HR) practices. But I found too many counter examples. For instance, profit-sharing was a common practice among the "100 Best," yet many great workplaces did not have profit-sharing while many bad workplaces did have profit-sharing. Clearly, another approach was needed.

As I examined the data more closely, I noticed that employees at these companies frequently used the same language to describe their workplaces. In particular, I saw that they used similar phrases to express their confidence and trust in the management—that they felt the management was believable, was competent, and had integrity, that they thought the management treated them with professional and personal respect, and that the management treated them fairly both in terms of pay and benefits and in providing opportunities for growth and advancement. These statements contrasted sharply with what employees said at the bad workplaces that I had written about as a labor reporter. That is, in bad workplaces employees did not trust the management. As a result, I saw that trust was key. In my book, *A Great Place to Work®: What makes some employers so good and most so bad*, I defined a "great place to work" as one where you "trust the people you work for, have pride in what you do, and enjoy the people you work with." Since that book was first published in 1988, I have seen this insight about trust being the heart of a great workplace confirmed again and again.

In 1992, I founded the Great Place to Work® Institute, along with Amy Lyman, a former college professor from the University of California, Davis, who specialized in issues related to family businesses. The mission of the Institute was "Building a better society by helping companies transform their workplaces." We developed an employee survey, called the Great Place to Work® Trust Index©, that specifically measures the level of trust between employees and management.

The 1990s witnessed a number of major changes in the business world that had a dramatic impact on the workplace. Women began entering the workforce in greater numbers, which led to companies offering a variety of new, so-called "family friendly" benefits, such as flextime and on-site child care. At the same time, the high-tech boom put an increasing premium on more highly skilled workers. A mantra heard throughout the world was "attraction and retention," pointing to the need to hire the best talent and keep them on board. And finally, globalization has led to more intense market competition. Senior executives have become much more aware of the link between the quality of the workplace and innovation and productivity. Or, in the words of Dan Warmenhoven, CEO of Network Appliance, "We see our culture as a competitive weapon."

As a result of all of these developments, managers became much more interested in the quality of the workplace than ever before. So it is only natural that business magazines would become interested in ranking companies according to quality of their workplaces. In 1997 *Fortune* called to ask if we would be interested in doing an annual list of the 100 Best Companies to Work for. That same year, we were contacted by a major business magazine in Brazil about doing a similar list in Latin America's largest country. So, 10 years ago this year, marks the first two best workplace lists with major national magazines.

It is important to point out that, in compiling our lists, our Institute uses the same methodology throughout the world—the Trust Index© employee survey and a questionnaire about a company's people policies and practices called the Culture Audit©. We have discovered that the essence of a great workplace, principally the level of trust, is a universal concept, not only across different countries but also across different industries. In other words, what employees consider a great workplace is basically the same whether someone works for a bank in El Salvador or an oil company in the United States or a retailer in the Netherlands or an electronics firm in Korea. We now have more than a decade's worth of survey data with more than 3,000 companies annually that conclusively demonstrate the universality of the desire for trust, pride, and camaraderie in the workplace.

We have also discovered that these best workplace lists actually do have an impact in raising the quality of the workplace. First, these lists raise consciousness about the existence of the genuinely excellent workplaces that currently exist in a country. That awareness makes it possible for companies to benchmark their own practices with the best. And the competition for a spot on the lists means that companies actively attempt to improve their workplaces.

We have seen this process repeated in every country where we have introduced best workplace lists. We look forward to this new list in Central America and the Caribbean helping to raise the quality of work life for employees in this important region of the world. Not only will the improvement in workplaces be good for employees, but it is good for businesses, which must increase their productivity and innovation in the increasingly competitive global marketplace. But most important of all, it is good for society as a whole because most of our waking hours are spent at work.

2009

SUSTAINABILITY AND EUROPE'S BEST WORKPLACES

By **Sandrine Lage**

[ANUÁRIO DE RH]

This article originally appeared in *Anuário de RH*. Sandrine Lage, Founder of Great Place to Work® Institute Portugal, shows how many of Europe's Best Workplaces are contributing to a more sustainable society.

Leading companies are gradually engaging as key stakeholders, along with employees, in improving the environment. The Best Places to Work for increasingly support their employees' involvement in sustainability issues. They take the first steps by reducing waste or by promoting recycling. And they focus on the implementation of energy efficiency, the preservation of buildings, or increasing the use of energy-efficient transportation. In the regions that allow it, employees are even given bicycles.

Some companies go even farther: they lobby the government on ecological issues. Internationally, most people value the practice of tying the Corporate Social Responsibility (CSR) to the employees' recognition and to remuneration packages. The goal is for all to be part of the socio-environmental agenda—including climate change concerns—in their everyday lives. For Europe's elite in the Best Workplaces list having the skills to build teams and the leadership to understand the strategic challenges of adopting sustainability, or even, social responsibility, is therefore the order of the day.

According to the Great Place to Work® Institute's evaluation, there are organizations that lead the market in the formation and leadership in sustainability, which have not only won the Sustainability Leadership and Formation award, but also received the special Health and Well-Being award was and were appointed to the list of the Best Workplaces list.

The winners maintain the commitment to minimize the environmental impact that may result from their business: normally, the company tries to have its business activity exert only a neutral carbon impact on air quality. To honor this commitment, Google, for example, invests in a three-step approach.

The giant bets on carbon offsetting schemes to compensate the balance of emissions that they do not directly reduce, while they work on the constant increase of energy efficiency in their own operations. They also resort to clean, renewable electricity sources.

Externally, the company makes it a high priority to lobby with international policymakers. Aiming to speed up the development of renewable energy technologies, Google privileges research for finding an effective energy-efficient cost. The goal is to reduce the emissions causing the greenhouse effect.

The company engages and encourages the team to adopt a healthful lifestyle and to think, in their everyday lives, of environment-friendly transportation alternatives. The organization offered (in 2007) a pair of "hot wheels" — a Google bicycle—to each employee (in the EMEA region).

The company translates the relevance of placing sustainability at the top of the corporate agenda: it is not limited to working effectively at a macro level (lobbying governments and rulers/decision-makers). The work is extended to a micro level, by supporting each employee in adopting practices that impact the environment as little as possible. Additionally, the commitment with key stakeholders is clear in what concerns sustainability-related issues, an action that establishes a valuable precedent in the market.

"Green policies passed beyond the 'so do I' phase and are now being gradually recognized as value-added benefit to the business. Leading employers acknowledge that not only do they have the obligation to promote sustainable policies in their own organizations, but also must take proactive steps to educate consumers and to lobby governments to create an actual change," said a person from Google, whose informal motto, "don't be evil," led to supporting more sustainable policies. Whether it is to offer organic meals in the restaurant or to introduce tribal leaders to the world scene in order to protect Amazon Basin, they show a green example to all of the googlers, inspiring simple changes in the teams' lifestyle that can make all the difference.

Making the difference inside and outside of the doors

Organizations stand out when the motto is "make the difference." A strong tradition of corporate social responsibility, an essential ingredient in how to do business, motivates people, who are more committed and productive when they respect the organizations they work for. CSR is, therefore, an element that has a growing importance.

In the case of a British company, the effort to commit to the stakeholders and the fact that they take the impact of their activity in key areas of their business into consideration made the difference. Examples of the best practices in this area include: conducting business based on global principles that establish requirements for suppliers, so that they comply with national and international laws; the collaboration with the Marine Stewardship Council, supporting the sale of only fish that is approved by the company's environmental evaluation; and the replacement of 99 percent of the PVC packages for the food products they commercialize.

The values are also integrated at all levels, which presumes the employees' engagement with initiatives in the community. Offering an opportunity to more than 2,500 people who face obstacles when looking for a job, including the homeless, people with special needs, young people, and parents of young children, were part of the Marks & Spencer's Marks and Start program, considered as the largest scheme carried out by an organization to provide professional experience.

Over 90 percent of those who took part in this program, in the first year, stated that a placement at Marks & Spencer, even for a short time, changed their lives and generated the confidence they needed to return to the work world. The participants found safe, permanent jobs, either at Marks & Spencer stores or in areas such as education, accounting, or security. During one year, about 1,000 employees at the company played the role of mentor and developed skills such as coaching and communication—all along with their work day.

Ethics wanted in the DNA of organizations

These are the organizations that the Institute looks for and evaluates in more than 40 countries, for over 25 years. Committed to finding companies whose profile incorporates in their very DNA, the search for management committed to improvement and excellence, the Institute has recently decided to reinforce the recognition of the organizations to whom ethics and innovation are the words of command. In Portugal and the United Kingdom, it highlights organizations by their Sustainability Formation and Leadership and by Social Responsibility. Initiatives adopted with the mission of reverberating the best practices and reference role models worldwide. We are hoping for a multiplying effect in the diverse markets.

2005

DIRTY AND **CLEAN** LAUNDRY

By **Milton Moskowitz**

[STRATEGY + BUSINESS]

Enron fooled a lot of people, including me. For two years in a row, 2000 and 2001, the former energy star made *Fortune* magazine's list of the 100 Best Companies to Work For. This list, which I co-developed, is based on an annual survey of employees. Enron's employees were enthusiastic about working there, which is why the company made the list. I visited Enron shortly before it imploded, and I also failed to detect anything amiss.

Certainly, it is different for outsiders to understand the inner workings of a large corporation. Even astute insiders frequently don't see trouble coming, especially when the problems have to do with culture and behavior. Note that Enron's board of directors, as the ship went under, included Robert K. Jaedicke, former dean of Stanford university business school, John A. Urquhart, former senior vice president of Industrial and Power Systems at General Electric, and Lord John Wakeham, former U.K.

Like many others, we were fooled by Enron. The company appeared on The Fortune 100 Best lists for three years from 1999 to 2001, the year it collapsed. In this article Milton Moskowitz considers Enron and two other companies that have appeared on our lists (Disney and Nike) in a discussion about the state of corporate ethics in the post-Enron era. The article appeared in Booz & Company's quarterly journal, strategy + business in 2005.

secretary of state for energy under Prime Minister Margaret Thatcher. Today, nearly four years after Enron declared the largest bankruptcy in U.S. history, reverberations from this financial tremor are still being felt. We are being inundated with books, films, and essays dealing not just with ethical breaches and badly behaved executives but also with corporate social responsibility (CSR). Meanwhile, there has been a surge of comprehensive corporate reports on social performance from large, influential companies.

With corporate behavior increasingly on display, the rules of the game have changed. Corporations can't hide their actions or true natures, and some writers are using dirty laundry of recent years to hold companies to a much higher ethical standard. Other books, chronicling the stories of implosion, suggest that human nature, as manifested in the character of the company's leaders, is the critical factor. And a few writers (including some who speak for companies) are articulating ethical standards for the private sector that could represent a significant change from the past.

Joel Bakan, author of *The Corporation: The Pathological Pursuit of Profit and Power* and an American on the faculty of the University of British Colombia's law school, believes he understands exactly what happened to Enron. He attributes the collapse to the characteristics common to all corporations: "obsession with profits and share prices, greed, lack of concern for others, and a penchant for breaking legal rules." These characteristics, he says, are a direct result of the system in which corporations are legally bound to put profit ahead of all other goals.

In his book, published in 2004 simultaneously with the release of the documentary film (now available on DVD), Mr. Bakan argues that the corporation is constitutionally unable to act in the public interest. Only the great expanded regulation by government can "[bring] corporations under democratic control and [ensure] that they respect the interest of the citizens, communities, and the environment."

This is a viewpoint one might find compelling after dipping into three new books by seasoned investigative reporters that chronicle the travails of Enron and the Walt Disney Company.

The authors interviewed hundreds of employees and ex-employees, and immersed themselves in massive numbers of documents disgorged as a result of regulatory actions, bankruptcy proceedings, criminal indictments, and—at Disney—on going litigation.

The stories, which are stupefying but not exaggerated, show the people running these companies behaving in mean, spiteful, petty, selfish, and childish ways. Although the egregious practices at Enron and the jealous infighting at Disney have been ventilated in the press, the devil is always in the details. These books are worth reading just to get the full force of the brazenness and the cupidity that were allowed to grow like weeds in the corporate garden. (Professor Bakan would say that these weeds are natural growth.)

Andrew Fastow, the chief financial officer of Enron, set up off-the-books partnerships to do deals, primarily with Enron assets, hiding Enron's debts and making money for himself and his friends. He took home more than $60 million before he got caught! Jeffery Skilling, an alumnus of Harvard Business School and of McKinsey consulting firm, who joined Enron in 1990, was the brains behind the transformation of Enron from a natural gas pipeline operator into a company free of physical assets that traded

> The rules of the game have changed. Corporations can no longer hide their dirty laundry.

natural gas future contracts the way Wall Street bankers traded bonds. The idea: stop making things, do smart deals, and securitize everything not nailed down. In short order, Enron traders saw themselves as Masters of the Universe, as portrayed in Tom Wolfe's sendup of Wall Street, *Bonfire of the Vanities*.

Mr. Skilling once told a colleague: "I've thought about this a lot, and all that matters is money. You buy loyalty with money."

Readers are likely to feel the same revulsion at corporations when they read *Disney War* as they did reading the Enron books. James B. Stewart, who was a lawyer at the white-show New York-based law firm of Cravath, Swaine & Moore before becoming a writer, has a lawyerly way of marshaling facts and stories to make his narrative come alive. This is not an Enron-like story, though, Disney has a reputation to protect, built over decades, that Enron never had. Its customers and the public at large see everything it does: movies, television, publishing, or the theme parks. And Disney's executives wrought destructive behaviors, which led not to the demise of the company but rather to the ouster of the CEO, Michael Eisner. Robert A. Iger, longtime head of the ABC network, which Disney owns, succeeded Mr. Eisner on October 1, 2005.

While chronicling Disney's growth and its achievements, Mr. Stewart takes us behind the scenes to describe how Mr. Eisner presided over a business rife with nasty arguments, backstabbing, politicking, spying, turf quarrels, lying, and belittling of coworkers. Mr. Stewart exposes a host of other brawls that are staggering in their frequency and ferocity. After reading this book, one comes away with the impression there isn't anyone Michael Eisner worked with to whom he did not first offer praise and promises, and, later offense and insult.

Mr. Eisner's ouster was never about financial performance, however. When he took over as CEO in 1984, Disney was close to being moribund, living on its past glory in animation and its two theme parks, Disneyland and Disney World. In 1983, the studio released only three films; annual revenue was $1.6 billion. In contrast, in 2004, Disney took in $30 billion. Its film library had grown from 158 titles to 900. The studio had won 140 Academy Awards. It owned ABC and cable channels like ESPN and the Disney Channel. It had Disney Resort Paris just outside the French capital. This book makes one wonder what Michael Eisner's behavior cost Disney shareholders, and how it constrained value creation opportunities.

Of course, the scandals and brazen behavior that rocked Wall Street and the business world globally in the first years of the 21st century hark back to the first stock market crash, in the 18th century, when the "South Sea bubble" marked the sudden rise and collapse of the artificially pumped-up stock price of a British trading company. Corruption and excess in business are recidivist. As a result, every generation has its watchdogs dedicated to exposing bad corporate behavior and thereby shaming companies into being better, and its regulations to keep wayward corporate behavior in check.

That corporations can be forced, nudged, shamed, or pressured into being good and doing good has been a preoccupation of mine for 37 years. On the basis of my own experience, I agree with the arguments mounted in Steven Lydenberg's *Corporations and the Public Interest* that suggest strategies for elevating corporate behavior through a mix of regulatory oversight and new voluntary standards and reporting systems.

In this slim book, Mr. Lydenberg traces the growth and impact of CSR and socially responsible investing (SRI)—both of which are inspired by the notion that public accountability leads to better corporate behavior. He also lays out a blueprint for a marketplace that rewards corporations for the pursuit of long-term wealth creation, which he describes as the "creation of value that will continue to benefit members of society even if the corporation was dissolved today."

As I was writing this review, another example of voluntary reporting surfaced—reinforcing Mr. Lydenberg's view (and my own) that public accountability is helping to change corporate behavior. For many years, Nike has been the bête-noire of activists who deplored the working conditions in contract plants, mostly in Asia, where virtually all Nike products are made. Nike at first stonewalled these protests, claiming that they were bringing badly needed jobs to developing countries. The company's 2004 "Corporate Responsibility Report" shows a complete about-face. Nike now has a strong code of conduct governing condition in these plants, a comprehensive monitoring program, grading system, and internal compliance staff of 90 full-time employees who make spot-check visits. Detailed description of noncompliance with Nike standards are presented in this year's report. For example, 25 to 50 percent of recent plant audits showed workers being paid below the legal minimum.

To create this report, Nike reached out to involve a committee of outsiders, including a labor union leader, the director of accountability at CERES, a labor rights consultant in the NGO field, and other social activists. At first, the company argued against releasing the names of specific factories because, it said, it would make operations too transparent to competitors, exposing sensitive information such as new product styles or production volume. But Nike now posts on its Web site the names and addresses of 731 contractors in 52 countries. Some 625,000 employees work in these factories—including 200,00 in 124 factories in China, and 84,000 in 34 in Vietnam. (Rival Reebok already published a list of its footwear factories on its Web site.) In introducing the Nike report, founder and chairman Phil Knight even owned up to having made a "bumpy original response" to activists, "an error for which yours truly was responsible."

1983

TRUMPETING THE NEW VALUES

By **Milton Moskowitz**

[COMMUNICATION WORLD]

Milton Moskowitz wrote this article in 1983, when companies were just beginning to write values statements, a practice that has since become commonplace. His reflections of what makes for a good values statement are as relevant today as a quarter century ago when he wrote this. The magazine, Communication World, is a bimonthly put out by an association of corporate public relations professionals, the International Association of Business Communicators.

American business has suddenly discovered that it pays to have values.

Oh, deep down, especially when they sat in a church pew on Sunday morning, business leaders always knew that values were important. But they managed to check them at the door Monday morning. Their behavior depicted in a recent Charles Addams cartoon in *The New Yorker*: A boss tells one of his subordinates: "I admire your honesty and integrity Wilson but I have no room for them in my firm."

Today, many companies are trying to find room for values such as "honesty" and "integrity." The surest sign that they are making this effort comes in the burgeoning sales of "In Search of Excellence" by Thomas J. Peters and Robert H. Waterman, Jr. This manual of "lessons from America's best-run companies" sold more than 500,000 copies in hardcover, at $19.95 apiece, much to the surprise of its publisher, Harper & Row, which had a small first printing, and the *New York Times*, which failed to review the book until it became a best-seller. The reason it has such a phenomenal sale is that companies have been ordering them by the case for their executives to read. Charles Brown, chairman of the soon-to-be-dismembered American Telephone & Telegraph, reportedly bought a slew of them for his people. And why not? If you're starting out life as a new corporation, you want to be thinking of what you are about—and you want to find out what has worked for other corporations.

The message that comes back again and again from the recent literature is that companies with strong cultures win. They have a zeal for product quality. They stimulate rather than stifle their imaginative employees. (And many of them are loath even to call their people "employees.") They give the people who work for them a stake in the business. They shower their customers with kindness. They are sensitive to the needs of the communities where they operate. They recruit, train, and advance minorities and women. They listen to their employees. As Peters and Waterman concede, many of these findings appear to be "motherhoods" or "platitudes." The difference comes in the intensity with which these ideals are practiced. That separates the good companies from bad ones, the achievers from the under achievers.

If you work for a company that has a strong sense of values—that has room, if you will, for "honesty" and "integrity" — you probably know it. You can tell in a myriad of ways — from the opportunities you have to speak up, from the way management addresses you, from the quality of lunch in the cafeteria, from the amount of pilferage that goes on, from the variety, or lack, of benefits offered to employees. I've been interviewing people across the country for a book tentatively entitled, *"The 100 Best Companies in America to Work For"*, and employees working for the good companies frequently tell me what impressed them first was the character of the people who interviewed them. They knew they wanted to work there because the people who interviewed them were smart, warm, and open. Stuffy bureaucrats will never turn anyone on. However, if your company is concerned with the issue of "management by values," sooner or later it will probably have to confront the question: "Do we need to write it down? Should we have a formal statement expressing our belief system? Or is it enough just to practice it?"

Judging from the number of codes of ethics and value statements being issued these days by American companies, more and more corporations are opting to write it down. Some obvious benefits flow from having a written statement. You're on record with your employees and the outside world on what you believe. You consider this area important enough to have a written statement. It's a benchmark. It has worked very well for Johnson & Johnson, which has had in print for 40 years a value statement called "Our Credo." It's included in recruitment booklets. It's given to all new employees. And it appears in numerous forms inside the company. In 291 words the J&J Credo spells out four responsibilities the company has, putting in last place "the responsibility to our stockholders" (customers, employees, and communities come ahead of that).

In a profile of J&J two years ago, *Fortune* found that this code "has a mystical but nonetheless palpable influence in the company." For one thing, since the shareholders come last in the pecking order, a Johnson & Johnson manager may sacrifice profits to satisfy customers. *Fortune* noted, for example, that J&J stopped advertising its baby oil as a tanning agent in the face of increasing evidence that overexposure to the sun could cause skin cancer. And J&J didn't pay much heed to cost in 1982 when it pulled back from store shelves and medicine chests of consumers every package of Extra-Strength Tylenol capsules after seven persons in the Chicago area died from cyanide-laced Tylenol capsules, the company credited its Credo with helping it to react quickly and decisively in the Tylenol crisis. Chairman James E. Burke said the Credo enabled the company to decide early on "that the welfare and protection of the consumer must come first, and all other considerations must come secondary."

The biggest danger in trying to put down your values is that you come up with a tinny statement, one that doesn't ring true. Then you may have on your hands a piece of hypocrisy. One important step taken by some companies is to canvass employees. Ask them what they think should be the corporate value statement. Atlantic Richfield went this route in the middle of 1983 when the companywide newspaper, the *AcroSpark*, carried a full-page "Dear Mr. Kieschniek" notice. William Kieschniek, who succeeded Robert O. Anderson as chief executive officer of ARCO in 1982, has been trying to articulate the values for the company. They include "aspiration for excellence" and concern for the "quality of life in our communities." Now Kieschniek turned around and asked employees to write him. "I'm asking for your thoughts on ARCO's style and values," he said. There was a form that employees could clip out and finish this sentence, "In thinking about the ARCO style and values, I feel that . . ." Some 125 persons in the company did respond to this invitation — and the responses, in a few cases, ran four-and five-page letters.

Borg-Warner also consulted with people before crafting a belief statement. In 1981, at a conference of the company's top 100 managers, Chairman James F. Bere asked them to define the company's basic principles. They were asked to think about what the company stood for and then to send their

> "Without people we have only idle factories and empty stores."

thoughts to Bere in Chicago. They did—and some were later interviewed. Even after you go through this "democratic" process, the drafting of a value statement is not easy. It's hard work getting the words to say precisely what the company name means without sounding fuzzy-headed or insincere or pompous or all of the above. The Borg-Warner communication people worked for many months before coming up in May 1982 with the final statement, entitled "to reach beyond the minimal." It's a felicitous expression of values because it states in simple, easy-to-understand language what the company believes in.

For example: "For Borg-Warner to succeed we must operate in a climate of openness and trust, in which each of us freely grants others the same respect, cooperation, and decency we seek for ourselves."

For example: "Though we may be better today than we were yesterday, we are not as good as what we must become."

And for example: "Borg-Warner is a federation of businesses and a community of people . . . true unity is more than a melding of self-interests; it results when values and ideals also are shared. Some of ours are spelled out in these statements of belief. Others include faith in our political, economic, and spiritual heritage; pride in our work and our company; the knowledge that loyalty must flow in many directions; and a conviction that power is strongest when shared."

Borg-Warner has to be ahead of the game for having put down these uplifting statements of belief.

Not so felicitous is a more recent statement, "The Road to Premiership," issued by another Chicago company, Hartmarx. This is the company that used to be known as Hart Schaffner & Marx. Having changed its name, it's now setting down its philosophy. This is a much longer statement that ". . .

to reach beyond the minimal." It's a 12-page booklet that covers the waterfront, mixing salesmanship with statesmanship. There's plenty of hyperbole. Here are some excerpts:

"HARTMARX is its people. People make the difference. They are the company. Without people, we have only idle factories and empty stores.

"Going beyond the law, we strive for physical working conditions that facilitate employee comfort and safety. Including a clean, attractive work area—consistent with the work use of that area. Clean offices. Clean factories. Clean stores. Sparkling clean!"

In the end, "The Road to Premiership" ends up saying all things to all people. It says the company is "committed to systems that keep costs down," and it says, on the same page that "human capital is as vital as financial capital." It promises its shareholders "a continuous and growing stream of dividends," while it also pledges to be a leader not only in charitable "giving, but in serving society."

"All our constituencies should perceive us as a quality business, operated by quality people, selling quality merchandise, and providing quality services. No compromises. Class all the way. Premier." And then it says: "We exist to earn profits."

You set down a statement of beliefs because you want the people who work for the company to live up to them. So this statement has to be credible. This means you have to devote a lot of time to finding out what the beliefs of the company are (not every company is just like the next one) and to articulating then in the clearest possible language. Done well, it should serve a company well.

The message that comes back again and again from the recent literature is that companies with strong cultures win. They have a zeal for product quality. They stimulate rather than stifle their imaginative employees.

1997

THE SPIRIT

By Milton Moskowitz

[MOTHER JONES]

A few months before *Fortune* published the first list of The 100 Best Companies to Work for, Milton Moskowitz penned this article for *Mother Jones*, a magazine considered to be on the political left in the U.S. Milton raises the question of whether a company can have a "soul." A number of the companies he refers to had appeared in either the 1984 or 1993 edition of The 100 Best Companies to Work for in America—Ben & Jerry's, Whole Foods, Patagonia, Digital Equipment, and Herman Miller.

When the Green Bay Packers won the 1997 Super Bowl, it was a triumph of soul. The Packers are deeply rooted in the Wisconsin city where they were founded in 1919. They were named after a local meat processing plant, the Indian Packing Company, which paid for the first uniforms. Starting in the 1920s, the Green Bay Football Corp. made a series of public stock offerings. In 1950, 1,900 local residents each put up $25 a share to buy the team. They and their descendants remain the owners. No one owns more than 200 shares of Packers stock. And it pays no dividends—every cent goes back to the team in pay or toward the improvement of facilities. The result is a community—and team—spirit that is unmatched in any other National Football League city. That's why Packer players who score touchdowns leap into the stands to enhance spectators [wc ok?]. That's why fans at Lambeau field sing "Amazing Grace" during timeouts. It's also the reason why a team from the small northern town of Green Bay could beat all the big, bankrolled teams from New York to Los Angeles—the Packers have soul.

Now, soul is in. *The San Francisco Chronicle* recently called it the "buzzword of the '90s," in a headline for a front-page story reporting that some 322 citations for the word appeared in the current edition of Books in Print. That's nearly four times the number in 1990. The notion has even permeated TV ads. Millions of viewers were exposed late last year to Nissan Motor's gaudy commercials introducing the 1997 Infiniti Q45 luxury automobile with the slogan "Everything changes but the soul." And this year Ford Motor is touting its top-of-the-line Lincoln Continental as a car that "gets into your soul, not your pocket."

So it may not be surprising that forces calling for an awakening of spirituality are now marching into enemy territory: the business world. If anything could be considered antithetical to soulfulness, it's humdrum, buttoned-up, make-a-buck commerce. Witness the long line of business villains in literature, theater, and film. (Just revisit Charles Dickens' *A Christmas Carol* or Arthur Miller's *Death of a Salesman*.)

But today, a particular malaise—a sense that business crushes the spirit and compels workers to suppress feelings—has become an opportunity for the spirituality gurus, who propose to bring soul unto the workplace.

There was a time when this effort focused on turning companies into more socially responsible corporate citizens. The movement arose from the civil rights struggles and counterculture of the 1960s, and it eventually spawned a new crop of companies (Ben & Jerry's, Tom's of Maine, Odwalla, Stonyfield Yogurt, Just Desserts,

Aveda, the Body Shop) and a new group of organizations (the Social Venture Network, Business for Social Responsibility, Students for Responsible Business, the Social Investment Forum) dedicated to moving corporations along a path of social responsibility.

The new endeavor, however, takes a different tack. It strikes me as being more about personal transformation than corporate transformation. It is a call for people not to sacrifice their souls for the corporation: They are urged to bring their innermost thoughts. By so doing, of course, they might well change the way business is conducted. But the literature I have seen and the talks I have heard are very short on prescriptive changes.

What is one to make of all this? First of all, it's a new variant on an old theme. The hunger that people feel today for cohesion, for some sense of belonging, for purpose—a hunger reflected on the booming sales of books by psychotherapist Thomas Moore and psychologist James Hillman—has long been the by-product of modern industrial civilization. Business has always had a bad name among moralists, and efforts to reform it go back a long way. Christ gave only one piece of advice to merchants: to abandon their work and follow him. Catholic theologians of the Middle Ages and the Renaissance largely regarded business activity as "beyond moral pale," according to David Vogel, a professor at the University of California at Berkeley Haas School of Business. Only with Reformation did the West find theological sanction for the workaday world, as the Protestant ethic accorded the market a place of grace.

More recently, Marxist critics brought a different theology to labor and commerce, advocating an overthrow of capitalism. But this idea has been discredited, and certainly none of the new reformers seeks to dismantle the commercial order—they just want to open the halls of commerce to spirituality.

Most of the people I talk to, however, are skeptical about the movement's chances. They see business still cleaving to the profit motive above all else. In a symposium on "African-American Art and Its Audience," held last fall at Washington University in St. Louis, Tricia Rose, an assistant professor at New York University stated: "Corporations don't have a vision for society, except for a profitable space for them to operate in, as freely as possible. They don't have a value system. They pretend to, when they get pressure. But they don't really have a value system."

The views expressed by certain captains of commerce confirm Rose's cynicism. In an interview in the October 1996 issue of *Fortune* magazine, Don Tyson, the head of the Arkansas company that ranks as the nation's largest chicken supplier, said: "If it makes money, we expand it. If it doesn't, we cut its throat." In the same issue, the magazine reported that Doug Ivester, the president of Coca-Cola, tells his managers to follow the words of McDonald's founder Ray Kroc: "What do you do when your competitor is drowning? Give him a live hose and stick it in his mouth." Now those are some authentic voices of business. And mind you, Coca-Cola has just signed up as a member of Business for Social Responsibilty.

For five years now I have carried around in my head an observation made by Alan Parker, who is director of investor relations for Ben & Jerry's ice cream. In an article I had asked him to contribute, for the 20th century edition of the quarterly, *Business and Society Review*, Parker wrote: "There is a saying in favor among 'New Age' caring capitalists that business is the most powerful force in society. They mean that business,

If anything could be considered antithetical to soulfulness, it's humdrum, buttoned-up, make-a-buck commerce.

by joining creativity and money, can create tremendous positive change in our world. If business is the most powerful force in the society, how come Bach cantata can move us to tears, but a healthy balance sheet cannot?"

I recently asked Parker if he thought it was possible for business to have a soul. "Business pressures will put strain on the soul," he says, "but it's still possible to preserve it. If people bring their souls to business, it will have a soul."

I put the same question to James Mackey, the CEO of Austin, Texas-based Whole Foods, the nation's largest operator of natural food stores. "Businesspeople shy away from talking about this responsibility because they don't want to be considered non-serious," he says. "They want to appear tough-minded. But business does have a higher purpose, a deeper purpose than making a profit. Making a profit is like breathing. You need to breathe to live. But we have a purpose connected to products, people, community, the environment, stakeholders."

Mackey quickly adds, however, that corporate spirit is inseparable from corporeal health. "Even if you have a soul, a spirit, that doesn't mean you will be safe from turns in the marketplace. You can have a certain essence, a reality that is greater than the bottom line, but that does not make you invulnerable to change."

Patagonia, the outdoor clothing company based in Ventura, California, may well be the most environmentally-conscious company in the land, and it has exemplary family-friendly policies such as on-site childcare and eight-week paid leaves for new parents. "We definitely have soul as a company, but we don't tend to be explicit about it," CEO David Olsen says. "And it would be difficult, if not impossible, to maintain, if we were not a privately held company." Olsen points out that at Patagonia, soul manifests itself in a number of ways—a belief that "sacred places" exist in nature and need protection; rigorous field audits of overseas plants to ensure that workers are not being abused; and mindfulness about environmental degradation that has resulted in the company using organic cotton to make its garments.

"We are not driven to look for commercial success," he explains. "We try to create value, and we feel that if you make value, you will be rewarded." To Olsen, that's soul.

In the end, I think, most corporate changes have occurred at the margin, and companies continue to sell their souls to the devil to make their numbers. This is especially true if your company is publicly held, with shares traded every day of the stock market. John Mackey calls Wall Street security analysts, with their short-term outlook, "the high priests of materialism." But even soulful companies are at risk from the prevailing ethos.

In 1984, when Robert Levering and I published *The 100 Best Companies to Work for in America*, we listed 10 companies with no-layoff policy. Today, only two of those companies—Johnson Wax in Racine, Wisconsin, and Worthington Industries in Columbus, Ohio—offer this kind of job security.

Even the most caring companies can sometimes lay off workers in a harsh manner. Herman Miller, the western Michigan furniture maker, has long had a reputation for treating its employees well, thanks in great measure to the De Pree family, which founded the company. Max De Pree, son of the founder, set down the company's egalitarian humanism in his 1987 book, *Leadership Is an Art*, wherein he spelled out the importance of "covenantal relationships." De Pree wrote that "words such as love, warmth, [and] personal chemistry" are relevant to the operation of a company. I remember seeing meetings at Herman Miller being opened by a prayer. They still do this at the annual meeting, but the past five years have bruised the company's spirit. A new CEO has come and gone. Profits have slumped, and in 1995 the company laid off 160 people out of a workforce of 6,500—brusquely and impersonally. It was a direct contradiction of De Pree's philosophy—and, in fact, the company now concedes that it botched that downsizing. The managers who were in charge of it are no longer with Herman Miller, and the company's new CEO, Michael A. Volkema, has reaffirmed the company's values. "Furniture is simply a way to support our families," he says.

Tough times will always try a company's soul. Elliot Hoffman, co-founder of the Just Desserts bakery company in San Francisco, has been wrestling with this problem for the past few years. If any company has soul, it's Just Desserts, reflected in its strong commitment to employees and the community. It has received national attention for its affiliation with the Garden Project, which employs ex-prisoners to grow vegetables. But the company has faced a financial crunch, provoked by the rise of the Starbucks coffee chain. Two years ago, in a talk at a Social Ventures Network conference, Hoffman reported that the venture capital people he had met with, including those with an alleged interest in social responsibility, didn't see "human returns" as a part of the return on investment. "Are there investors out there who value the importance of multiple returns," he asked, "a multiple bottom line that includes human, community, and social returns?"

We would all like a workplace to embrace such concerns. That's a business with soul. But soul may not last, even in a company with a conscience. In 1985, I addressed a meeting of salespersons at Digital Equipment Corp., and I was impressed with the session, which opened with taped excerpts from Martin Luther King Jr.'s moving address at the March on Washington in 1963. That certainly revved up the troops, but it didn't help the company's management escape miscalculations on the future of the computer industry. Digital's workforce has gone from more than 120,000 down to 51,000, and its stock has dropped from an all-time high of $199 to its current price of $31. The fact is, in business, when you are doing well, it's easy to persuade yourself that soul is a component of your operations.

Undoubtedly, businesspeople would be uncomfortable with the intrusion of spirituality into discussions of ongoing business operations. Soul is not part of the language of business. There is no entry for it on the balance sheet. And it will take little short of a miracle from above to have business executives recognize the existence of soul. Of course, if they could be convinced that it does help the bottom line, they would quickly embrace it. But that's not what soul is about.

GREAT PLACE TO WORK® INSTITUTE WORLDWIDE

- CANADA
- USA
- MEXICO
- GUATEMALA
- EL SALVADOR
- COSTA RICA
- PANAMA
- ECUADOR
- COLOMBIA
- PERU
- BOLIVIA
- CHILE
- PARAGUAY
- URUGUAY
- ARGENTINA
- HONDURAS
- DOMINICAN REPUBLIC
- PUERTO RICO
- NICARAGUA
- VENEZUELA
- BRAZIL
- DENMARK
- GERMANY
- NETHERLANDS
- UK
- IRELAND
- BELGIUM
- SWITZERLAND
- FRANCE
- PORTUGAL
- SPAIN

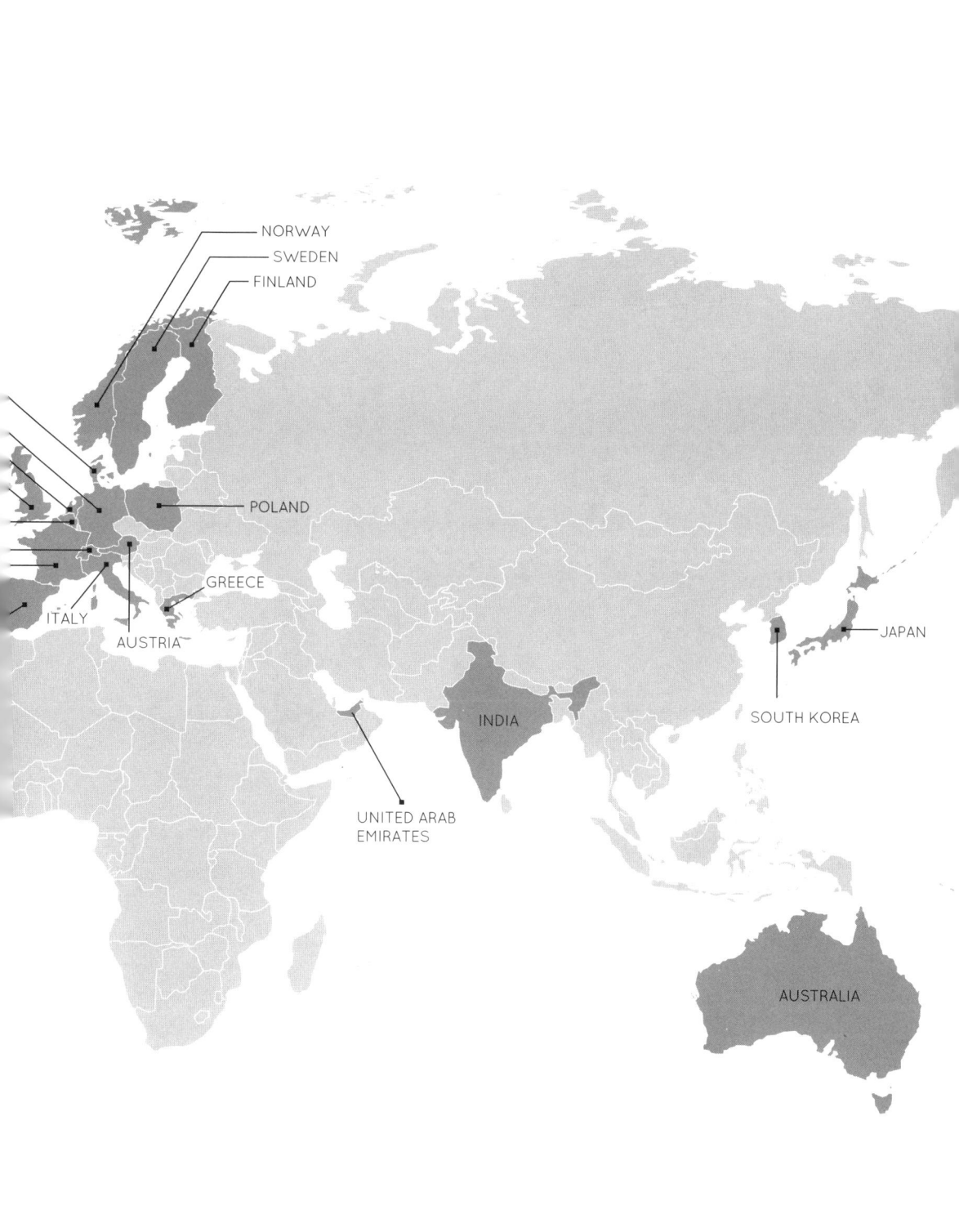

- NORWAY
- SWEDEN
- FINLAND
- POLAND
- GREECE
- ITALY
- AUSTRIA
- JAPAN
- SOUTH KOREA
- INDIA
- UNITED ARAB EMIRATES
- AUSTRALIA

INDEX OF ALL ARTICLES

17 WHERE IT ALL BEGAN

18 The 100 best companies to work for in America
Robert Levering, Milton Moskowitz, Michael Katz

25 Beyond good policies and practices
Robert Levering, Milton Moskowitz, Michael Katz

30 Working for the best
Robert Levering, Milton Moskowitz

40 The 100 best companies to work for: one year later
Robert Levering, Milton Moskowitz

49 What makes some employers so good — and most so bad
Robert Levering

54 The 100 best companies to work for In America (second edition)
Robert Levering, Milton Moskowitz

58 The first list
José Tolovi Jr.

62 We love our jobs. Just ask us.
Milton Moskowitz

67 IMPORTANCE OF TRUST

68 Even a prison can be a great workplace
Robert Levering

75 Deutschlands beste Arbeitgeber 2005
Frank Hauser, Tobias Schmidtner Introduction By Robert Levering

	78	**Leadership in a great workplace** Robert Levering
	81	**The care and nurturing of employees** Robert Levering
84	**Trust, not happiness, is key to workplace success** Robert Levering	
	89	**Values, violations and viable workplaces** Prasenjit Bhattacharya
	95	**When the owl takes flight** Horacio Bolaños
	98	**Trust is scary!** Palle Ellemann
	102	**The economy of empowerment** José Tolovi Jr.
	105	**Born to command: why less is more** Williams Johnson
	110	**The emotional bond** Ana Maria Gubbins
	112	**What did we do wrong?** José Tolovi Jr.

117 MODELS FOR CHANGE AND GLOBAL PERSPECTIVES

118 GREAT PLACE TO WORK® MODEL

119 **Five case studies**
 Lisa Ratner

137	Today's employees expect more: a good workplace Robert Levering
141	Many of Latin America's best are also good citizens Robert Levering
147	Money does not make people, people make money Raciel Sosa
150	Owner-led small and medium-size companies Prasenjit Bhattacharya
166	GIFTWORK®
167	How the best workplaces create "giftwork® cultures" Robert Levering
174	What distinguishes great workplaces is giftwork® Robert Levering
180	GLOBAL PRESPECTIVES
181	How Do India's best workplaces compare With the best in the U.S.? Robert Levering
186	Balancing work and family Mexico's best workplaces Jennifer Amozorrutia
191	On Tolstoy, business startegy and corporate culture Robert Levering
196	The key to organizational transformation Adriana Souza

200   Chile and global workplaces trends
Robert Levering

206 The catalyst for organization excellence
Jennifer Amozorrutia

209   Are multinationals better places to work?
José Tolovi Jr.

213   "Diffuse creativity" and innovation:
lessons from italy´s best workplaces
Gilberto Dondé

223   TRUST MAKES COMPANIES STRONGER AND MORE ABLE TO HANDLE BAD TIMES

224   THE BOTTOM LINE

225   Creating trust: it's worth the effort
Amy Lyman

262   Consumers, employees and the trust barometer
Amy Lyman

269   Why great workplaces outperform competitors
Robert Levering

272   German study: culture counts
Frank Hauser

276   Business benefits: an Indian perspective
Prasenjit Bhattacharya

282 MANAGING IN DIFFICULT TIMES

283 Maintaining trust in difficult times
Amy Lyman

287 Keeping employees loyalty during tough times in Australia
Trish Dagg And Chris Taylor

293 How best workplaces in U.S. handle layoffs
Leslie Caccamese

300 How Brazil's best handle crises
José Tolovi Jr.

305 BUILDING A BETTER SOCIETY

306 Rating corporate social responsibility: Minumum standards vs. Competition
Robert Levering

311 How best workplace lists benefit society
Robert Levering

317 Sustainability and Europe's best workplaces
Sandrine Lage

322 Dirty and clean laundry
Milton Moskowitz

329 Trumpeting the new values
Milton Moskowitz

335 The spirit
Milton Moskowitz

TITLE **TRANSFORMING WORKPLACE CULTURES**
Insights from Great Place to Work® Institute's first 25 years

© 2010, Great Place to Work® Inc.

PUBLISHED BY PRIMAVERA EDITORIAL

Editorial Team LOURDES MAGALHÃES AND TÂNIA LINS
Design Concept PAULA PARON
Design Application MARIANA CARBONELL AND PAULA PARON
Review CAMILLE CUSUMANO
Cover Picture GETTY IMAGES

Dados Internacionais de Catalogação na Publicação (CIP)
(Câmara Brasileira do Livro, SP, Brasil)

Transforming workplace cultures : insight from
Great Place to Work Institute's first years /
edited by Robert Levering . -- São Paulo :
Primavera Editorial, 2010.

Vários autores.
ISBN 978-85-61977-16-0

1. Administração de empresas 2. Administração
de pessoal 3. Ambiente de trabalho
4. Comportamento organizacional 5. Cultura
organizacional 6. Qualidade de vida no trabalho
7. Satisfação no trabalho 8. Sucesso em negócios
I. Levering, Robert.

10-03669   CDD-658.4

Índice para catálogo sistemático:
1. Gestão empresarial : Administração executiva 658.4

PRIMAVERA
EDITORIAL

Rua Ferreira de Araújo, 202 - 8º andar
05428-000 – São Paulo – SP
Telefone: (55 11) 3034-3925
www.primaveraeditorial.com.br
contato@primaveraeditorial.com.br

All rights reserved and protected by the brazilian law 9.610 of 19 February 1998. No part of this publication may be reproduced or distributed in any form or by any means, or stored in a database or retrieval system, without permission of the publisher.

TRANSFORMING WORKPLACE CULTURES
Insights from Great Place to Work® Institute's first 25 years

printed in São Paulo
by gráfica Bandeirantes,
for Primavera Editorial in
july of 2010.